The Evaluation Enterprise

~~~~~~

A Realistic Appraisal
of Evaluation Careers,
Methods, and Applications

William R. Meyers

The
Evaluation
Enterprise

~~~~~~

Jossey-Bass Publishers
San Francisco • Washington • London • 1981

THE EVALUATION ENTERPRISE
A Realistic Appraisal of Evaluation Careers,
Methods, and Applications
    by William R. Meyers

Copyright © 1981 by: Jossey-Bass Inc., Publishers
                433 California Street
                San Francisco, California 94104
                        &
                Jossey-Bass Limited
                28 Banner Street
                London EC1Y 8QE

Library of Congress Cataloging in Publication Data

Meyers, William R.
        The evaluation enterprise.

        Includes bibliographical references and index.
        1. Evaluation—United States. I. Title.
AZ193.U6M49   001.4′0973   81-81961
ISBN 0-87589-503-4   AACR2

Manufactured in the United States of America

JACKET DESIGN BY WILLI BAUM

FIRST EDITION

Code 8119

The Jossey-Bass
Social and Behavioral Science Series

Special Adviser
Methodology of Social and
Behavioral Research
DONALD W. FISKE
University of Chicago

Preface

This book should prove useful to practicing evaluators and to program managers and administrators, in both the public and private sectors, in planning, conducting, and using program evaluations. The issues considered are sufficiently generic that the recommendations should be applicable to all sorts of programs, not merely to traditional social programs. It is hoped that both evaluators and clients will gain an improved conceptual understanding that will make the day-to-day practice and use of evaluation less tormented, more manageable, and more fruitful for everyone.

This book is written from the multiple perspectives of my experience and training. I have been a practitioner of evaluation for almost twenty years: five years as a full-time industrial consultant, two years as a federal research administrator, and ten years as a professor of psychology. Since I also have some training in law, sociology, and history, and some background in urban planning, I have a broader approach to evaluation than that of many practitioners. As a practicing evaluator and as a user of evaluation, I have been struck by a number of issues that repeatedly cause serious and needless difficulty for evaluators and clients served by evaluators. This book is an effort to clarify and resolve those issues.

Chapters One and Three address certain misunderstandings about the profession of evaluation that lead to career difficulties for evaluators and conflicts between evaluators and clients. Chapter Two examines the social systems nature of programs and the counterintuitive character of program functioning, offering evaluators and administrators a realistic assessment of how programs interact with their social context.

I have found that many users of evaluations lack a basic understanding of how to commission and guide evaluations and how to ensure that the results are used by their agency. Chapter Four presents detailed and blunt advice on these subjects. I have also observed the understandable but painful inability of many evaluators to cope with the federal system of contracts and grants for funding evaluation. Chapter Five considers strategies in these areas in a frank and detailed way. Most of my recommendations are applicable to coping with state and local systems as well. Chapter Six attempts to resolve many of the perplexities that face evaluators and clients concerning the nature of program goals and the various ways of taking account of program goals in an evaluation.

Chapters Seven through Nine address specific problems in experimentation, data collection, and data analysis. Chapter Seven responds to the usual approach to field experimentation, an approach that often yields experiments that are massive, expensive, and labor-intensive efforts, by presenting a model for an alternative kind of evaluative field experimentation that remedies some of these shortcomings. Chapters Eight and Nine clarify several basic confusions about the qualitative and quantitative methods and data in evaluation. These issues are recast in understandable terms so that evaluators and clients can make sensible choices among various evaluation methods.

The regrettable technocratic emphasis in evaluation has led evaluators and administrators to overestimate the value of the results that can be achieved by using various managerial and administrative analyses as models for evaluation. As a result, evaluators become technicians and their clients become mystified. To remedy that situation, Chapter Ten helps the reader form a balanced appreciation of the proper role of these methods.

Throughout this book, the understanding of societal factors and methodological insights are equally stressed. Clearly, the future of evaluation will be shaped as much by broad social changes as by methodological developments. Chapter Eleven forecasts some of the impending social changes that will affect the practice of evaluation, the training of evaluators, and the needs of their clients.

This book owes a great deal to my teaching. For ten years I have taught a graduate course in evaluation, and I have been fortunate enough to have had an extraordinary number of very good students from a variety of disciplines, including practitioners and many full-time business and government people. Most were far more knowledgeable and proficient in some area or another than I, and I learned a great deal from them. The ideas in the book also have been refined in the crucible of my consulting work and my observations of the trials and triumphs of colleagues.

A number of people have been kind enough to read and comment in detail on various chapters of this book. They include Thomas Banta, Saul Benison, Ronald Boyer, William Dember, Joseph Foster, Goldine Gleser, Richard Honeck, Steven Howe, Paul Karoly, Edward Klein, Samuel Mantel, Zane Miller, David Ricks, Donald Rohner, Donald Schumsky, Marvin Schwartz, R. Joel Senter, Samuel Sherrill, Mary Stefl, Frank Tepe, Alfred Tuchfarber, Joel Warm, and Albert Yates. Their insights have greatly improved the book, and it is hoped that the reader will benefit from the broader perspective that their willingness to help me has provided.

A very special debt is owed to William Dember, who kindly read and commented on several versions of the entire manuscript and who gave steady encouragement and help over the entire course of writing the book.

I would also like to thank *Science* and Aaron Wildavsky for permission to quote extensively from a fine book review Professor Wildavsky published there ("Consumer Report," *Science*, 1973, *182*, 1335-1338). Thanks are due also to the *Journal of Applied Behavioral Science* for permission to use (in a revised form) portions of my article "The Politics of Evaluation Research: The Peace Corps" (*Journal of Applied Behavioral Science*, 1975, *11*, 261-280) in Chapter Five.

Special thanks are owed to the stalwart, patient, and conscientious people who typed the many versions of the manuscript: Garnett Pugh, Rebecca Lytle, Olive Beard, and Eve Ruppert. Cyma Khalily gathered together from my files the several hundred bibliographical references for this book and faithfully tracked down the missing ones. I am very grateful to her. The references cover a broad range of material from a variety of fields, and the reader will find them helpful in delving further into the issues addressed in this book. Since programmatic efforts of many kinds, such as training programs, executive development programs, and procedures for improving productivity, exist in business and industry, the references and the analyses and suggestions in this book should be helpful to business and industrial managers as well as to administrators of programs in the public sector.

Gunnar Myrdal, in "Diplomacy by Terminology," one of the many scintillating appendixes to his *Asian Drama* (1968), describes the debilitating effect of excessive politeness and of the use of euphemisms on the analysis of economic and social problems. I have tried not to err in that direction.

Cincinnati, Ohio   William R. Meyers
September 1981

Contents

~.

The Author

~~~~~~~~~~~~~~~~~~~~~~~~~~~~~~~~~~~

William R. Meyers is professor of psychology at the University of Cincinnati. He received his A.B. degree in history from Harvard College (1955). He completed two years at Harvard Law School and then received his M.A. (1960) and Ph.D. (1963) in clinical psychology from the Social Relations Department at Harvard University. From 1962 to 1967 he worked for Arthur D. Little, Inc., specializing in program evaluation in the public and private sectors. From 1967 to 1969 he was research director of the Peace Corps, responsible for all Peace Corps research in sixty-seven countries, and from 1969 to 1971 he was a lecturer on psychology in the Psychiatry Department at Harvard Medical School.

Meyers' research interests focus on program evaluation and have covered a broad span of programs. He has published work on alcoholism treatment, social ecology, urban renewal, health planning, industrial development, and the methods and politics of program evaluation. He coauthored, with Robert A. Dorwart, *Citizen Participation in Mental Health: Research and Social Policy* (1981). Meyers is an active evaluation consultant.

To my wife Susan, and my children, Steven and Sally.

The
Evaluation
Enterprise

A Realistic Appraisal
of Evaluation Careers,
Methods, and Applications

1

How Real Is the Need for Evaluation?

Evaluation is the effort to understand the functioning and effects of a program, which is a planned sequence of activities intended to achieve some goal. In this book, we will consider a range of programs far broader than is usual in discussions of evaluation. Most of the programs we will discuss, however, are social programs, that is, programs intended to ameliorate societal problems. Our initial question is, Is there a need for program evaluation? There is certainly a demand for program evaluation, but is it an appropriate demand and thus a true need? One's answer depends on whether one considers social programs as serious activities worthy of evaluation. That is the complex issue which we consider in this chapter and the next. For the moment, let us defer the question of whether social programs are worthy of evaluation and look at the evidence of the demand for program evaluation.

The Growing Demand for Evaluation

Prior to 1969, the federal government showed relatively little interest in evaluating federal programs and funded relatively few evaluations (Horst and others, 1974), but by 1972 a

1

great deal of funding was allocated to federal program evaluation. In 1969, the literature on program evaluation was very small; today it is extensive. These changes reflect political developments rather than advances in evaluation methodology. Taking office in 1969, the Nixon administration wanted to cut programs, partly in revenge against the Democrats and partly to save money. The new administration immediately showed a strong interest in evaluation, since it appeared to be a legitimate way to abolish programs. They believed that most social programs do not work and that logical analyses of costs and benefits would demonstrate that fact. Consequently they pressed for evaluation of existing programs; for example, the Nixon administration pressed for early release of the Westinghouse–Ohio University Head Start Evaluation, a program the administration wanted to discontinue. Nixon referred to these adverse findings in his first inaugural address.

A second motivation for the sudden interest in evaluation was the development of the planning-programming-budgeting system (PPBS), and its component cost-benefit analyses and cost-effectiveness analyses, at the Pentagon under McNamara during Johnson's presidency. The intellectual roots of this effort lie in the business world and in the business schools—McNamara was a former president of the Ford Motor Company and teacher of accounting at the Harvard Business School. After the use of PPBS at the Pentagon, Johnson issued an executive order, in 1968, requiring its use in all federal agencies. The data needed for the cost-benefit analyses required the evaluation of the outcomes of programs; indeed a major problem in implementing PPBS was that the necessary data were not available. Evaluation looked like the answer to that need.

A broader source of the increased demand for program evaluation is the growing public demand for accountability, an outcry that expresses the increasingly bitter antibureaucratic sentiment in the United States. Concurrently, protesting taxpayers object to programs designed to redistribute some of the nation's wealth by offering social benefits to poor Americans. Adherents of this view do not require that social programs be shown to be ineffective in order to oppose them, but if evaluation can help discredit some programs, so much the better. The taxpayers' revolt, the general antibureaucratic sentiment, and the traditional American wish to be free of external controls, fuel criticism of public bureaucracies that fund social programs. Those who demand evaluation in order to identify ineffective programs and thereby reduce bureaucracy point to two facts: The most frequent finding of an outcome evaluation is that the program did not work; and, in some programs, administrative costs approach the values of services provided to program recipients.

In assessing the causes of the new frenzy for evaluation, we must not neglect the growing conservative sentiment in the United States. This conservatism includes an antiintellectual, antiuniversity, anti-Ivy League, and antiliberal animus. Evaluation is one way to apply conservative, businesslike realism in order to abolish programs. In a sense, evaluators are hired guns, intellectuals paid to police the work of other intellectuals.

Clients' disappointment with social programs also has increased the demand for evaluation. Grandiose promises of equal opportunity, economic opportunity, the war on poverty, model cities, and the great society were followed by program failures. The clients, the target populations, felt deceived by the bureaucracy and then wanted to wrest control of the programs from the bureaucracy, or at least to find out whether the programs were good ones. Representatives of disillusioned client groups are a major force for the evaluation of programs so that the necessary reforms, for example, in welfare, can make them effective.

The results of all these forces on the evaluation field have been staggering. Wortman (1977) notes that between 1967 and 1972 Congress passed at least twenty-three acts requiring evaluation of federal programs; since 1972 all federal executive departments are required to conduct program evaluations. During fiscal 1975, according to Wortman, the federal government allocated over $130 million for evaluation. Federal funding of research on evaluation methodology and evaluation policy issues is growing, most notably in funding by the National Institute of Mental Health, but also by the National Science Foundation, the Peace Corps, the National Institute of Education, the Law

Enforcement Assistance Agency, and others. More recently, sunset laws have been proposed, which would require that each federal program terminate at a specific date unless Congress is persuaded by evaluative evidence that the program deserves to continue. A congressional bill proposing that all federal programs be evaluated at least every two years failed to pass, but a similar bill is expected to pass at a future session.

Some centralized evaluation activity is now undertaken by the federal government. The Office of Management and Budget (OMB) does not usually perform evaluations, but it enforces the policy that each agency is responsible for evaluating its own programs, and it reviews agency evaluations. In 1974, OMB established a central Evaluation Division to help with these tasks, as part of the agency's overall budgetary supervision and coordination. The General Accounting Office (GAO), which oversees fiscal matters on behalf of the Congress, conducts some evaluations for the Congress and appraises evaluations carried out by the federal agencies. If these are inadequate, of low quality, or overdue, the GAO conducts an evaluation.

Quality has been a serious problem in the evaluation field. The Law Enforcement Assistance Agency (LEAA) was forced to set up a committee, headed by a well-known methodologist, to evaluate the quality of the LEAA evaluations. As a result of the gross defects in evaluations carried out by agencies, legislatures are skeptical and the state audit, originally financial only, has expanded to include outcome-oriented evaluation. Audits by state legislatures of state programs are now of three kinds: a financial audit, to ensure that the money was legally and properly spent; a performance audit, to gauge the effectiveness or accomplishment of the programs; and a management audit, to assess the efficiency of operations.

Efforts at zero-base budgeting have also fostered evaluation. One of the first uses of this budgetary method was by the state of Georgia, during the term of Governor Jimmy Carter. During Carter's presidency, federal agencies were urged to introduce this method. Earlier efforts at zero-base budgeting in the federal government, notably in the Department of Agriculture (Wildavsky, 1975), and their marked lack of success pose questions that are examined in Chapter Ten. Essential to zero-base budgeting is the knowledge of which programs are effective toward what ends. This budgeting method therefore requires evaluative data and thus contributes to the evaluation boom.

The present wave of conservatism has implications for the growth of evaluation. A report of the Heritage Foundation, drawn up by some of President Reagan's staff, is analyzed in *The American Psychological Association Monitor,* January 1981, to which this discussion is indebted. The report, widely regarded as a manual for cutting programs and agencies, discusses the desiderata for evaluation under the present administration. It expresses concern that a high proportion of evaluations for the Department of Health and Human Services are designed to produce results favorable to programs dear to that agency. The report asserts that evaluations should focus on outcomes and not on the process by which programs function. The report notes that in general, "Program evaluations directed toward substance questions—does this program actually enhance self-sufficiency in the target population—should take precedence over process questions—how can the Meals-on-Wheels program delivery network be more efficiently established—in initial allocation of both research and evaluation dollars" (*In Transition,* 1981, p. 11). The report states that evaluation "should be directed toward discovering which programs have intrinsic merit, no matter how shabbily administered, and which could not do the job even if run by Peter Drucker [a leading management theorist]." In Chapter Two, we return to this distinction between program merit and program implementation, and discuss the difficulty of defining "intrinsic merit."

As a result of these various sources of demand, the evaluation profession is flowering, and this in a time of academic depression and marked antiintellectual sentiments in the population. In the 1960s, only two books on evaluation received much attention (Suchman, 1967; Hyman, Wright, and Hopkins, 1962). Now there are at least a dozen such treatises, new journals, and at least two annual reviews. The *Handbook of Evaluation Research* (Guttentag, 1975; Struening, 1975), in two volumes, is reputed to have sold over 15,000 copies in its first year; several similar compendiums have now appeared. A new professional society, the Evaluation Research Society, was formed in October 1976; by the end of the first meeting, it had several hundred members, and it is growing rapidly. A number of universities now offer doctoral and master's degree programs in evaluation research and postdoctoral and nondegree programs for experienced administrators. The National Institute of Mental Health has funded a series of summer workshops on evaluation, for professionals.

Thus, although evaluation once lacked academic respectability, now many social science disciplines claim it as a major concern. The growing interest in evaluation has attracted some very able people and led to a number of advances in methodology. It is apparent that many social programs do not work, and there is strong interest among scholars, the public, and government administrators in finding out which ones do work, and why. In this sense, social programs are being taken more seriously than previously, that is, their outcomes are deemed worthy of examination.

But there is another sense in which we must ask whether social programs are to be taken seriously: Are they seriously intended? The question arises because so many seem to fail. Programs to lift the poor from poverty have not changed the status of vast segments of our society. Programs to eliminate slums have failed. The problems of urban transportation are unsolved, for congestion increases daily. The white and middle-class flight to the suburbs continues unabated. Racial tensions continue high, despite some gains by some minorities. Programs to help Native American Indians have been counterproductive. The prisons go unreformed and remain violent schools for crime. The streets of central cities grow more dangerous. Billions of dollars have been allocated for programs to remediate these problems, with little apparent result. What is worse, ineffective programs continue to receive funds. We must ask how serious our social programs are if we tolerate repeated failure of the same program. Certainly no business firm would continue to finance the manufacture of products that did not sell; even if it wished to, clamor by the shareholders or impending bankruptcy would force a change of course. But the government need not fear bankruptcy; aloof from the marketplace, it seems content to repeat failures endlessly.

Social Programs

Some programs are doomed by their very nature, while others have a good chance of success if permitted to benefit from the self-correcting feedback provided by competent evaluation. A typology of programs may prove useful in understanding the need for evaluation and its likelihood of success. We distinguish four types of social programs: opportunity, restitution, redistribution, and holistic.

Opportunity Programs. The rationale for opportunity programs is that the poor or the disadvantaged are unable to take advantage of the opportunities presently available to them. Opportunity programs provide training or education intended to enable the disadvantaged person to cope with society. Such programs, of course, do not attempt to reform the institutional features of our society that produce poverty and oppression, such as racial prejudice by unions and corporate employers, discrimination in housing, and unequal school systems. Some observers charge that by locating the social inability in the disadvantaged person, opportunity programs are, to some extent, "blaming the victim" (Ryan, 1971); that is, the program's concept postulates that the moral shortcomings or emotional or cognitive deficits exist in these people, rather than in the institutions that keep them poor.

The notion of blaming the victim is not new, nor need we subscribe to it unreservedly. Any individual's cognitive or other deficits may have been produced by his having been exploited or treated in a discriminatory manner. If a society's institutions keep a group of people in a disadvantaged state, for example, by discrimination against blacks in hiring, then the institutions are likely to overwhelm the effect of the training program on individual blacks. The program may help a few to do better than they otherwise would have, but most will be unable to surmount the societal barriers. Thus the rationale for opportunity programs reflects either the planners' faulty understanding of social causation or their wish to do nothing while appearing to create change.

The scope of this defect of opportunity programs is broad and subtle. Head Start is in part vitiated by it, since the most important effect on these children's education is the unemployment or underemployment of their parents. But because opportunity programs try to create social change without changing institutions, the distribution of wealth, or discriminatory social arrangements, changes in employment practices, which may be essential to children's education, are taboo. Another feature of opportunity programs is a reluctance to give the disadvantaged anything tangible such as money or jobs. The only thing given is the opportunity to remedy some deficit that may not exist. Even if a deficit does exist—for example, a lack of skills—remediation is likely to be insufficient since trainees still must face the unchanged institutional structure. For example, evaluators discovered that after children finished Head Start, they still faced the unchanged school system.

Opportunity programs reflect middle-class moralism, which finds it convenient to locate the blame for exploitation in the victim, and the American individualistic bias, which says that anything can be achieved by a determined individual. Related to this bias is economic individualism, by which some economic theorists disguise the economic power of monopolies and oligopolies by analyzing the economic system as a free market of equal individuals operating with perfect knowledge. Opportunity programs also assume psychological individualism, which considers the individual the most appropriate unit of social analysis. A surprising number of social programs are based on the thinking, sometimes construed third-hand, of economists and psychologists of unalloyed individualistic persuasion.

We can expect that opportunity programs, because of their flawed conception of social causation, will be found by competent evaluation to be largely ineffective. Opportunity programs, unaccompanied by the necessary institutional changes, are largely a farce and a deception; Alinsky (1969) describes the War on Poverty as political pornography.

Restitution Programs. Restitution programs attempt to return people to a former status or to restore to them something they once had but have lost through no fault of their own. One instance is federal disaster relief, that is, aid to communities, individuals, and businesses that have suffered loss through earthquakes, floods, hurricanes, or other natural disasters. Mental health programs could be considered opportunity programs, locating the cause of the disadvantage within a person, but they can also be viewed as attempts to restore people to a healthy status they once had or are postulated to have had.

The rationale for restitution programs seems more realistic than that for opportunity programs, because the aid given to the recipients is specific, the deficit they have is verifiable, and recipients are to be helped to achieve a level of functioning they have already shown themselves to be capable of. Institutional reforms are not necessary, except those involved in the giving of the aid itself, such as financial assistance for businesspeople whose place of business was destroyed, or substitute housing or housing loans for householders whose homes were destroyed. No moralistic strictures cripple or constrict restitution programs, unlike opportunity programs, since the deficit is attributed to natural events rather than to the fault of the recipients.

In general, therefore, evaluators can expect that restitution programs are seriously intentioned and likely to succeed. One limitation on their success is any permanent or long-lasting psychological damage (depression, grief, survivors' guilt) produced by the natural catastrophe that cannot be remedied by material aid. But in most cases, one can expect that the material aid will have discernible and marked effects in restoring people to their former status.

Perhaps the largest restitution program was the very successful Marshall Plan to rebuild war-torn Europe. However, subsequent foreign aid programs to developing nations, although modeled on the Marshall Plan, have largely failed. These later programs were not restitution programs; rather they tried to lift nations to a status they had never before attained, a much more difficult undertaking, analogous to that attempted by opportunity programs and redistribution programs.

Redistribution Programs. Redistribution programs take resources from the more favored to give to the less favored, as with the negative income tax; or take from all to give to the favored few, as with tax breaks for business lunches and subsidies to the airlines. The essence of these programs is the redistribution of wealth. Redistribution programs differ from opportunity programs in that a direct benefit is given, not a promise of possible opportunity for some future benefit. Redistribution does not rely on the principle of restoration, but rather on principles of equity or moral duty, as with the negative income tax, or on claims that redistribution is beneficial or essential to the nation as a whole, as with airline subsidies.

The concept is simple and concrete: the transfer of assets to a favored group. The fact of the transfer is usually easy to establish, while the outcome of the transfer may be more complex to unravel. (For example: Would the airlines be more competitive and efficient without a subsidy? Would a negative income tax reduce the recipients' motivation to work?). But the evaluator is likely to have an easier time than with opportunity programs since the benefits conferred are tangible and not contingent on future opportunities. However, these programs are likely to be ineffective if social and institutional arrangements must be drastically altered for the transfer of assets to be successful. For example, for aid to developing countries to be effective, major reforms in land tenure and the reduction of corruption are essential.

Holistic Programs. Holistic programs use resources for the benefit of the community as a whole. They offer tangible benefits, not conditional opportunities in the future, and they do not aim to redistribute assets by taking them from some groups and giving them to certain other groups. Holistic programs benefit a community or society as a whole, as an interacting system, rather than benefiting favored groups. Examples are public health immunizations, programs for eliminating infectious diseases through water purification, and sewerage systems. Other examples are large-scale construction projects that seek to benefit a nation as a whole, like the Aswan Dam.

Evaluators analyzing holistic programs must realize that

the community, region, or nation—that is, a very large-scale interacting entity—is the unit of analysis for the evaluation. One may study particular individuals, as in immunization programs, but the central unit of analysis is the social system. Consequently, evaluators must develop some of their methodology from sociological and anthropological models.

If the scale of a holistic program is too small, or if insufficient resources have been committed to it, or if the wrong social system unit (or an imaginary one) has been chosen as the program's target, then evaluators should question whether the program is seriously intended. Consider Model Cities as an example. The program's goals are holistic, to benefit the community, but the areas chosen for the program are not natural communities; they are too small, and the determinations of the residents' socioeconomic status (occupation, income, employment, and housing segregation) are made by employers, unions, and slumlords who are not residents of the neighborhood. Consequently, it is questionable whether knowledgeable people ever really expected Model Cities to work. The analogy on which the program is based suggests the difficulties resulting from too small a program scale: Model Cities was entitled "Demonstration Cities" until the urban riots of 1968. Agricultural demonstrations pool a variety of program inputs (such as new seed, new fertilizer, new irrigation and cultivation patterns) in the same way that Model Cities combined inputs from a variety of earlier, more fragmentary programs. But agricultural demonstration programs, like Model Cities, typically have had great difficulty creating spontaneous change outside the demonstration area if they rely only on imitation and diffusion of innovation. Instead, additional resources are needed for each area that adopts the package of innovations.

Institutional Change. Some programs directly change the major social institutions that produce social disadvantage and social pathology. These programs are clearly serious and hence worthy of evaluation. An example is land tenure reform. This is a serious issue in underdeveloped areas like India and Latin America since many economists believe development cannot take place in these nations without giving landless workers a

share of land ownership. A contrasting program, whose seriousness can be questioned, is rural community development. Myrdal (1968) suggests that without land reform, rural community
development (and also the Green Revolution, incidentally) will
benefit primarily those who are already well off. In the United
States, a successful effort to better the living conditions of sizable groups—for example, the extension of constitutional voting
rights to blacks in the South—is not considered a social program. One wonders whether such efforts are not called social
programs because they are serious. Another melancholy and disturbing possibility is that programs that involve marked institutional change are not called social programs because social programs are expected to leave institutions as they are. Under this
view, social programs are programs designed to—and restricted
to—effect whatever changes are possible, if any, without disturbing the basic social institutions.

Can Evaluation Improve Programs?

The evaluator must face political conservatives, who view
evaluation as a means of cutting programs, and program proponents, who hope that an evaluation will testify that illusory programs are real and that ineffective programs are effective. There
is evidence of lack of seriousness about evaluation and about
the program in those program designs where the evaluation
component is added as an afterthought at the last moment, or
drastically underfunded. By drastically underfunded is meant
characteristic sums like three percent, or one percent, or even
less, of the program budget. Since we very rarely know in advance that programs will work well, a much greater share of the
program budget is needed for evaluation, to assess the wisdom
of the overall expenditure, and to suggest program improvements.

Certain categories of programs may not be intended seriously, and evaluators are called upon merely to supply the win-
dow-dressing. However, program evaluation has, at times, been
useful in improving programs. Despite the impracticality of
some evaluators and the sedulous reluctance of social agencies

to change anything, some evaluations are used by decision makers.

At the Cincinnati General Hospital Outpatient Clinics, thousands of patients are seen each month. There are long waits, misunderstandings, people waiting in the wrong line, and other reflections of an overloaded system whose clients are unsophisticated about the functioning of the system. An administrator assigned a social worker to wear a large button marked "Ombudsman" and roam the area, seeking to answer questions from befuddled patients, to direct them to the right clinic, and so forth. This innovation appeared to be of some help. A careful evaluation, by the social work staff, however, disclosed that a large proportion of the patients did not know what *ombudsman* meant. A new button bearing the legend "May I help you?" greatly increased the usefulness of the roving social worker.

Let us consider a larger program, the Peace Corps, which at any given time had community development programs in most of the sixty or so nations to which it sent volunteers. These programs were repeatedly evaluated, through a variety of methods, including questionnaires filled out by volunteers, visits by journalists, and case studies by social scientists. Results of the rural community development programs varied a good deal, depending on the culture, on governmental support, on the current political situation in the particular country, and on the staffing of the specific program.

There was a persistent trend, however, for community development programs in urban areas to be conspicuous failures. The urban environment was clearly less supportive of the volunteers' efforts than was the rural community. The urban community development programs were not abolished as a result of the first evaluations, scathing though they were. But a long series of negative evaluations, over several years, finally persuaded the Peace Corps to abandon urban community development efforts (which had failed in areas as diverse as Bombay and Guayaquil), and concentrate its community development efforts in rural areas, where they were often successful.

A more tangled illustration from the Peace Corps is the evaluation of the full-field background investigation (Meyers,

1975). Only a very simple security investigation of volunteer applicants is required by the Peace Corps enabling legislation, consisting mainly of inquiries at the local police station to determine whether the applicant has an arrest or criminal record. However, the Peace Corps in its early days informally assured Congress that a more thorough "full-field background investigation" would be carried out for each applicant being seriously considered. This procedure involved interviews by Civil Service investigators with people who knew the applicant at various stages of his or her life, at a cost of about $450 for each applicant, or some $4.5 million a year paid to the Civil Service Commission by the Peace Corps. Since the Peace Corps had to process and interpret the results, the total costs were greater still.

At congressional hearings in 1968, Senator Fulbright, on learning that only about ten persons were rejected each year *solely* on the basis of the full-field investigations, calculated that the cost per selectee was about $440,000, a figure he considered unreasonably large. The Peace Corps promised to continue research to compare the worth of the full-field investigation and the routine check of local police records; the latter cost only $15 per applicant, a savings of 97 percent.

Since the full-field background information was a factor, though not the sole or most important one, in many selection decisions, one can argue that the annual cost should have been measured against a larger body of rejected applicants than the ten rejected solely on the basis of the full-field. The research question is then whether the full-field had sufficient extra validity in predicting volunteer performance overseas to warrant the extra expense. Peace Corps overseas staff strongly objected to abandoning the full-field investigation, even for research purposes, since each overseas director feared receiving unsuitable volunteers.

Jones' (1969) study, using as a control group several hundred volunteers whose full-field reports arrived too late to be used in the selection decision, failed to show any difference in the overseas performance between those volunteers and a large sample of volunteers who had been selected partly on the basis of the full-field information. The Peace Corps' research division, which had been skeptical about the full-field on the grounds of redundancy and hostile to it because volunteers regarded it as a spylike intrusion, praised the study as a good justification for abandoning the costly full-field investigation. Other groups within the agency attacked the study because the control group was not randomly selected. But it was clear that careful evaluative research had failed to prove the value of the full-field, and that the burden of proof could reasonably be expected to be on the full-field, since it cost so much. After about a year of internal wrangling, the Peace Corps dropped the full-field, with some trepidation. Almost $5 million a year was saved, and there was no discernible decrement in the effectiveness of the selection procedure.

A domestic example of an evaluation used to improve a program comes from an evaluation of a system of citizen catchment-area boards concerned with mental health and retardation in Massachusetts (Meyers and others, 1972, 1974). The study assessed both the outcome of the efforts of these citizen boards to improve services and the process by which they functioned. The researchers report that the political activities of the boards were even more efficacious than overall planning, private fund raising, coordination of existing services, or independent efforts to create new services. Political lobbying by the boards resulted in changing previously crippling legislation, in producing sizable increases in state funding, and in obtaining large federal grants. A second finding was that the boards were in a condition of pluralistic ignorance; that is, each board was unaware of the efforts of the others and so could not learn from their experiences. Circulating the evaluation study findings to the boards increased their efforts at joint action and their political lobbying. One major reason the evaluation was used to change the system was that some board members had helped design the evaluation.

Let us conclude with an instance of an evaluation of a novel type that promises to be useful: a study of the functioning of a central city square, Fountain Square in Cincinnati (Howe, 1980). Complete with fountain statuary imported from Italy, the square is the focus of psychic identification with the city. It is the place most Cincinnatians would name as the center of the city and is the main gathering place for crowds to celebrate public events. As such, it is a modest member of a larger class of urban public squares, including Times Square, La Place de la Concorde, and Trafalgar Square. Fountain Square contains innovations in urban design, such as a very large and impressive system of elevated walkways, and the usual assortment of benches, balustrades, an arcade, and an atrium.

The findings indicate that the square functions in several ways unintended and unforseen by the designers. First, although the balustrades were not intended for sitting and do not meet the public engineering minimum specifications for that purpose, more people sit on them, because of their elevated viewpoint, than on the benches. Second, the walkways and arcade are functioning in the daylight hours as intended, to facilitate shopping; in the evening hours, however, they are the site of muggings and rapes. The evaluators recommend modifications in lighting and police patrols to improve public safety. They also recommend that future designs for seating in public squares recess some seats and benches and elevate them to give sitters an eye-level viewpoint slightly above the waist level of pedestrians. As this example indicates, a considerable range of social interventions could be improved by evaluation data.

Are Programs Seriously Intended? Is the Demand for Evaluation Serious?

If one accepts the conclusion that evaluation can and sometimes does improve programs, some interesting corollaries follow. Since a large proportion of social programs miscarry seriously or fail outright, in the opinion of the recipients and the general public, one would expect that social programs are regularly and expertly evaluated to effect improvements. But that is not the case. Despite increasing legislative and administrative pressures for evaluation, the quality of the vast majority of evaluations is lamentably low. Some are whitewashes of the program, others are evaluations in name only; many are conducted by people without research training or experience; most are drastically underfunded and subject to unrealistic deadlines. Some are subject to absurd constraints on method, such as limitations on who may be interviewed, and many are formulated by the funding agency in such a way that threatening questions cannot be addressed. The incidence of program difficulty or failure and the deplorable quality of the evaluations suggest that funding agencies are neither entirely serious about the programs nor entirely serious about evaluation. Evaluators therefore must take care that—in the formulation, design, and funding of the evaluation—they are not being co-opted by the agency. Evaluators cannot take good will for granted or disregard ulterior motives. Agencies may view evaluation as a form of advertising or public relations, and the evaluator must be careful not to become a flack as well as a flak-catcher. Evaluators face difficult problems in determining the seriousness, and even the intent, of the program drafters, legislators, administrators, and staff. Furthermore, the constituents who pay for the program and the recipients of the program may define the program differently than do the program designers and staff, and they may expect different outcomes from it. For example, one indicator of a fundamental flaw in the Model Cities program was that the recipients never expected it to do what the designers said it would.

We have sketched the history and development of the clamor for evaluation, and also examined the reality of the need for evaluation and the role it can play. In Chapter Two, we turn to a salient and infrequently discussed aspect of the need for evaluation, one which arises from the counterintuitive functioning of social programs. This concept is fundamental to this book and requires careful discussion.

2

Why Programs Fail

~.

Even when social programs are seriously intended, the nature of modern society is such that a large proportion of social programs function counterintuitively; that is, their results are quite different from the expectations of the program planners. For this reason, there is much social benefit to be derived from the evaluation of what a program is doing and how it is doing it. Let us consider the evidence that social programs frequently or typically function counterintuitively. In so doing, we will also deepen our understanding of what a social program is.

The proposition that social programs function counterintuitively is a corollary of the more general proposition that the world itself is an interacting social-technical system in which most interventions function counterintuitively. As subsystems within the larger world system, social programs interact with the larger system and with other subsystems in ways so complex that their results are unpredictable and counterintuitive. This assertion takes us into deep and murky waters that are unfamiliar to many evaluators. To make our case, we must examine the writings of some harsh, saturnine, insightful, and helpful thinkers. A review of these ideas will not solve evaluators' problems. Rather, our review will give us a more sophisticated and realistic understanding of how programs work.

Systems

In this chapter, we view social programs as subsystems in a poorly controlled world system. Ackoff's (1973) useful definition of a system comprises four characteristics. First, a system "has two or more parts. Therefore it is not an ultimate element or an indivisible part. It is a whole which has parts and may itself be part of a larger whole." Second, "Each part can have an effect on the behavior or properties of the whole." Third, "The effect that each part can have on the whole depends on at least one other part. . . . This is the property of interdependence." Fourth, any subgrouping of parts yields *subsets,* which have the same properties as *parts*: each can affect the whole, and the effect of each on the whole depends on the other subsets. "If the subsets are combined into larger subsets, they have the same properties" (p. 2).

Ackoff then wryly defines another concept: "A *mess* is a system of external conditions that produces dissatisfaction. A problem is an ultimate element abstracted from a mess. A mess can be conceptualized as a system of problems. Problems, even as an abstract conceptualization, do not exist in isolation: they are elements of a system" (p. 2). From the systems nature of messes follow some important conclusions. For one, the optimal solution to a mess is not the sum of the optimal solutions to its component problems treated independently of each other. As Ackoff points out, decision makers must cope with messes; problem solving is not enough, for problems do not stay solved, or they change while being solved, and each solution gives rise to new problems. Ackoff thus distinguishes problem solving from "mess management."

One may disagree with Ackoff's faintly quietistic emphasis, implied by his emphasis on management (which smacks of system maintenance) rather than solution. However, his fundamental insights are correct, supported by the abundant evidence that old problems are often transformed by their alleged solutions into new ones. Piecemeal approaches have proved futile. As Mannheim might have observed from a sociology of knowledge viewpoint, the systems formulation is what one would expect as the world in fact grows more interdependent and the autonomous Jeffersonian freeholder is no more.

Counterintuitive Consequences

The second component of the intellectual tradition from which we derive our view of the nature of social programs is the notion of counterintuitiveness. A prime exponent of this idea is Jacques Ellul, the French sociologist and a former leader of the French Resistance in World War II. In the English translation of his book *La Technique* (1965), the title was interestingly rendered by a less disturbing one, *The Technological Society* (1965). His book is an exposition, in trenchant prose and overwhelming detail, of the nature of technique. He defines a technique as "any complex of standardized means for attaining a predetermined result most efficiently" (p. vi); that is, the greatest result for a given effort, or a given result for the least effort. And "Technique itself is the totality of methods rationally arrived at and having absolute efficiency" (p. xxv). Thus, a technique is a rationalized method and it need not be mechanical. Examples of techniques include administration, city planning, propaganda, political campaigning, sales engineering, concentration camps (protective detention and reeducation as well as extermination), torture (we note here that Amnesty International has found that in at least thirty-two of the many nations practicing torture of political prisoners, there is medical supervision of torture), applied science, behavior modification, psychoanalysis, time-and-motion study, public opinion polling, sports and mass entertainment, Montessori, human engineering, personnel testing, motivation research, human relations, and vocational guidance, among others. Thus social programs of all sorts are techniques, and clearly, program evaluation itself is also a technique. Indeed, we can define evaluation as a measurement and feedback technique to improve and control other techniques.

Ellul depicts the state as the overall coordinator of technique. He notes that many techniques require state control, since they are inherently monopolistic and universalistic, such as propaganda, agricultural planning, city planning, and family planning. Too, a technique is inherently self-augmenting, for several reasons: because so much of a technique is under state control, because each technique begets others (for example, a technique may require computers, or modern administration, or training, or evaluation), and because each technical solution begets more and bigger problems. Garbage disposal units pollute the rivers, since the garbage goes down the drain. DDT kills insects but poisons animals who eat them; later in the food chain, people are then poisoned, and meanwhile DDT resistant strains of insects develop. A further illustration is the phenomenon of addiction to methadone. Addicts use it as a rest period before going back to heroin; also they sell it to get money to buy heroin. Ellul argues that solutions create new problems because we cannot possibly foresee the consequences of a given solution. Although this position may sound extreme, newspapers and history books provide many illustrations of Ellul's view. For example, public health programs in underdeveloped countries have lowered infant mortality rates, which has led to a population explosion, one of whose consequences is mass starvation. New agricultural technologies, such as so-called Green Revolution ("miracle wheat" and "miracle rice"), greatly increased crop yields for a while (and also increased agricultural unemployment), but when the price of oil quadrupled, fertilizer prices increased dramatically, and fertilizer imports by underdeveloped countries decreased. Since the new crop varieties required substantial amounts of fertilizer, many farmers were worse off than they would have been had they continued to use the old varieties that needed less fertilizer. At the same time, the denuding of wooded areas for firewood for fuel, a major phenomenon in Africa and Asia, increased erosion; in India, the increased use of cow dung for fuel left less available for fertilizer.

A large-scale example is the Aswan Dam in Egypt. As Sherrill (forthcoming) and Owen (1975) point out, the purpose of the Aswan Dam is to restrict the flood waters of the Nile, saving the water for release during the dry season into irrigation channels. Planners hoped to increase the agricultural production of Egypt, and, in fact, a 40 percent increase was achieved. But there were unintended consequences also. Owing to the year-round presence of water, the mosquito and black fly populations increased; in turn, the incidence of malaria and river blindness increased among people living or working near the irrigation channels. The aquatic snail population also greatly increased, causing an enormous increase in cases of schistosomiasis, a debilitating parasitical disease carried by the snails. About 80 percent of the villagers in the irrigated areas have schistosomiasis, and this figure is expected to rise to almost 100 percent. Already, about one death in ten in Egypt is caused by schistosomiasis (Sherrill, forthcoming).

Another major and very somber example can be taken from public health programs. In a classic article, Gruenberg (1977) argues that medical innovations and discoveries in disease control have raised the prevalance of certain diseases and disabilities by prolonging their average duration. For example, a disease increasing rapidly in prevalence owing to the great reduction in pneumonia is senile brain disease, which produces the mental condition known as senile dementia. Gruenberg speculates that this disease may have been the reason that the noted physician, Osler (1935), referred to pneumonia as the old man's friend. Gruenberg's conclusion is that the efforts of medicine to concentrate on abolishing killing diseases must now be supplemented with efforts to prevent the diseases and conditions that produce the chronically disabled. The evaluator would do well to examine programs whose dramatic successes may, in addition, entail such somber outcomes.

A final example is provided by a 1973 drug law in New York State that mandated life sentences for adult drug pushers. As a result of the law, according to the police, more adolescents, ages 9 to 16, have become engaged in the transfer and sale of addictive hard drugs. For them, the rewards are high and the risks low. The drug traffic, of course, continues unabated, and more children have become pushers. This case, like our earlier examples, shows that a program does not exist in isolation. A program exists in a context of other social forces, in a social system, and in an environmental and ecological system. Since program planners cannot foresee the overall consequences of a program, programs typically have unforeseen, counterintuitive, counterproductive consequences. (See Mosteller [1981] for some statistical studies that have concluded that low percentages of various classes of innovations have worked out as expected.)

Models of World Systems

Social programs must be understood as components of a complex system. When they are designed in isolation, evaluation will find that they function counterproductively. This proposition has been stated in mathematical form by Jay Forrester of M.I.T. Through computer modeling, Forrester gives mathematical expression to the ideas of systems and counterintuitive consequences. He argues that social systems belong to the class called "multiloop nonlinear feedback systems"; that is, there are many channels (loops) through which a result in the system can affect a cause in the system (feedback). As a result, a clear differentiation between causes and results is not possible. Also, the patterns of causation are nonlinear: a given increment in a causative variable will produce different amounts of effect on a second variable, depending on the initial level of both variables. Relationships between variables must therefore be expressed as complex curves, not as simple straight lines. Forrester believes that the human mind has not been adapted by evolution to understand multiloop, nonlinear feedback systems, which have become crucial only in very recent times. As a result, Forrester concludes, social programs often have effects the reverse of those intended.

Since we cannot think without models (overall conceptions of causes and effects) of some sort, and computers can process more complex models than our minds can, Forrester suggests that we ought to model social systems by computer before implementing them. If we do not know enough to construct such computer models, then we do not know enough to enact the program. For example, Forrester's (1961b) computer models show four urban programs to be useless or counterproductive: the creation of jobs by bussing the unemployed to the suburbs or by government as the employer of last resort; training programs to increase the skills of the lowest-income groups; financial aid to a depressed city, as by federal subsidy; and construction of low-cost housing. The model indicates that the fundamental problem is an excess of low-income housing in the central city; the moment conditions improve, population rises until the standard of living falls again. The solution is one opposite to that which is intuitively appealing. Instead of increasing the amount of low-income housing in the city, decrease it and increase income-producing land uses in the central city.

Not only is the construction of low-income housing in the central city counterproductive, but so are highway construction and loans for suburban housing, since they help the middle class to leave the city. While Forrester's solution might seem unfeeling toward the urban poor, one must remember that the financial disaster that has repeatedly confronted New York City is, in part, a result of its humane welfare policies. The city's shorter residency requirements and higher welfare subsidies attract a disproportionate share of welfare families. That problem can be solved only by a national welfare policy or partial municipal insolvency that forces New York to decrease welfare allowances to or below those of surrounding areas.

Forrester's model, *World Dynamics* (1971b), was presented at the first conference organized by the Club of Rome, a group of fifty leading industrialists, government administrators, and experts in crucial world problems, such as food, population, and economic development, who were concerned that the world's problems had never been considered in their interrelationships. Forrester concludes that "industrialization is a more disturbing force in the world ecology than is population. In fact the population explosion is perhaps best viewed as a result of technology and industrialization. I include medicine and health as part of industrialization" (1971b, p. 65). He suggests therefore that we may need to limit industrialization as the first step in gaining control of the runaway world ecological system. This viewpoint, consistent with that of Ellul, implies that evaluation is not simply a matter of seeing whether the program goals were met, for, if they were, that success may itself cause systemwide counterproductive consequences.

Ellul's and Forrester's views also suggest that the relevant time period for evaluation is much longer than popularly supposed, perhaps a decade or two, since undesired consequences may not appear immediately. Some programs have counterproductive consequences that pose difficult value conflicts for the evaluator. Public health programs that reduce infant mortality may later cause misery and loss of life through starvation because the population explosion outstrips the food supply. Forrester asserts that, by computer modeling of social programs, counterproductive and counterintuitive consequences can be foreseen and avoided; a proposed program can be redesigned until the computer model shows it to have a net balance of desired effects.

Critics of Forrester's approach point out that computer modeling is highly dependent on the assumptions underlying the model, many of which concern important properties of society about which there is no consensus. Under different assumptions, a program that has been modeled will appear to have entirely different consequences. A safe approach might be to use modeling for the purpose of stimulating thought about programs, not for reaching firm conclusions about how a program will work.

Limited Resources

Garrett Hardin, a biologist at the University of California at Santa Barbara, discusses the effects of limited resources within social systems. Hardin's law states simply that "you can never do merely one thing" (cited by Mesarovic and Pestel, 1974, p. 21). The fact that a program cannot do merely one thing makes the evaluator's life difficult. Programs are not nasty, brutish, and short; they are deceptively appealing, subtle in their operation, and their intended and unintended consequences are long-term.

Hardin's (1971) short discussion of a 1970 typhoon in East Bengal, which killed half a million people, illustrates the theme of limited resources. Pakistani parents replaced the net population loss in just 40 days, but the deaths were real. Hardin attributes these deaths to overpopulation, and views the typhoon as merely an intermediary cause. His argument runs as follows: Because of population pressure on the available land, people lived in the delta, which was so susceptible to flooding that it was unsuitable for human habitation. Similarly, in other countries, overpopulation leads to malnutrition that weakens people sufficiently to make many diseases so often fatal. Thus overpopulation—not flood or disease—is the true cause of many deaths in Asia and Africa.

Hardin's formulation gives pause to planners and evaluators. If these diseases are intermediate causes, with the primary cause being malnutrition, then if these diseases are stamped out, malnutrition will still weaken people, and other diseases will replace them as the listed cause of death. If, as Hardin argues, malnutrition is an inevitable result of overpopulation then the eradication of certain diseases will not decrease mortality rates unless the population increase is also abated. If malaria is wiped out, measles, dysentery, or even the common cold and respiratory infections will become greater killers.

Hardin's view is essentially a social and ecological systems view, in which a developing nation is a complex social system that returns to an equilibrium of susceptibility to disease (or floods) as long as the social programmatic intervention does not reduce the rate of population increase. Overpopulation and consequent pressure on agricultural resources create a reservoir of human misery which expands to fill any vacuum left by remedying any specific human ill.

The Commons, the Lifeboat, and Triage

Hardin has advanced other ideas important to evaluators. In "The Tragedy of the Commons," Hardin (1968) discusses the important ecological concept of the commons. For example, an individual farmer protects his land from overgrazing. But if public land is treated as a commons, that is, a place all may use freely and without regulation, then each farmer will graze more sheep on it until there is not a blade of grass left. Moreover, the more considerate farmer suffers more than the less considerate. If one farmer adds one more cow to the already overgrazed common, all the cows already there suffer, including any that he already has there, but the gain to his additional cow is greater than the loss to his other cows.

The commons is a generic situation in the ecological and economic context, Hardin points out. Air and water are now polluted because they are treated as a commons, and mechanized fishing fleets are depleting the oceans beyond their ability to replenish themselves. As Brown (1978) and the World Watch Institute note, people all over the world are using firewood faster than nature can replenish this resource, with increased erosion as an important side effect. Hardin believes that a proposed world food bank, currently being urged by developing nations, is a commons in disguise. The bank would be a food stockpile, under international control, to which the rich nations would contribute and from which the poor countries would freely draw. Hardin argues that nations would have more motivation to draw from it than to add to it. Population will grow in the less provident countries up to the level permitted by the food drawn from the food bank, and the more provident nations will suffer to pay for the improvidence (defined here as the absence of an effective population control policy) of the poorer nations, dragging all nations down to the level of the poorest. Population in the poorest nations will rise to consume the amount in the food bank, no matter how much there is. The world, Hardin says, is not a spaceship with all parts of the system on an equal footing. Rather, we and the other rich nations are in a lifeboat, surrounded by the drowning, poorer nations. If we let everyone, or too many, into the lifeboat—by sharing all food, or allowing free immigration into the rich countries—the lifeboat will sink and we will drown as well as those who would have drowned anyway. The underlying cause of the lifeboat situation (a particular conception of the world social system) is the different reproduction rates in different parts of the world. Hardin argues that if we share with all, we imperil posterity. We must save at least some parts of the world from environmental ruin. His overall prescription for the general benefit of the world is that everyone relinquish the freedom to have as many children as they wish. Failing this (and it does not seem likely to be adopted soon), Hardin advances as the next best solution his most disturbing conception of all: food triage.

Triage, derived from the French verb, trier, to sort, was a term used by French doctors in World War I to describe their procedure for allocating scarce medical resources at the battlefront. The wounded were divided into three groups: those who would survive without treatment, those who would probably die even if they received treatment, and those who would live only if they received treatment. The first two groups were given no medical treatment, and the scarce medical resources were given to the third group. It is harsh to refuse a dying man medical help, but with the great overload on medical services in the battlefield, triage probably saved more lives than a more evenhanded policy would have. In the modern equivalents of the battlefield, the emergency rooms of large metropolitan hospitals, the term triage is also used to decide whom to treat first.

Triage can be conceived of as a method of allocating the few available places in the lifeboat among the many claimants, given the premise that if all are taken aboard, the lifeboat will sink. Triage thus raises a profound question about the design and evaluation of social programs. If resources are scarce, either in actuality or in practice, should not scarce resources be allocated to those who appear to have sufficient vitality to benefit from them? Although the equal treatment and due process clauses of the Constitution would seem to prohibit triage as a deliberate policy in social programming, many programs function along such priority principles. Most programs reach a group of higher social status than the intended target group, partly because of the bias of the staff (less disadvantaged groups are easier to work with) and partly because those worst off are so overwhelmed by the environment that they are not aware of or are unable to take advantage of what help is available. Thus, the poorest usually have difficulty even getting transportation to the hospital emergency room or out-patient clinics.

Hardin applies triage to the world system, arguing that we should give food aid only to those who can be helped by it to self-sufficiency. He argues that food aid is wasted when given to India, whose population is growing by twelve million a year. Because food aid makes possible greater population growth, it enables more millions to reach the starvation level. Hardin's view is that, compared to a more even-handed policy, triage makes more help available to those who can become self-sufficient. This argument has produced rage and consternation among economic development programmers, who are strongly motivated to help those who need it most; that is, those who have least.

Hardin's position can be applied to development aid of all sorts, for the effect of any development aid on nations with uncontrolled population growth may be to subsidize greater population increase by enabling more people to survive long enough to reproduce. In support of the triage idea, the economic historian must admit that while the United Nation's "decade of development" fizzled in the 1960s with the developing nations falling further behind than before, the greatest success in the history of economic development aid is the Marshall Plan. In rebuilding war-torn Europe, this plan gave aid to those most capable of using it, nations with a large base of skilled workers and low rates of population growth.

Hardin is not alone in this sombre triage view. Forrester (1961b) also argues that food aid is not humanitarian, because it increases population. But there are strong proponents of the opposing view. Myrdal (1968) argues that food aid will increase productivity since malnutrition and illness now depress productivity. This reasoning is irrefutable, but it requires us to accept one further premise, that increased productivity will operate to lower the birthrate. At present this point is disputed.

For domestic social programs, one must ask if scarce resources (limited congressional appropriations and limited taxpayer generosity) are directed where they will do the most good (to people who can thereby become self-sufficient), or to the most needy (and perhaps least likely to become self-sufficient), or to those constituting the strongest political pressure groups. The evaluator, knowing that resources are limited, must judge whether a program is aimed at the appropriate target group. Some groups, such as preschool children, have no votes and no political power. Someone must assess and balance the interests of these groups against other groups.

The concepts of the commons, triage, and the lifeboat have great relevance for evaluation. Triage asks whether it is reasonable and moral to direct a program to those other than the most needy, to attain greater effectiveness in the use of scarce resources. The lifeboat image reminds us of the tendency of the givers to go under if they try to give enough to meet all the unmet needs, with the result that no one is saved. The notion of a commons emphasizes the tendency of population pressures to be increased by the act of giving, so that the commons can never be sufficient. Since pollution of the air and water can be conceived of as dumping into a commons, the commons analogy is very broadly applicable.

The evaluator must take into account the systems consequences of limited resources. Programs whose existence increases demand—so that no matter how fast the program expands, demand rises to outstrip it—must be evaluated somewhat gloomily. An example is the one chosen by Forrester: the more low-income housing is constructed in the central city, the more low-income people are attracted there, swelling the ranks of the unemployed. Differential migration of the poor to those areas of the country that offer the best social services, namely the already overloaded major central cities, may sink the lifeboat through urban insolvency. At the national level, Hardin points out that unrestricted migration between nations would swamp the rich nations and reduce all to poverty. It is no accident that the United States has since 1922 restricted immigration from the poorer nations and is currently endeavoring to close off the annual tide of 800,000 illegal immigrants from Mexico.

The Club of Rome Models

The proposition being considered here is that social programs exist in a systems reality, and program consequences, often counterintuitive and counterproductive, are determined by the program's interrelations with the other parts of the social system. Meadows and others (1974), in the first of three reports commissioned by the Club of Rome, have stated this proposition in its most general form. Meadows conceives of the world as a complex system which has become so deeply interrelated that any major social intervention, such as a nation's population policy, energy policy, or agricultural policy, has effects highly dependent on the rest of the system. Meadows and his colleagues define a model as an ordered set of assumptions about a complex system; their proposed model is precise and quantitative, so that a computer can play it out.

The work of Meadows, like that of Forrester, can be described as sired by Malthus out of a computer. The importance of the influence of Malthus is aptly put by Hardin (cited in Cole and others, 1973, p. 217). "Malthus has been buried again. (This is the 174th year in which that redoubtable economist has been interred. We may take it as certain that anyone who has to be buried 174 times cannot be wholly dead.)" Malthus' central idea is that population increase will outstrip resources. Meadows and Forrester go one step further, arguing that the exponential growth of resources, even if it could keep up with population growth, would itself undermine the world system. In Meadows' model, the five basic factors that determine growth on this planet are population, agricultural production, natural resources, industrial production, and pollution. Meadows and his colleagues argue that if something serious goes wrong with the world system, local programs will collapse, so it is foolish to concentrate only on local problems. To the evaluator, this position means that the world system is a program or combination of programs (raising children, growing food, producing goods and services) that needs to be considered as a system as well as evaluated separately.

The model considers general behavior modes, not exact results; it uses a high level of aggregation, such as treating all pollutants alike, using general population trends, and so forth. The key determinant of the model is a feedback loop that relates causative variables to each other, such as the influence of population growth on industrial production and vice versa. The exact numbers used in the model to quantify variables are not crucial in determining the outcome of the model. Meadows' group asserts that the quantification of variables may affect the *period* of an oscillation in the system, or the *rate* of growth, or the *timing* of a collapse but does not affect the fact that the basic mode of behavior of the system is oscillation, or growth, or collapse. The aim of the model is to predict behavior modes, not exact timing.

The conclusions of Meadows' model are that the limits to growth will be reached within the next hundred years, if present trends continue. When the limits are reached, or before, the world system will collapse into chaos, starvation, and industrial breakdown. Specifically, the standard run of their model predicts overshoot (excessive growth of some system components) followed by collapse as the behavior mode for the world system. The depletion of nonrenewable natural resources will lead to collapse of the agricultural and industrial production systems; as the food supply decreases, population will decline. The results do not vary much under assumed changes that might result from technology, such as increased natural resources or reduced pollution. Reruns of the standard model, with various of the initial quantitative assumptions changed, still result in collapse. For example, if we double the amounts of natural resources assumed to exist, collapse of the world system occurs at about the same time (in less than a century), this time from pollution and lack of food. If we assume that nuclear power will double the resource reserves that can be utilized and that there is extensive recycling and resource substitution, a new run of the model shows that the system will still collapse within a century because of pollution. Finally, a run of the model with doubled resources, reduced pollution, increased land yields, and perfect birth control still shows a collapse at about the same time owing to gradual resource depletion and pollution.

In sum, all the runs of the model show that the basic behavior of the world system is exponential growth of both population and capital, followed by collapse. The inevitable delays in the feedback loops between each cause and its ultimate effects are the cause of overshoot. System components such as population or capital or pollution grow before the rest of the system can react to stop the growth, and these components rise to levels intolerable to the rest of the system, causing the system to collapse.

Meadows argues that there are no technological solutions to the problems of the world system; social changes are necessary. Although some technological changes can be instituted rather quickly, the social system cannot adapt to them in time to prevent unforeseen and unwanted consequences, often greater than the original problem. For example, Meadows points out that widening inequality is among the "side effects" of the Green Revolution, since the new crops give a differential advantage to the larger farmer. Other side effects are agricultural unemployment since the machinery needed is labor displacing and since the smaller farmers fail to compete successfully. Increased urban migration is a result, and ironically, there even may be increased malnutrition owing to increased unemployment. The Meadows team quotes Hardin's definition of side effects as "effects which I hadn't foreseen or don't want to think about" (Meadows and others, 1974, p. 146). They argue, as he does, that the side effects are as direct a consequence of the systems nature of programs as are any other kind of effects. More systems-oriented social planning and evaluation is required.

Thus technical improvements, including social and economic programs, are insufficient and may even be counterproductive, unless capital growth and population growth are halted. Evaluators must understand not only a program's immediate effects but also its interaction with the world system. Public works programs, such as highway building, may be successful in reducing unemployment, but may act to hasten the collapse of the world system by accelerating the depletion of nonrenewable resources like oil. Alternative public programs, such as forest conservation, may have a smaller immediate effect on reducing unemployment but a more positive effect on the world system and on this subsystem, our nation, in particular.

There is another way of showing that the world system cannot be saved by purely technical solutions. Let us look only at the current situation, ignoring both continuing population growth and the effect that Hardin says a world food bank would have on accelerating that growth. Current technology has already "solved" the present world food crisis: all that remains are the social reforms to distribute the food properly. Lappe

(1978) notes that world grain production alone (not counting meats, vegetables, root crops, nuts, and other foods), if evenly divided and distributed, would provide 3,000 calories a day for every man, woman, and child in the world. The problems are ownership and distribution of the food.

Critics of Meadows' model have not been convincing. For example, Cole and others (1973) argue that pollution-free solar energy is possible. But they do not consider that an infinite amount of solar energy would be needed if the population increases exponentially. In addition, there would be heat pollution from the spill-off of solar energy, so it would not be pollution free. Cole also argues that birthrates will decline before the system collapses, owing to the lower quality of life or to improved economic status. But those two reasons are mutually contradictory.

Meadows' model indicates that since all production involves some use of land, some pollution, and some depletion of nonrenewable resources, exponential capital growth or population growth will eventually overwhelm any technology. Indeed, Meadows' conclusions are a logical and necessary consequence of the nature of exponential growth. Any system will collapse under exponential growth. Evaluators must realize that many programs increase, not decrease, the rate of exponential growth, particularly in capital growth and resource utilization. Examples are construction programs, most economic development programs, and many public health programs. Among the programs that do not operate in this way are those that increase services rather than the production of goods, since services usually require less capital formation and hence less depletion of nonrenewable resources. Manpower training programs for computer programmers may have better long-run system consequences than the training of construction workers or auto assembly line workers.

The Second Report. The second report to the Club of Rome (Mesarovic and Pestel, 1974) views the world as a global system with ten well-defined regional subsystems, rather than as a homogeneous system. Instead of a collapse of the world system in the middle of the next century, as Meadows predicts,

Mesarovic and Pestel predict that regional collapses could occur, possibly much sooner, and such catastrophe would profoundly affect the world system and perhaps cause its collapse. By analogy, consider a table that is subjected to ever increasing weight. Meadows predicts the whole table will collapse at once; for Mesarovic and Pestel, since the legs are of unequal strength, some will collapse far sooner than others, bringing down the whole table.

To avoid regional collapse followed by world system collapse, Mesarovic and Pestel believe concerted global action is necessary. Instead of a halt to growth, as urged by Meadows, or exponential growth as is the current trend, Mesarovic and Pestel urge organic growth. Organic growth they define as differentiated growth, with some parts of the world, the developing nations, growing for a while, while others stop growing now. The report addresses in some detail the economic changes that will have to be made—for example, the resort to "intermediate technology" (small-scale decentralized industry) as propounded by Schumacher. It also devotes some attention to the political steps that will have to be taken to bring about the needed policies. A reformulation of the world system with more attention to the subsystems gives the evaluator all the more reason to appraise programs in terms of their systems effects. Since some subsystems are more vulnerable than others, the danger to the overall system from programs that miscarry or from the absence of needed programs is greater than if marked subsystem differences did not exist.

The Third Report. The third report to the Club of Rome (Tinbergen, 1977) focuses on the disparity between rich and poor nations in the world system. The message of the report is that the long-term interests of all nations are tightly interlocked. Unlike Hardin, Tinbergen believes that if the rich nations neglect the poor ones, armed conflict and the invasion of the rich nations by the poor are inevitable. Food and energy are the most crucial items to be shared. Because of the interdependencies between rich and poor and the disparity between them, a new international economic order is needed. Tinbergen favors a gradual reduction of growth in the rich nations and an accelerated growth rate in the poor ones, so that in forty years the disparity of income between them will be reduced from about 13:1 to about 3:1.

Tinbergen believes that the new world economic order will work only if there is much less conspicuous consumption in the rich countries. For example, insulation should be used instead of fuel, and soybean products substituted for most of the meat consumed. His report argues that drastic changes are essential since economic analysis shows that the fate of the rich and the poor nations are interlocked and that continued neglect of the poor nations will bring on the collapse of the world system.

Implications for Evaluation. Whether or not one believes such reforms are likely, several principles impress themselves on the evaluator. A program must be evaluated not only with respect to its own stated goals but also with respect to a larger system. In looking at the effects on a larger system, one acquires more insight into unintended consequences, since many of these occur because of the program's interaction with the larger system. One also better understands the meaning of the program goals. It is important for the evaluator to view the announced program goals as intermediate steps in a causal sequence and examine the subsequent steps in that sequence by looking at the larger system. For low-income public housing in the central city, one needs to consider how the economy of the city is affected by potential increased migration into the central city or deferred emigration out of it, by isolation of residents from job opportunities, by stigmatization of residents based on where they reside, and by increased economic and racial ghettoization. The viability of the urban economy has regional implications, and urban public housing programs have to be evaluated in a regional context. Social programs can have metropolitan, regional, and even international consequences.

A new element that is emerging from the interactions of the world system is programming by compulsion, as when the developing nations attempt to force the developed ones to establish a world food bank by threatening to increase oil prices. Recently, the international community has taken a more lively interest in each nation's internal programming. For example, the weakness of the dollar in international markets in 1980 was due, in part, to other nations' reactions to the lack of an effective energy conservation policy by the United States. The day is apparently approaching when some of a nation's internal social programming may be dictated by compulsion from outside. Evaluators may have to take into account international repercussions of program outcomes.

Counterintuitive Implementation

There is evidence that the larger social system affects not only the consequences of a program but also its actual implementation. As a result, the program as carried out may bear little resemblance to one designed by the administrators or enacted by the legislature. Alternatively, implementation may fail entirely, that is, the program designed may never be carried out. Pressman and Wildavsky (1973) have addressed this issue in a book entitled *Implementation: How Great Expectations in Washington are Dashed in Oakland; Or Why It's Amazing that Federal Programs Work at All, This Being a Saga of the Economic Development Administration as Told by Two Sympathetic Observers Who Seek to Build Morals on a Foundation of Ruined Hopes.* The book is appropriately illustrated with Rube Goldberg cartoons showing the absurdly roundabout ways that can be devised to achieve everyday objectives (like pouring a glass of water or lighting a cigar). Since the failure of a program to be implemented as envisioned is a major analytic problem confronting evaluators, let us summarize Pressman and Wildavsky's findings.

They consider two Economic Development Administration (EDA) programs in Oakland, California: a public works program to construct an aircraft hangar and a marine terminal, and a small business loan program. The programs were designed and begun in 1965; the terminal and hangar were still incomplete five years later even though $20 million had been committed by EDA for their construction. The purpose of the programs was to produce jobs for hard-core unemployed minorities, yet the construction program produced only about 800 jobs for

$20 million and the loan program produced 43 jobs for over $1 million expended by EDA.

Pressman and Wildavsky contend that implementation is very difficult, even in "normal" circumstances like these. The greater the number of clearance points needed, the lower the probability that the program will succeed. They calculate that even if there is a 90 percent probability of approval at each point, if seven clearances are needed the probability of program completion is less than .5. If seventy clearances are needed, as with the public works program, the probability of success is about .0006. This holds true even though all parties agree on the program goal, reflected in the high probability of each individual clearance.

Why do some clearances fail, killing the program or holding it up until they can be renegotiated? Competing and conflicting program commitments by the parties involved, dependence on some parties with a low sense of urgency, and the appearance of new and unforeseen participants—all contribute to delay. Also involved are differences of opinion among and within the parties about leadership, organization, and legal and administrative differences. These problems are mostly concomitants of the very indirect way in which a public works program functions. Instead of providing capital grants and loans to contractors in exchange for their promises to employ minorities in the resulting construction projects, the EDA could have simply subsidized the payrolls of local firms with minority employees.

A host of problems afflict the implementation of programs even when the causal chain is short. These include undue speed, that is, the haste to spend the budget before the end of the fiscal year, so that Congress will not reduce future appropriations. Turnover in personnel, vague legislation, severe understaffing, racial tensions, conflicts between local field offices and Washington, conflicts between local government and federal government—all these factors affect implementation.

Pressman and Wildavsky argue that many urban programs represent a kind of foreign aid within America, with all the usual problems besetting foreign aid. One side has limited resources to donate and the other has limited ability to spend aid wisely, but both err in the direction of the grandiose, partly because both are panicked by the need to do something immediately, owing to the atmosphere of crisis. In Oakland, the crisis was the fear that unemployed blacks would riot, as in Watts. As with foreign aid, the criterion of success for the funding agency seems to be the ability to spend the allotted budget on time. One implication for evaluators is that evaluations of long-term effects need to be accompanied by evaluations, using special methods, that give very early feedback on how the program is doing. Another common error is for the funding agency to overestimate the degree of local support for the program; often local pressure to make the program work is not forthcoming.

In addition to federal grandiosity and inadequate local support, the divorce of implementation from policy causes programs to fail. The way to avoid the last is to incorporate implementation, which is not merely a set of technical details, in the initial formulation of policy; the plan for implementation must be part of the program design. How does one do this? Pressman and Wildavsky suggest planners find more direct ways of accomplishing the desired ends, with fewer clearance points and fewer organizations. They also suggest planners pay as much attention to designing organizational machinery for implementation as they do to creating the organization that designs the program. For example, the high-powered people who designed the program should remain for the implementation. High turnover in the federal government adversely affects programs. In the federal government, the fastest way up the career ladder is to change jobs every eighteen months, a period just long enough to establish that one has held the job, but not long enough to face the consequences of the failed programs. High federal turnover means that an agency loses its memory as people depart, and new people have little stake in making other people's programs work but much in establishing their own new programs.

Pressman and Wildavsky suggest that programs start with "local unity, federal modesty, and an excess of resources over requirements" (p. 146), rather than the opposite. But if cities continue to be internally disunited, and urban problems continue to be major, there will continue to be pressure to program hastily. Although some difficulties can be avoided by good planning, a number of difficulties are inherent in the federal and local political structure, in the socioeconomic system (conflict between interest groups), and in the world system (shortage of resources to meet needs).

I believe that the difficulties of implementation notwithstanding, there is a more fundamental cause for the failure of the Oakland programs: The program designers did not understand the problem they sought to remedy. The programs were intended to reduce unemployment among minority hard-core unemployed, but planners did not have a clear idea of what causes unemployment, and consequently could not know at what point in the causative chain to intervene. It is the absence of a clear theory behind the program that necessitates the use of elaborate, flawed, seventy clearance-point, Rube Goldbergian program designs. Pressman and Wildavsky perceive the theoretical difficulties in the programs but they do not see them as causative of the implementation difficulties.

The EDA was experienced in aid programs for depressed rural areas but had little urban experience, and consequently failed to recognize that Oakland was not a depressed region, but rather a depressed neighborhood in an affluent region. Therefore the EDA's offer of low-cost capital to capital-intensive industries would lead to more capital intensiveness, that is, automation, and fewer jobs. A depressed region, such as Appalachia, has both a surplus of cheap semiskilled labor and a capital shortage, so additional capital there would create more jobs. But in Oakland, a depressed neighborhood in the midst of the prosperous East Bay region, any new jobs would go to the more highly skilled members of the work force, not to the untrained minority unemployed. Poor implementation was a result of the lack of adequate social theory, not a factor in addition to it.

Advice for the Evaluator

What can we learn from this chapter? Programs are often not meant seriously. Programs usually fail to achieve their aims. Programs often operate counterintuitively. Programs are often counterproductive. And programs are tough to implement. The root cause of all these failings is the same: poor program designs. Designs are poor because we sometimes lack adequate theories about social causation that would enable us to design effective programs, or we disregard the theories we do have. As programmers, we often do not know what we are doing. And sometimes we lack the courage, the determination, or the power to design workable programs even when we do have the necessary theory. While good evaluation cannot give us courage, it can tell us why programs are succeeding or failing, and so help us formulate some of the needed social theory. Good evaluation, like good programming, is not primarily a technical matter; it must be informed by substantive social theory. That view forms a central theme of this book.

3

Economics of the Profession

~·

In Chapter One, we discussed the need for evaluation, and in Chapter Two, we considered the nature of the social programs that give rise to this need. In analyzing that need, we looked at the recent growth of evaluation as a career field and the current pressures for continued growth of the evaluation profession. In this chapter, we examine in more detail the economics and sociology of the evaluation profession. Our purpose is to help the reader understand more about how evaluators usually function, and how they must or should function in order to be able to evaluate programs helpfully and without too much hazard to their own careers or those of the innocent. This presentation lays the basis for Chapter Four, in which we examine the political and administrative settings of evaluation. Our broad goal is to provide insights that will help the evaluator evaluate better and help the administrator use the evaluation results more intelligently.

The Scope of Evaluation

It is not at all obvious that the proper scope of program evaluation is exclusively governmental, as is often assumed. There is substantial opportunity for the practice of program evaluation in the business community. Over half of our gross national product is in services, and the quality of the services provided and the process by which they are provided are appropriate fields for evaluation. For example, How effective is life insurance coverage? How well do the insured understand the policies? How are the proceeds of life insurance usually spent? Groups such as Nader's Raiders, who do a rough-and-ready sort of evaluation, apply this approach not only to industrial products, such as automobiles, and to government programs, such as those of the National Institute of Mental Health, but also to business service activities. But more objective, scientifically defensible methods can also be applied in this area, with improved results.

Although evaluation is not exclusively governmental in its potential scope, the great bulk of the current demand for evaluation concerns governmental programs. In Chapter One, we discussed the political forces that create a demand for evaluation, such as the taxpayers' lobbies and the growing conservative climate. Also important in creating a market for evaluation are sellers of evaluation—the consulting firms and the evaluation profession.

Consulting Firms

A large proportion of evaluation for federal agencies is not done in-house by research staff but under contract or grant to outside persons or institutions. Generally, the government prefers to deal with firms or institutes rather than individuals, on the grounds that firms and institutes have more flexibility of talents available and are less subject to the difficulties caused by illness or scheduling. Firms tend to be less affected by the vicissitudes that plague individual careers. And the federal government increasingly prefers to fund evaluation by contracts rather than grants because contracts give the agency greater control over the nature of the work and over the content and timeliness of the final report (see Meyers, 1975).

A key factor affecting the evaluative performance of consulting firms is profit. The social research industry is more extensive than usually realized (Kalish, 1969), comprising at least

500 firms, scattered throughout the nation, with heavy concentrations in Cambridge, Santa Monica, Palo Alto; and especially Washington, D.C. Those in Washington are often called the "beltway bandits" because so many are located on the circumferential route surrounding Washington, and because of their entrepreneurial willingness to accept assignments bearing little relation to their previous competence. The intense competition for contracts, leading to work overload and much inefficiency, is an important factor in low quality. Let us trace the operation of these economic pressures.

Federal agencies are required to hold competitive bidding on all government-sponsored research contracts, except when the agency can make a strong showing that a particular firm is the sole source of the expertise and experience needed, based on unique or pioneering work in a particular area. An agency usually cannot make a case for a sole-source evaluation contract that will stand up to the claims of rival research institutions. Thus an agency may receive scores of bids and proposals for a given contract. The agency's staff must choose one proposal as better than all others on explicitly stated, legally defensible criteria. This system leaves all but one of the bidders disappointed, perhaps irritated, and usually uncertain as to why they failed. It leaves the agency staff with the guarded attitude of people under siege, wishing to divulge as little as possible that might give an unsuccessful bidder ammunition to challenge the fairness of the selection process. Suspicion and confusion result on both sides.

The standard consultant's view appears to be that government administrators are imbeciles or bumpkins, while government and industrial clients perceive the research firms as sharks in a feeding frenzy (Meyers, 1975). This mutual distrust inhibits collaboration and makes for lower-quality evaluations. During the rush at the end of the fiscal year, agencies try to spend the remainder of their allotted budgets lest Congress reduce subsequent years' appropriations by an amount equal to the unspent funds. At this time of year, pandemonium reigns, with rushed and silly requests for proposals and equally rushed and silly proposals in response.

The bidding system, with so many bidders for each contract, compels a firm to make many bids on a broad spectrum of topics in order to win enough contracts to stay solvent. It is not unusual for more than half of the professional hours spent by a firm to be devoted to writing proposals and bids. These costs must be recouped from any contracts won. The result is less time for the firm to work on contracts it does get, and lower quality in that work. However, if a firm consistently manages to do a good job, word spreads among research administrators in related agencies, and subsequent proposals by the firm are viewed favorably. The firm will then find its sales costs rapidly diminishing because a high percentage of its proposals results in contracts. The savings in sales time makes available more professional time for working on the contracts, thus strengthening the firm's ability to produce high-quality evaluations.

Considerations of profitability often lead consulting firms to attempt to be jacks-of-all-trades, with the result that they master few. Lacking substantive competence in a particular field, the firm (if awarded the contract) must try to teach itself that field, such as economic development, race relations, or public health, while it works on the contract. Firms often try to compensate for their inexperience by hiring specialist consultants for the evaluation team, but specialists are more expensive than employees and are thus used irregularly.

Grants and Contracts

Today most evaluation for governmental agencies is done under contract, although formerly grants were often used. The distinction between a research contract and a research grant has many consequences for evaluation, including the nature of the product and the staffing. Legally, the recipient of a research grant must pursue the general purposes and adhere to the scope of the grant. However, the grantee has considerable latitude in modifying the methodology specified in the grant application and in modifying the scope of the work. The grant system is ideal for basic scientific research because there is a very large element of the unknown, and the problem may need to be redefined drastically during the research. Because grants have comparative freedom and flexibility, federal agencies usually do not award them to for-profit firms. When grants are given at all, they tend to be given to nonprofit institutes and to university research teams. Even in the awarding of contracts, many agencies prefer to work with nonprofit groups.

The precise legal nature of contracts has an important influence on the evaluation process. There are at least two main types of research contracts: one commits research contractors to deliver a specified product at a specified date; the other commits them to use their best efforts to produce a specified product at a specified date, but does not commit them to produce the product successfully. Under both contracts, the researcher is accountable for the exact nature of the product specified and for using the exact research methodologies specified in the contract; a contractor is not permitted to deviate from the contract without a written authorization from the agency. Any unauthorized change or failure to meet a deadline subjects the contractor to one or more modes of redress by the contracting agency, including cancellation of the contract, withholding of payment for work already performed, or suit for breach of contract.

In contrast, a research grantee is rarely held to the exact date of delivery and is often accorded extensions of time. If a grantee fails to produce, the grant may be terminated early, or may not be renewed, but the grantee is rarely subject to suit for breach of contract or to withholding of payment for work already performed or expenses already incurred. Because the grant provides greater freedom, as well as lesser financial risk, it is usually easier to involve academics directly in the grant system. Because university people are more likely to be nationally known specialists in a particular field than are research firm employees, the grant system is used to involve experts, although some firms do use expert scholars and academics as consultants on a regular basis. And some nonprofit institutes, such as Brookings, have a permanent or temporary staff of widely known specialists. But as research money is scarce, universities are becoming more willing to accept contracts when grants are unavailable.

Other aspects of research contracts deserve note. The provisions giving the agency the right to cancel without notice, to withhold payment for nonperformance, and so forth, are not subject to individual negotiation by the contractor. Rather, the federal government has standard provisions, called "boilerplate," which are preprinted and attached to every research contract. These provisions, however, are rarely rigidly enforced in research contracts. Contractors, especially university people, often deliver the product, the final research report, after the deadline, usually without penalty. The practical problems of holding a research contractor to the time provisions of a contract are so great that many contracts require interim reports, with funding conditional on receipt of an acceptable interim or progress report.

A more intractible problem is quality. Sometimes a consulting firm delivers its report on time, but its quality is often lamentable. Occasionally, the agency returns the report for revision, but this is usually of cosmetic value only, as it is too late to remedy defects in the quality of the data gathered. If the data-gathering methods are inadequate, the report is useless, misleading, or uninterpretable.

Sometimes a basically sound report is returned to the consultant for additional analyses of the data in order to clarify certain issues. Such collaboration between evaluator and agency is constructive. More often, however, evaluation reports are "sanitized," that is, the report is changed to please the agency. Material adverse to the program or the agency is dropped; sometimes material complimentary to the agency is substituted. Sanitization is sometimes done by the evaluator at the request of the agency. To facilitate this process, many agencies require the evaluator to submit a draft of the report for approval or consultation before the final report is submitted. Some agencies sanitize the final report themselves before "disseminating" it. Others do not release final reports or release them only to a select in-house audience. By a standard clause, some research contracts explicitly limit the right of the contractor to publish the report, even in scientific journals, without prior approval of the agency. Such approval is sometimes contingent on the evaluator's acceding to requested changes in the report. All these provisions and practices have the effect of intimidating evaluators, as well as directly and indirectly censoring their work. Agencies have more control over the final report of a contractor than a grantee, since most grants in effect promise a best-efforts attempt, not an acceptable final product.

Although grantees are often experts and in addition are less susceptible to intimidation or to having reports rewritten, there are inherent disadvantages to the grant system as a method of funding evaluation research. Since research grants are deliberately vague about the product promised, to allow the researcher freedom to explore the problem and change strategy as new facts emerge, the agency has little control over the course of the research, much less the content of the report. As a result, the research product may express the interests and career needs of the researcher but, through subtle and usually unintentional misformulations, may not provide the needed evaluation information to the agency. Grants are more suited to basic research than to answering questions about specific decisions that need to be made by the agency.

Policy questions fall somewhere in between specific questions and basic research explorations, and some evaluative research, like the guaranteed annual income experiment, falls into the policy area. But much evaluative research is related directly to improving agency operations in specific ways and must be tailored to meet the agency's particular decision criteria and information needs. Consequently, a grantee who deviates from the original research aims or delivers the results too late to influence program decisions poses problems. As many writers note, if the evaluation report arrives too late to influence decisions that need to be taken at a specific time, it may be useless to the agency.

The contract system has its own problems. The best-efforts type of contract protects the evaluator from an agency's desire to control the conclusions of the report, but it does not guarantee the agency that an acceptable product will be produced. An ideal system would protect the researchers' need to be flexible as more is learned about the problem and their right to present their findings without agency censorship, and at the same time protect the agency's right to receive a relevant, competent, and timely report.

Because of agencies' wishes to exert some control over the final report, the best-efforts contract is not nearly as frequent as the fixed-price contract. The latter, because it requires a highly specific product to be achieved by a fixed methodology, is not well suited to research, given its inherent uncertainties. Fixed-price contracts are more appropriate for buying material objects, such as pencils or typewriters, whose physical or performance characteristics can be specified in advance. It reflects the bargaining power of the funding agencies that they can require a fixed-price contract for evaluation research. Agencies often describe the product desired in ten or twenty pages of turgid single-spaced text, detailing the required research procedures with ridiculous specificity. In this way, the agency's research administrators enforce their ideas of the evaluation's scope and design. This amount of detail is very undesirable as it precludes the evaluator from taking a fresh, outside look at the topic, and the agency's research design may bias the study's conclusions.

A recent example was a federal request for proposals on research on unwed teenage mothers, specifying at great length the demographic data to be sought, but expressly forbidding the researchers to talk to such mothers. There seem to be few means by which evaluators can counteract an agency's desire to treat them as technicians compelled to follow a prescribed procedure. Agencies that prescribe design or method are intruding on a professional's integrity and status, since the essence of being a professional is to make independent judgments on matters within one's expertise. Such agency controls also deprive evaluators of the opportunity to make ethical judgments about the desirability of certain approaches to the evaluation, a situation that further threatens the professional's function.

The evaluator and the firm need not always be caught in a difficult choice between grants and contracts, however. A third type of arrangement, called a cooperative agreement, whose characteristics are midway between those of a grant and those of a contract, was devised under the Childs Act, passed by Congress in 1980. The cooperative agreement is particularly designed for situations where some of the work on a project will be done by the agency and some will be done by an outside party. It is to be hoped that this arrangement, created to make collaboration and flexibility easier, will indeed have that effect.

Evaluation Is Research

A major issue in understanding the economic and sociological position of the evaluation profession is posed in the literature by attempts to distinguish evaluation from research. The issue is important because if one posits that evaluation is not a form of research, then one may argue that evaluation can be done by people who are not trained researchers. The growth of one-year master's programs in evaluation indicates that some institutions have accepted this position; it is difficult to believe that such institutions hold that a research specialty in the social sciences can be taught in a one-year program. A proliferation of how-to-do-it workshops for the layman similarly implies that a great many practitioners do not view evaluation as research. Certainly, workshops that enable administrators or other users of evaluation to become more knowledgeable, or specialized workshops for persons who have advanced social science training are fine. But a workshop cannot teach evaluation, a social research specialty, to the person with no research training.

The latest development in the frenzy to oversell evaluation is the appearance of do-it-yourself evaluation guidebooks sold through the mails by various publishers. This is doubtless better than do-it-yourself brain surgery, but one fears for the careers and well-being of those involved in programs, whether as staff or recipients, so unfortunate as to be evaluated by people whose only training is such a guidebook. Research talent, research training, and research experience are needed to do a good evaluation. An understanding of the substantive social phenomena involved in a particular program is also vital. None of these is quickly imparted.

In addition, the claim is now being made that anyone can easily be taught to do evaluation, but that different techniques are required for different programs, that different handbooks are needed for evaluating mental health programs, public health programs, and so forth. Such methodological specialization is largely unwarranted. It is perhaps true that some kinds of instruments (such as attitude scales or observers' ratings) or some research designs (such as interrupted time series) are more useful for some programs than others, but these differences are of degree and do not apply to all instances of the program. The important differences among different kinds of programs are the social phenomena involved, such as contagion, primary prevention, psychopathology, and so forth. These are not covered in most of the specialized approaches being sold.

Against this background of entrepreneurship in selling evaluation, the attempt to define evaluation as a nonresearch activity becomes worthy of scrutiny, since the more different evaluation is from research, the more one may argue that evaluators need not have research training. For example, one finds ads in the *New York Times* and the *Chronicle of Higher Education* for evaluators to be hired by state departments of mental health and departments of education at salaries of about $8000 a year, a salary that suggests a low-level clerk. Evaluation has become a buzzword.

Let us, therefore, look critically at five arguments for distinguishing evaluation from research, since that proposition has crucial implications in the training of evaluators and the status of the profession. First, it has been argued that evaluation differs from research in that, instead of being leisurely and hypercritical, evaluation is fast-paced, politically charged, and criterion oriented (Sommer, 1977). Actually, field research has many of these qualities. As a classic example of field research, consider Liebow's (1967) *Tally's Corner,* a study of unemployed black men on a street corner in southeast Washington, D.C. Studies of street gangs, of policemen at work, of Japanese-Americans in wartime-relocation camps, of hospital emergency rooms, and of public housing projects are also fast-paced and politically charged, though not criterion oriented in any simple sense. But process evaluation, the study of the ongoing social process by which a program actually operates, is not criterion oriented either.

Second, some writers argue that evaluation means "determining the worth of" and hence involves value judgments; they also argue that research, which they define as the generation of new knowledge, does not require the making of value judgments (Sommer, 1977). This view flies in the face of the entire body of thought known as the sociology of knowledge. In choosing a research problem one views as important enough to work on, one makes a value judgment. If one researches one topic, one is choosing not to study something else. To study individuals rather than groups, for example, is a value choice reflecting one's beliefs about society and about causation. The approach one takes to a problem, the aspects one views as central, the methods used, and the audience addressed—all involve value judgments, even though these are often not explicitly stated.

So research cannot be distinguished from evaluation by the assertion that research does not involve value judgments. Myrdal (1969), Gouldner (1968), Becker (1970), and many others have pointed out the necessary role of values in research. Researchers should acknowledge the value assumptions they are making and hope that others will study the same problem from different points of view and, therefore, different value premises. Insight into the truth emerges from comparisons of the results.

Third, some writers assert that research is self-generated with originality being important or even required; in evaluation, the problem is presented to the evaluator, and there is no premium on originality (Sommer, 1977). It is true that the evaluation researcher has a client who has rather specific ideas and often even a research plan, proposed methods, limitations on what may be studied, and a plan for sampling instances of the program. But rarely mentioned in discussions of evaluation is the fact that basic issues of social causation and of social policy may have to be addressed to evaluate a particular program. If an income maintenance experiment shows a tendency for blacks to work harder than whites when they receive income support, evaluators will ask what might explain this tendency.

Social programs being what they are (confused) and social theory being what it is (incomplete), evaluation almost invariably involves basic social phenomena, social causation, and social issues. Consequently, evaluation research findings are often of interest beyond a specific program if the research is well done. For example, consider a study of whether Peace Corps teaching programs are more or less effective in fostering economic development than Peace Corps community development programs. Involved in this evaluation are theories about the importance of skills and attitudinal change, the nature of communities and of social change, the role of elites and the middle classes in developing nations, and the nature of economic development. Evaluators with theoretical training will not fail to see the bearing of their data on social theory and social causation.

It is regrettable also that agencies are often rigid and constricted in their formulation of the research design they wish to fund. An agency should not unilaterally decide on the research design but should collaborate with the outside researcher. Because the agency is so close to the forest that it can only see the trees and because the agency has specific biases about the program, collaboration is essential.

Fourth, it is often stated that deadlines are critical in evaluation, because decisions depend on the result, while in research there are no deadlines (Sommer, 1977). Sommer also notes that since evaluators examine ongoing programs, they often have only three or four weeks for a survey from inception to report. Such cases, however, are not models for evaluation; they are inadequate, flyweight studies. Evaluators who do a quick study and call it an evaluation are using their credentials in a way that misleads the client and the public. It is true that deadlines can be more important in evaluation research since the client expects the results at a specific time. However, since agencies repeatedly make the same programming mistakes, information late for one program cycle can be used in later ones. In fact, the premise that evaluations are primarily important to aid in decision making is itself subject to question.

Katzenmeyer (1979) points out that evaluations can be more generally thought of as a means of resolving conflicts among the various parties that have interests in the program, rather than being intended for a specific decision. Evaluations may be used by agency staff to call the attention of the agency to certain programs, reduce agency complacency about a particular program, or force the agency to rethink a program (Katzenmeyer, 1979). It may in fact be the exception rather than the rule that a particular decision hinges on the evaluation. Consequently, deadlines are not always characteristic of evaluations. Moreover, the idea that research other than evaluation has no deadlines is mistaken. Social research is often constrained by limitations on the availability of the people to be interviewed and by the duration of funding.

Fifth, it is sometimes alleged that research is a continuing effort leading to further research and more publications, while an evaluation report is probably the only time the evaluators will write on that topic (Sommer, 1977). This is often true for brief studies in which the evaluators do not have time, inclination, or opportunity to examine the problem profoundly. It is not the case for large-scale evaluations. Very often evaluators perform studies with an eye to later publications in journals or books. One may do an evaluation and move on to other projects, but if an evaluator looks deeply into the underlying issues in a well-done evaluation study, scholarly or even popular publications may result.

Sommer (1977) argues that the final report in a research project is a formality—the ensuing publications are important, while in evaluation the final report is crucial and no other publications are envisaged. It is true that the final report to the funding agency for a typical research project is less important to the researchers, and even to the agency, than are the resulting publications in scholarly journals. But the fact that agencies often attempt to limit the right of independent publication by the evaluators indicates the importance agencies attach to the possibility of scholarly or popular publications. In evaluation studies, the question sometimes arises about who owns the report. Evaluation contracts often state that the data are the property of agency and give the agency the right to veto publication elsewhere. If these provisions were challenged in court, the controlling decision would be Snepp v. U.S., 1980, in which the Supreme Court decided that such provisions were enforceable against a former Central Intelligence Agency employee, even though all parties to the suit stipulated that no secrets were involved. It is not clear whether a similar ruling would be made in the case of the Department of Health and Human Services or other agencies not involved in national security matters. It is possible that by signing such an agreement the researcher waives the rights that would otherwise be protected under the freedom of speech and of the press provisions of the Constitution. Signing such an agreement is unwise, since the right of publication is extremely important in maintaining the viability of evaluation as a scholarly, research-based discipline as opposed to an impressionistic effort or a free-wheeling consultation.

Distortions Produced by Market Pressures

The pressures to make a sharp distinction between evaluation and research, for example, to accept unreasonable deadlines and forgo ownership of one's research findings, are to a major extent pressures exerted by the marketplace on the evaluator. The need to sell one's services in order to survive puts tremendous pressure on the evaluator to promise too much, too fast, too cheaply, and too well-tailored to the views of the client. Chatterjee (1975) has deftly satirized the evaluation profession in a description of a mythical evaluation work group that is designing an evaluation of the death penalty for a state government. Each member of the interdisciplinary research team tries to twist the research to suit his or her particular career interests, and members make concessions about the design in order to get concessions for themselves. The resulting project is poorly designed, poorly done, and biased to please the funder, the state legislature.

In the satire, the researchers' ingenuity in biasing the research was due to their eagerness to get funding. The means they employed to bias the evaluation are widely used for this purpose by evaluators, and include the use of peculiar measures: for example, the social value of the death penalty is taken to be the number of votes in the state legislature in favor of it. Though their method is patently ridiculous, it is worth specifying what is wrong with it. The measure was chosen to achieve a certain end, that is, to make the death penalty look good, in order to please the state legislature. It is also a fractional measurement (Etzioni and Lehman, 1967): it measures only a part (in this case, a minuscule part) of the social value of the death penalty. Further, it is measurement by fiat, that is, the number of votes is a measure of social value because the researchers say it is and not for any other reason. Lacking a good measure, that is, one that relates to the phenomenon being studied and to other measures, the evaluators call something a measure because it suits their convenience to do so.

A further problem with this particular measure is its seeming objectivity, that is, it is numerical. Federal requests for proposals frequently ask for objective evaluations, by which they mean an evaluation whose results are quantified. But the proper meaning of objective in the social sciences, as applied to a measure or to a study, is "susceptible to consensus among observers." The use of easily quantified indicators, although no one can agree what they indicate, is not objectivity; it is concrete thinking that, in the clinical sense, suggests a disinclination or disability for abstract reasoning. Another characteristic of this measure is that, though a product of concrete thinking, it is peculiarly abstracted from human feeling, human meaning, and social context.

Unfortunately Chatterjee's satire is a faithful representation of some important trends in the social sciences. As Campbell notes (see Salasin, 1973), the abstractions of PPBS helped promote the body count as an indicator in Vietnam. Officials felt that since territory changed hands from day to night as the guerillas reinfiltrated, territory captured was not a good measure of whether one was winning or losing the war. The body count, the number of the enemy killed each day, replaced measures of battles won, territory lost, and so forth. But, as so often happens, the measure was viewed by some not as an indicator, but as the thing striven for. Press reports indicate that one cause of the My Lai massacre was the wish to produce an acceptable body count.

Gouldner (1968) examines some of the distortions produced by the nature of the market on social research, and we can extend his analyses to evaluation research. He notes the bias of conservative sociologists like Parsons: Their model of society takes equilibrium and homeostasis as normal, considering social change as deviance which the social system tends to control in order to return to stable equilibrium. Gouldner also discusses studies of local programs funded by the central federal bureaucracy. These reports often blame the local caretaking agencies for mishandling programs, while the bureaucracy, which is comprised of the institutions of society that produce the social problems, accepts no responsibility for those problems. Gouldner's list of national institutions that control our society includes government agencies (the Pentagon, the Department of Housing and Urban Development, the Department of Transportation, the Bureau of Indian Affairs), the medical and legal systems, and the huge corporate employers. Gouldner argues that many liberal sociologists, by studying the oppressed rather than the oppressor, and by blaming local caretakers, are distorting social reality as a result of their self-interest in pursuit of a career.

It is not hard to find such distortions in the evaluation field. In the community mental health literature, little attention is paid to unemployment as a major cause of mental illness and emotional disturbance in men, and of severe stresses for their families. Researchers prefer to evaluate the effectiveness of local community mental health centers rather than the employers who lay off or fire workers. Although prevention is a major tenet of the community mental health philosophy, in the literature prevention is most often taken to mean early diagnosis of individual disturbance so there can be individual intervention. Evaluations of community mental health programs rarely ask whether a community mental health center can possibly be expected to remedy unemployment, racial discrimination, or discrimination against the aged.

Coexisting with, and in odd contradiction to, the opportunistic strand in the thinking of evaluators is a marked concern with an ideal society. Although the literature is replete with discussions of the political aspects of evaluation, these discussions are mostly evaluators' laments or assertions that many vicissitudes must be undergone and many bureaucrats propitiated before evaluation results are used by policy makers. The literature depicts the individual power struggles and countervailing currents within a client agency, but does not provide a concept of broader social conflict that acknowledges that the self-interest of differing groups in the population (such as white ethnics, white suburbanites, and inner-city dwellers) may be in conflict. The assumption is that there is an overall social good that always can be found and that conflicting interests can always be reconciled by proper program design, by proper understanding, and by proper politicking. At the base of this kind of thinking is the desire to wish away social conflict. There are, however, marked exceptions to this point of view, such as Sjoberg (1975) and Gouldner (1968).

The Evaluator's Bargaining Position

Our analysis of distortions in evaluation owing to market pressures on the evaluator suggests that a closer look be taken at the bargaining position of evaluators in various contexts. Rodman and Kolodny (1964) detail the difficulties faced by the applied researcher working in a setting he does not control, as for example a social scientist doing a study in a hospital. The authors note the conflict between researchers who conduct the research in the client agency and the agency's operating staff. They treat the conflict between researcher and practitioner as a special case of the conflict between line and staff people. The evaluator is treated by operating people as a staff person who offers advice but is not responsible for the program outcome. Moreover, the agency people, both line and staff, suspect that the researcher is doing the study for publication credit only, not to help the organization. Rodman and Kolodny note the consequent hostility toward the researcher.

Although all evaluators have experienced resentment from some agency personnel, Rodman and Kolodny's analysis does not hold in all situations. For example, during Peace Corps evaluations (Meyers, 1975), the problems they describe were not salient. The Peace Corps had many different programs in about sixty-five countries and limited evaluation resources.

Thus the research and evaluation staff were able to choose primarily those programs that took the initiative in requesting evaluation. Furthermore, the operations people had high self-esteem and were recruited on a noncareer basis; staff were limited to five years of service. Consequently, the people hired were not career bureaucrats, but rather successful business, academic, or professional people, and they tended to be less defensive than career administrators. Moreover, unlike the applied researchers studying hospitals, described by Rodman and Kolodny, these evaluators were not threatening the professional status of the Peace Corps staff. But evaluators who are in a subsidiary profession within the organizational setting under study do have a poor bargaining position.

A very different arena of experience is discussed by Downs (1971). His consulting firm makes research-based recommendations to business about industrial location, that is, where to build a proposed factory or shopping center. He also advises local governments about matters of economic development, that is, how to lure new industries to the area. Downs' experience with clients is quite positive. What does this imply for the evaluator? Note that Downs' evaluations are oriented to the future; they analyze and weigh factors predictive of the success of a proposed program. Since the program decisions have not been made yet, the client's defensiveness is less. Moreover, his clients do gain from the evaluation a more lucrative or cost-saving location than they might have otherwise chosen. Since Downs' clients expect pleasure rather than pain as a result of the study, they are more forthcoming. These clients seek out the consultant, not vice versa, which adds to the bargaining power of the evaluator. Too, the evaluator for an industrial location study has direct and continued high-level managerial contact, access denied to most evaluators.

For business clients, the income benefits from the evaluation accrue to the client. Evaluations of government agencies or nonprofit groups rarely yield income consequences, since there are no revenues. Any decreased costs may be reflected in a decrease in the next year's legislative appropriation. Benefits from the evaluation accrue not to the agency but to the target population, the agency's clients, in the form of impoved services. All the evaluation can do for the agency itself is to make it look better and thus strengthen its case for appropriations or defuse public criticism. Since the benefits of evaluation for a public agency are more contingent and less tangible than for a business client, it is not surprising that evaluators with business clients have more bargaining power.

Evaluators oriented to the private sector usually have many clients, while those who deal with public programs generally become heavily involved with one or a few agencies, often because of the scope of the programs involved. But having many clients gives an evaluator a better bargaining position. Since Downs, for example, has a multiplicity of clients, he is free to turn down those who are too demanding, unrealistic, or demeaning. This freedom is reflected in the tone of his reports, which are noteworthy for being candid and refreshing, as compared to the overly tactful tone of many evaluation reports. Myrdal (1968) notes the impairment of social scientific inquiry caused by the ethic of politeness. It is only one step from politeness to sanitization.

Unlike government agencies, potential business clients are often able to decide rather quickly whether they wish to purchase evaluation services. Private clients need not conduct open bidding, need not conform to interagency guidelines for contractual obligations. Evaluators and their private clients are free to negotiate a contract for the specific project at hand.

Evaluators in the public sector usually have more freedom and a better bargaining position with public agencies that have a large variety of programs of modest scale; in those cases, the agency is less defensive. For example, the Peace Corps was more open to evaluation, and less resistant to the results, than most agencies precisely because it had so many programs in so many countries. A negative evaluation of any one program did not threaten the entire agency. For example, when urban community development failed (and in fact it failed everywhere it was tried), more effort was put into teaching programs, rural community development (which was found to work often), irrigation, poultry, road-building, fisheries, inoculation, and so forth.

In contrast, Head Start was a single program. All local programs followed one basic design: a learning experience in a school situation. The design was differently implemented in different parts of the nation, but these differences (class size, type of facility, qualifications of teachers, and urban versus rural setting) were not systematically planned. The only systematic difference in program design was that some of the programs were held during the summer and others during the full school year. Thus Head Start either stood or fell as a unit. The Ohio University-Westinghouse Learning evaluation results suggested that any gains produced by the program faded quickly once the children were in elementary school. Since there was little program design variation, the evaluators could not find successful instances of the program and thus could not tell the operations people anything positive.

The evaluators' finding that a monolithic program was a failure led to political attacks on the evaluators. Had there been many clients involved, or many program designs, the bargaining power of the evaluators would have been greater. As it was, the Head Start evaluators were forced into the role of hatchet men, with the vulnerabilities that creates. The evaluators' bargaining position was further worsened by their not studying the process by which the program functioned, with the result that they were unable to tell the client why the program failed or what should be done differently next time. By taking an outcome-only approach to a unitary program, the evaluators were put at maximum risk.

Competition Among Professions

Another manifestation of market pressures is that, because of the availability of funds in the evaluation field and the scarcity of other research funds, various professions are competing for the evaluative dollar, each claiming unique competences. It has been argued, for example, that psychologists have more to offer as program evaluators than do political scientists, sociologists, economists, other behavioral scientists, or psychiatrists, because psychology is more rigorous (Bernstein and Freeman, 1975; Campbell, 1979; Sechrest, 1976). Why is psychology more rigorous? The reason given is that psychologists are trained in the experimental method. But this assumes that the experimental method is the best one. It is also argued that psychologists are trained in quantitative research. But this assumes that, in evaluation, quantitative methods are to be preferred to qualitative ones. Moreover, sociologists are trained in quantitative methods and so are economists.

The problem is that although many approaches are useful in evaluation, each profession in the competition for funding tends to claim that its own approach is the central one. In this debate, Kaplan's "law of the instrument" (1964, pp. 28-29) comes into play. This law holds that if you have a hammer, everything will seem to need hammering. Each of the social sciences has insights and methods to contribute to evaluation. From each profession comes a certain bias, a perspective or way of looking at the world, that reveals some aspects of a program and obscures others. The biases and perspectives contributed by psychology are a quantitative emphasis and a concentration on individuals and individual differences to the neglect of social structure, as pointed out long ago by Mannheim (1936).

The competition among professions for a primary role in evaluation raises the question of whether evaluation is itself a separate profession with its own claims to primacy. Individual practitioners of evaluation and consulting firms constitute the major groups involved in the evaluation field. It is hard to know whether evaluation is a profession, that is, whether it meets the sociological criteria ordinarily used to define a profession. These criteria include possession of specialized knowledge, regulation by a society of peers, adherence to ethical standards formulated by these peers, adherence to standards of certification to practice, regulation of entry into the profession on the basis of merit, communication among members in a regularized and formal way such as by journals and annual meetings, socialization of new members into the field in a systematic way, means for expelling from the group members who violate the norms (self-regulation), recognition by the wider society that the members constitute a separate group, renunciation (or the claim of renunciation) of the maximization of profit or income as the most crucial criterion of behavior, pursuit of knowledge to advance practice in the field and to further the public interest, and defense of the group against attacks from other groups or the society as a whole.

Certainly many occupational groups aspire to become professions or to be treated as though they are: computer programmers and X-ray technicians among them. Evaluators are no exception. The Evaluation Research Society holds regular meetings and seeks to promote the advance of knowledge in the field. Several journals devoted to that purpose have been started, and graduate programs have begun to appear. However, there is no generally accepted or formally enacted code of ethics. Most evaluators claim a primary loyalty to another profession, such as psychology or economics, with evaluation treated as a specialty area.

The journals speak optimistically of the evaluation profession. Although the Evaluation Research Society claims to be a professional society, the field is still in transition from a target of opportunity to a recognized discipline. One issue is that the methods are largely borrowed from other fields (as we will discuss in Chapters Seven through Ten). Another issue is that the field has burgeoned primarily because the money is there; an opportunistic tone marks much of the recent surge of enthusiasm for the evaluation field. The behavior of some consulting firms, discussed earlier, reflects this tone.

The Evaluator as Technician

To the extent that evaluators are not functioning as professionals, and yet have specialized knowledge that they use in their work, evaluators function as technicians. While professionals have considerable control over how they use their specialized knowledge, technicians do not. Bross is a statistician who has published research critical of cancer treatments; in the essay "The Statistician: Scientist or Shoe Clerk?" (1974), he reports pressure exerted on him by medical cancer researchers (to whom he was a consultant) to make his interpretation and write-up of their findings conform to what they wanted to find, rather than what the data showed. Federal officials threatened to withhold further research contracts if he persisted in interpreting the data contrary to their wishes but in line with the facts. Bross attributes some of this attempted censorship to the medical profession's tendency to view other professionals as technicians subject to the judgment of the physician and not to their own professional judgment. Bross believes that to avoid being treated as a shoe clerk or technician, the statistician must act as a scientist, taking scientific responsibility for his or her conclusions. To combat intimidation Bross believes the support of a strong professional organization is needed. For statisticians, the American Statistical Association works to support and protect its members from pressures to act unprofessionally.

Such intimidation of the researcher is not unknown in evaluation. Intimidation may take place before the report is written—as for example, when the statistical or other data analyses are conducted, or yet earlier, when certain topics, issues, or bodies of data are excluded from the investigation. The leverage exerted on the evaluator is economic: the threat of withholding of contracts and research funds, or job dismissal. The appropriate means of protection is again the professional organization.

Economic Pressures on Evaluators

We have looked at the issues of bargaining power, intimidation, and interprofessional rivalries. Now it is worth taking an overall look at the economic problems of evaluation as a career. Evaluators in the consulting firms face economic pressures that may lower the quality of their work. For example, Head Start asked the Ohio University-Westinghouse Learning group to evaluate the national Head Start program in eleven months. Although no evaluator likes to work that fast, the amount of the proposed contract was $500,000, and few consulting firms could turn down such a lucrative offer. Evaluators working in consulting firms report that such pressure to sell often compromises the quality of evaluations.

The behavior of the agencies contributes to the problem

and undermines efforts at quality. Evaluation budgets are often ridiculously small. Restrictions on realistic formulations of the evaluation issues result in evaluations that are not useable—they are not publishable and not intended to be. The evaluator feels degraded by the knowledge that no one will read the final report. A picture of the timidity and formalism of governmental funding sources is given in Schwartz's marvelous parody, "A Modest Proposal" (1974) in which Lord North, having received Thomas Jefferson's draft of the Declaration of Independence, writes to him asking for certain revisions and additions. These include measurable goals, statements giving proposed indicators for goals, a flow chart, an impact assessment, an organizational chart, and an evaluation design ("required since Queen Anne's War"). This list is not so different from the formal lists imposed by federal agencies on proposal writers. The requirement for an evaluation of any funded program is sometimes just one more item in the list of bureaucratic requirements, rather than something the agency is deeply concerned about.

In-house evaluators have another set of problems, whether they are full-time evaluators or staff members with other responsibilities. In-house evaluators are captives of the organization. They cannot be sure their evaluation reports will be read or acted upon nor that they will not be rewritten, edited, sanitized, or deliberately misinterpreted by superiors. The form, use, and interpretation of an in-house evaluation depends upon the top administrator's intentions, priorities, and attitudes.

Owing to such pressures, evaluators are often susceptible to intimidation, and as a result, evaluation is often a troubled career. We have mentioned the unfortunate fact that there are no credentials necessary for evaluation. The underqualified person who accepts a job as an evaluator has a particularly poor bargaining position and may be forced to act as a shoe clerk. Economic competition undermines the bargaining position of other evaluators and reduces their ability to insist that evaluations be of high quality.

To cope with these many difficulties inherent in an evaluation career, we strongly suggest that the evaluator establish and maintain a strong identification with another career area in addition to evaluation, whether it be psychology, economics, statistics or another field. This will provide a source of professional support and intellectual enrichment, a sense of solidarity, and an alternative career if things go badly in evaluation.

Job Mobility and Security

As the previous recommendation indicates, job mobility is an important area of career concern for evaluators. In order to be able to leave an evaluation job for an equivalent or better one if the circumstances of the job become insupportable, evaluators need to maintain their professional credentials by finishing any degrees they have begun and maintaining memberships in professional organizations. They should attempt to produce evaluations that are of publishable quality and should try to obtain the administrative clearances needed for such publications. Mastering several evaluation methodologies is also wise. For example, psychologists familiar with experimental and quasi-experimental methods should learn survey research or case study methods.

To attain job security, evaluators must gain access to high-level decision makers and seek to establish a relationship of trust and confidence with them. Decision makers interpret reports in the light of what they know about the evaluator. If a decision maker does not respect the evaluator, even the best evaluation report may be ignored or its recommendations dismissed. Thus evaluators need to understand the phenomenology of decision making and, without stooping to excessive tact, frame the report in terms that the decision maker can understand. For example, if the decision maker is an economist, the evaluator's explanations should be presented in economic terms.

Another way to gain trust is through self-disclosure. Many psychological studies confirm our experience that self-disclosure helps create trust. A client feels safer when he knows or can predict what is going on in the evaluator's mind; he feels more in control and less like a passive recipient of help. Organizational development consultants have long recognized the value of self-disclosure and the value of evaluators' including in their report some indication of their own reactions to the program. Not only does such information make the rest of the report more understandable, it also enables the reader to calibrate, and therefore trust, the evaluator.

To increase job security and mobility, evaluators should retain personal and formal ties to the academic community, such as adjunct faculty status. These links help the evaluator continue to learn and provide a source of consultants and intellectual stimulation. Academic institutions, though rarely able to offer the evaluator an appointment, still function as job clearinghouses for their alumni, even at the higher professional levels in the social sciences. And, even though public agencies may disparage universities as ivory towers, they use university affiliations, training, and publications to judge and legitimize the evaluator as a competent professional rather than a technician.

Evaluators should acquire a very strong substantive knowledge of the kinds of programs they are evaluating, whether they be health programs, economic development programs, or the like. Although some evaluative skills and techniques can be applied to a variety of programs, evaluators need to understand the particular program, institution, and culture in which they are working.

To take advantage of the benefits of specialization, evaluators should cultivate cross-disciplinary collaborators. Any friction caused by the differing viewpoints is compensated by the quality of result, and collaboration is more efficient than trying to be a one-man band. For people in different fields to collaborate successfully, both must know something of the other's field. Unfortunately, people who are able to do this are hard to find, for such an understanding usually results only from a long history of interest in the second field.

A travel budget is important to the economic viability of the evaluator. One should negotiate for it before accepting a job, for it enables one to meet colleagues, clients, publishers, prospective employers, and agency administrators. To be without one is to risk becoming intellectually provincial, which reduces one's economic worth. One might also become isolated from the markets for one's talents, and from colleagues who could help serve that market. There are essential transportation costs involved in offering intellectual services.

Evaluators in academia should publish their evaluations. The university reward system aside, faculty members who do not publish face loss of their colleagues' esteem. One should involve graduate students in evaluations, since they have good ideas, need any money they can earn, and require such supervised experience in order to learn evaluation. Graduate students can do some of the less difficult tasks at a lower price than an evaluator would have to charge for his or her own time. If one's teaching and consulting overlap, each enriches the other and there are savings in personal time and a reduction in role conflict.

Evaluators in a consulting firm or research institute, in addition to being perforce generalists, should cultivate a substantive specialty within evaluation. Although they may also have a methodological specialty, such as quasi-experimentation, clients more easily recognize their need for substantive specialists than for methodological ones. Clients know that their field of activity, whether it be mental health or economic development, is different from others, but they may not be aware of methodological specialities within evaluation research. Further, the logic of methodological choice is that the evaluator should understand the particular problem being studied, and choose the methodology to suit that problem, rather than trying to market a particular methodology as a multipurpose solution.

Evaluators working in consulting firms need to develop a long-term relationship with clients. The costs to be saved by not having constantly to sell work to new prospects have been detailed earlier, and long-term clients are also a source of job offers. These precautions are essential, for life in consulting firms is very unpredictable. In economic downturns, the firm may fire staff. Moreover, some evaluators cannot reconcile themselves to the mediocre or uneven work many firms produce. It is wise for evaluators to be especially vigilant about keeping their career options open. Because evaluation involves assigning a worth to other people's work, it is fraught with political conflicts and economic risks that can imperil the evaluator's job.

A Competitive Advantage: Writing Readable Reports

One small additional suggestion may help the beleaguered practitioner. An evaluator whose reports are readable has a major competitive advantage, and it is worth briefly examining this factor. Social science prose suffers from the twin maladies of overcompression and pretentiousness. Evaluators trained in the social sciences write in this style and produce boring reports. Readers are great hedonists. One reason evaluation reports go unread and unacted upon is that administrative decision makers have the well-founded idea that the reports are excruciatingly dull.

What makes something interesting to read is emotionality, which can often be achieved by relating material to the reader's own experiences and feelings. One way to achieve this emotional impact yet retain objectivity is to give carefully selected examples. Some researchers mistakenly denigrate these as anecdotes, but if the instances are chosen to illustrate, not to prove, they aid understanding without sacrificing objectivity. The researcher must ensure that the examples or anecdotes selected are representative, not necessarily in a statistical sense, but representative of the overall tenor of the program.

Another way to foster readability is to undertake systematic case studies as part of the evaluation, and include write-ups of these in the report. Case studies bring phenomena to light in a richly realistic, evocative way and are the most enjoyable parts of any research report. The training of many social scientists mistakenly prejudices them against the scientific value of case studies, and unfortunately most evaluators receive no systematic training in case study methodology.

A further suggestion to aid readability is to discuss in the report one's own emotional reactions to the program and one's personal perceptions of it. Students of evaluation often do not understand that their feelings and observations constitute data. They look for unbiased data, rather than recognizing that all social scientific data have biases that must be taken into account. Objectivity results from the comparison of these biases and the systematic analysis of them. Evaluators who try to be completely impersonal become technicians, easily dispensible and easily replaceable. Since technicians do not strive to influence people, they typically write poorly, further lowering their usefulness and bargaining position.

Each report should present its conclusions first. The report should be preceded by two summaries, one of three pages and one of one page. Busy administrators and managers have little time to read. If they have to rummage for the conclusions, they may not read the report. If they are left to formulate a concise summary themselves, they may fail to do so, and thus forget what the report said, or they may unintentionally misinterpret the conclusions. Some administrators will not read documents longer than two or three pages. Administrators may not be entirely mistaken in these proclivities. Managers face difficult problems in the administration of evaluation, and to this topic Chapter Four turns.

4

Managing Evaluations

~·

In this chapter, we give counsel to the administrator on political and administrative issues with respect to the commissioning and use of evaluations. In later chapters, we will consider questions of research methodology, but here we seek to make suggestions about organizing and managing the evaluation process that are applicable no matter what the research design or instrumentation. Our recommendations concern choosing evaluators, guiding an evaluation, reading an evaluation, and using an evaluation. Some of these issues are of interest to evaluators, too, because of their implications for their own role.

Many of our recommendations are frank and stated in the imperative mode. The extent to which each is appropriate and feasible in the administrator's particular situation is a matter for him or her to decide. As in all matters managerial and administrative, the role of judgment is very important, and the administration of evaluation cannot be reduced to a purely technical matter or a fixed set of prescriptions.

In-House and Outside Evaluators

The choosing of people to do the evaluation is crucial since an evaluation cannot be better than the insight and acumen of the evaluators permit, even if they use the most suitable method from the repertory of formal methodology. Our first recommendation to a research administrator with the responsibility for obtaining evaluations is that few evaluations should be done entirely in-house. In-house people are employees whose careers and income are highly dependent on the agency. In-house evaluators are needed for evaluations that require an understanding of the personalities of the key agency people and of the byzantine intricacies of its internal administration. In-house people can provide political awareness and knowledge of the agency, and internal perspectives on the program (such as its real purposes, its internal history, and its constituencies). But in-house evaluators should work closely with outside consultants, who bring perspective and objectivity to the evaluation.

Should all evaluations be done partly in-house to give this internal perspective? No. In-house evaluators inevitably reflect agency bias, even when working in collaboration with outside consultants. Moreover, an in-house staff is not likely to be large enough to play an active role in all the needed evaluations. Even if a large staff of in-house evaluators were employed, such a group would inevitably develop a group bias of its own, related to the agency bias but not identical to it. Furthermore, even a large group may not have the diversity of specialized talents that an agency could obtain, as needed, by choosing consultants to perform evaluations on a grant or contract basis.

In-house evaluators ought to have access to a few very experienced and able researchers who can give ongoing consultation to the agency evaluation staff on matters of research planning and design. The research administrator should find a few such people and set up limited but continuing consultations with the in-house research staff. The danger of the in-house staff becoming biased and parochial is great, despite their contribution based on their knowledge of the program and on the trust they can generate in operating staff. Also, in some circumstances the internal evaluation staff come to be feared or distrusted by program people, so that the latter are more ready to view an outside evaluation group as more objective and more neutral with regard to internal agency politics.

Thus, most of the evaluations of a large agency have to be done by outsiders, owing to the amount of work involved. In discussing how to choose these evaluators, we begin with the legal requirements binding federal agencies in letting evaluation contracts. As noted in Chapter Three, some evaluations can be sole sourced, to use the federal phrase. That is, the agency can argue that one firm has unique competencies for this particular evaluation, so that competitive bidding is not required. In practice, agency research administrators have some leeway in deciding to make a case for awarding a proposal on a sole-source basis, and they choose to do this when they particularly respect the competence of the firm as well as their arguably unique experience. A firm's unique experience may simply consist of previous evaluations for this same agency. The administrators' appreciation of the quality of their work sometimes results in sole sourcing to a favored firm whose competencies are not unique. The agency and the firm may both falsely claim that the firm has distinct, unique competencies (an illegal but not rare procedure discussed in detail in Chapter Five).

If a firm submits a proposal that has not been solicited by the agency, the proposal and the ideas in it remain the property of the firm provided the firm states explicitly that the proposal constitutes "proprietary information." Such a proposal must not be shown to competing firms. The agency can accept or reject the proposal, or accept it in modified form through negotiation with the firm, but it cannot (legally) take the ideas in the proposal and make them the basis of a request for proposals circulated to other firms. This is sometimes done illegally, however, and the original proposer may find his or her proposal appearing in the *Commerce Business Daily* as a request for proposals. In some of these cases, the original proposer is not even awarded the contract.

A related procedure is also unethical and is more widespread. A firm has a lengthy discussion of its own ideas with the agency, but has not put the ideas in writing nor formally claimed ownership. The agency, instead of recognizing the discussion as the beginning of an unsolicited proposal, requests proposals based on the firm's ideas and awards the resulting contract to someone else. This procedure is unethical and should be avoided.

More frequent, however, is a different phenomenon in which an agency administrator is very pleased with a firm's evaluation work and informally discusses various issues and needs with the firm. From this discussion emanates the subtly solicited, unsolicited proposal, which frees the agency from the complex and lengthy competitive bidding procedure. In some sense this process is a boon to other potential bidders, since it obviates the very frequent situation in which the agency, having already decided whom it wants to do the evaluation, puts out a request for proposals because it has no basis for a sole-source award. Since the agency has already decided whom it wants, the bidding is in effect foreclosed and other bidders have no hope of winning. This practice of "wiring in" one firm to do an evaluation causes intense resentment among the other firms, which have wasted their time. This procedure is very unethical and should be forsworn. Owing to its prevalence, however, in Chapter Five we discuss the theory and practice of wiring, and how the prospective bidder can cope with it.

Agency administrators should show great liveliness in encouraging unsolicited proposals, without stacking the cards by telling the firm what to propose and without appropriating their ideas for a request for proposals (RFP). The agency should also be alert to those circumstances when a sole-source contract is justifiable. The competitive bidding procedure is often inefficient and wastes the time of the firms and the agency.

An important reason for the administrator to try to establish enduring relationships with a cadre of reliable evaluators is that some kinds of studies require a stable research team. As Gruenberg (1977) notes, one reason some valuable research methods such as clinical trials of medical procedures are underused is that the federal project system does not easily permit the maintenance of the stable research teams that are so necessary to these methods. Long-term followup of program outcomes is another method underused for this reason.

Tandem and Advocate Evaluations

Whether bidding is competitive or not, the administrator should split the evaluation budget, if adequate, and contract with two sets of outside evaluators. Tandem evaluation is particularly important with major programs, when a great deal rides on the outcome of the evaluation and when the results of the evaluation will get considerable publicity. The use of two groups of evaluators, who should not be allowed to consult together, allows some correction for experimenter bias, as the idiosyncracies of one set of evaluators will not be duplicated by the other team. Bias is a crucial problem in evaluation, and one important source of bias is the evaluator. Weiss and Rein (1969, 1970) provide an example of the usefulness of a second evaluation team after the first team has gone awry.

To reduce bias, should the administrator require that the two evaluation firms (or groups) pursue divergent methodological approaches to the evaluation? Divergent approaches would correct for the bias inherent in a given method, a correction that is very desirable. But a disadvantage of using two approaches is that it confounds (blends or renders indistinguishable) the bias of the evaluator with that of the methodology. Thus, in comparing the two evaluation reports, one cannot ascertain whether the differences between them are owing to differences in the evaluators or to differences in the methodologies. Since it is the job of the research administrator to study the program, not the evaluators, this confounding is not a serious defect. The additional richness given by the use of divergent methodologies outweighs the inability to separate evaluator bias from method bias. Moreover, different evaluators ordinarily prefer different methods for studying the same problem—a fact not entirely separate from their own biases about the program itself —and are more competent in some methods than in others. These facts argue for encouraging the two sets of evaluators to use different methodologies.

Should the two groups study the same instances of the program or different ones? For example, if the program is enacted in many sites, should the two groups study the program at the same location or at different locations? Having two sets of evaluators interact with the same field staff would drain the staff's time and energy, and might produce test-retest effects. Using stratified random sampling or other appropriate sampling methods such as cluster sampling, the two evaluation groups should choose different but equivalent samples of program instances. Sample-to-sample variations will be confounded with researcher and method biases, but the reduced strain on the operating staff and the greater diversity of instances examined make such sampling well worthwhile.

An alternative suggestion is that the research administrator consider funding an advocate evaluation, that is, a study done by an evaluator chosen by the program recipients and working in their interests. The evaluator would be responsible to the recipients but funded by the agency. Such an evaluation must be accompanied by a more orthodox evaluation by another set of researchers responsible to the agency itself, since the advocate evaluation is designed to optimize bias of a certain kind, namely, the viewpoint of the recipients. The perspective of the recipients rarely attains much expression in orthodox evaluations, but this viewpoint is important to improving the program. All viewpoints contain information; what from one point of view is bias, from another is a perspective containing partial insight. The fact that the advocate evaluator is chosen and employed by the clients minimizes the extent to which he or she is subject to the control of the agency, although the research administrator will have to require that the advocate evaluator being funded have appropriate research credentials.

Advocate evaluation reduces one distortion in evaluation, the portrayal of the program recipients as passive and helpless. The recipients are unlikely to hire evaluators holding this view, and advocate evaluation permits the clients to be active and initiating. Some clients will in fact ask the evaluator to consider the role of the funding agency in causing the problems the program is designed to cure. This approach lessens another bias, namely, the steadfast refusal to study the central societal institutions themselves.

The idea of advocate evaluations derives from the advocate-planning movement within the urban planning profession. Decisions by housing agencies, redevelopment agencies, and highway departments often benefit one group at the expense of another. Residents on the site of an urban renewal project sometimes form citizens' groups to oppose the demolition of their homes. Sometimes they hire urban planners as advocates to present the residents' point of view. This requires the planners to draw up counterplans for the proposed highway or housing project. Advocate planning now forms part of the curriculum of many graduate urban planning departments (see Peattie, 1970).

Can the administrator of a small local agency afford tandem evaluations or advocate evaluation? Bias of evaluators is just as much a problem for small programs as for large, and just as important to correct for. Instead of two teams, the small agency can have two evaluators, each with perhaps only one research assistant, examine different instances or different aspects of the program. The administrator will have more faith in the evaluation results if the findings of two evaluators converge. Advocate evaluation is even more useful for a small local agency, such as a family service agency, than for a large federal one. Because funding is a crucial problem for local agencies, advocate evaluations are helpful in generating the community support needed to influence local politicians and lawmakers (see Dorwart and Meyers, 1981).

The National Institute of Mental Health, in promoting citizen evaluation of mental health services, issues manuals telling citizens how to carry out such evaluations. These evaluations, however, would be more trenchant if designed and performed by a professional hired by, reporting to, and collaborating with the citizens. Together they would not miss very many skeletons in program closets. Similarly, residents of a housing project, members of a manpower training program, or residents of a community mental health center catchment area could employ evaluators, funded by the agencies, to help them carry out citizen or client or consumer evaluations. The administrator of a small agency is especially wise to consider funding advocate evaluations, because they both generate citizen support for good programs and provide a helpful supplementary perspective to traditional evaluations.

The recommendation for sampling program instances can be adapted by a small agency that has few instances to sample. Some agencies are administratively linked to other agencies with similar programs, as with community mental health agencies in a county or a state; others are loosely federated with private agencies like the Jewish Family Service or Community Chest; still others are members of a class of such programs that exist nationwide, as with health maintenance organizations (HMOs), or federally funded community mental health centers. In all these cases, a local agency has much to gain by pooling its evaluation resources with those of similar agencies. The administrator should attempt to arrange pooled evaluations in order to take advantage of economies of scale in evaluation.

Choosing Evaluators

The administrator should heavily weigh credentials and experience in choosing evaluators. In most cases, it is wise to avoid choosing as the chief evaluator, or chief of the evaluation team, a person fresh out of graduate school. No matter how talented, such a person is likely to be too inexperienced to comprehend sufficiently the important political and administrative dimensions. An inexperienced person may also have difficulty in establishing rapport with program staff. If possible, also avoid choosing as the chief of an evaluation team a person whose experience is limited to evaluation, since that person's viewpoint will be too limited. When possible, favor evaluators with field experience in analogous programs, for they are likely to better understand the program and have better rapport with the program staff on whom they must depend for some of the important data and insights.

Weigh also a prospective candidate's past performance in the evaluation role. If an evaluator has already done very good work for the agency, consider whether it is justifiable to offer him or her the pending work. We made some suggestions for doing this earlier, under the rubrics of unsolicited proposals and sole-source contracting. In industry, of course, and to a lesser extent in a private foundation, nonprofit institution, or other nongovernmental setting, administrators have more freedom to choose evaluators according to the dictates of their best judgment, without the restrictions placed on governmental contract officers. In any case, obtain from the candidates a list of clients familiar with their evaluation work. Telephone past clients, usually research administrators or managers, to ask their opinion of the quality of work done for them. Keeping a record of these calls is desirable and a record may be necessary if you are a government administrator. Ask the evaluator for samples of past work. Such elementary precautions should not be ignored in choosing evaluators.

Most evaluation teams should be interdisciplinary, for most programs raise issues from several disciplines. For example, law, economics, and anthropology are disciplines that can contribute to many evaluations. The best evaluation teams offer a broad and balanced view. Therefore, beware of technicians willing to do anything you ask. One of the things they will do is give you the answer they think the agency wants, whether or not the data justify it, and whether or not it is really helpful. Also beware of technocrats who try to snow clients or themselves with complex statistical analyses and mathematical models. If the prospective evaluators cannot clearly explain the methodology in the proposal, they will not be able to explain it in the final report of their evaluation. Moreover, if the evaluators cannot clearly explain the technical procedures, the chances are good that they do not understand what they are doing or they will not be able to make the research procedure work, or both. .

Lack of rapport with the evaluation team should not be treated as an individual or interpersonal trait that is merely a temporary phenomenon. It is more likely to stem from an enduring ideological, intellectual, or emotional view toward the agency or its programs, a view that carries with it the substantial probability of producing a tendentious, negativistic, or aborted evaluation. For example, I once hired an evaluator to carry out an overseas research study for the Peace Corps. He was soon summarily deported from an Asian country by the American ambassador there. This dismal result was probably caused more by the evaluator's social views about the Peace Corps and American efforts abroad than by any abrasiveness of personality.

Selecting an Evaluation Approach

Contrary to the predominant federal practice, the administrator should not dictate the evaluation design in the request for proposals. Mandating the research design too often strictly defines the product that the agency would like to produce and precludes the evaluators from reaching certain conclusions. An evaluation whose design is specified by the agency may be an attempt to elicit a product favorable to the program, while giving the appearance that the evaluation is the work by an independent outsider. Again, contrary to the frequent practice in requests for proposals, it is unwise to forbid the evaluators to investigate certain questions or to collect certain kinds of data. To constrain an evaluation is to prevent the discovery of unexpected information that might be helpful to everyone.

Conversely, avoid choosing a prepackaged approach, whether it be evaluability assessment or multiattribute utility analyses or whatever. Also avoid a proposed evaluation design that is a simple derivation of the evaluator's life work. Seek a hand-tailored approach from an open-minded evaluator, not a nostrum. Do not choose an evaluation of the cost-benefit or cost-effectiveness type if the evaluators directly or by implication claim it is value-free. Such a claim indicates that they do not understand what they are doing. Similarly, do not select an approach in which the evaluators assign values to outcomes by fiat or by some other arbitrary method.

It is wise to urge the evaluators to take a multimethod approach, particularly if only one evaluation is to be commissioned. In line with this, and for reasons of good quality in general, make sure that, in the requested budget, the evaluation team has allotted enough money to hire outside consultants to them. For reasons discussed in Chapter Three, evaluators are often forced to be generalists, and they can save time and money in the long run by hiring the specialized competences they need.

Guiding an Evaluation

Once the evaluation team is chosen, the administrator must guide them in their task. Government administrators are expected to monitor evaluations; in practice, monitor may mean keeping vaguely aware or controlling every detail. Administrators should try to take an active role in fostering the evaluation without dictating its outcome. The administrator should consider promising to release the evaluation report exactly as drafted by the evaluators, without changes or editing. This pledge precludes sanitization and other more subtle forms of coercion of the evaluators. It enables the administrator to take maximum advantage of the acumen of the evaluators: If they know their report will not be distorted or eviscerated by the agency, they will be much more highly motivated to do an intelligent, perceptive job.

Administrators should list for the evaluators, in as much detail as possible, any decisions that the agency plans to make based on the evaluation, along with the probable timing of the decisions. Such information gives the evaluators the rationale for the evaluation and increases their self-esteem and their motivation. It also gives them reason to meet the contractual deadlines, or to inform the agency well in advance if they will be unable to do so.

An administrator should tell the evaluators what the agency decision makers consider believable data and credible evidence. This guideline helps prevent the evaluators from collecting only the kind of evidence that the agency may later term irrelevant. Data the agency considers believable should be collected as part of the evaluation, though the evaluators should not be limited to such data. Similarly, tell the evaluators what you would consider successful and unsuccessful outcomes of the program. Suggest indicators for these, and insist that some of these indicators be included. Again, evaluators should not be limited to these indicators.

The administrator should obtain from his or her administrative superiors (or, in a small agency, from the board of directors) their own list of appropriate indicators of program outcome and a list of the kinds of data they believe to be probative. The same information should be obtained from operations people, too, including those in the field. Also seek out the skeptics within the agency and obtain their suggestions for indicators of program success or failure and, more broadly, for believable sources of data and probative kinds of data. These suggestions should be shared with the evaluators, who should be asked to include some from each category in the evaluation. Ask them to state in the evaluation that they have done so and which indicators were suggested by which groups. These procedures help ensure that the agency will consider the resulting evaluation relevant, insightful, and probative. But the evaluators must not be limited to these indicators, these sources of data, nor these realms of discourse about the program, lest the agency unintentionally foreclose the outcome of the evaluation. The evaluators must suggest some measures of their own, for the agency is paying for their professional judgment as well as their methodological ability.

As a separate task, the administrator should write a detailed prediction of the probable outcome of the evaluation and the findings and recommendations of the evaluators. If at all possible, get predictions from the operating people, too. Seal all the lists and file them, and do not tell the evaluators of their existence. After the evaluation report is completed, administrators can consult these lists in defending against any accusations that the evaluation merely documented the obvious.

The administrator should consult with the evaluators in the preparation of the final research design. Make sure that the evaluators understand the agency's position, but do not intimidate or co-opt the evaluators. If there is strong disagreement about the research design, let the evaluators do it their way, but require that they collect some of the data another way or that they do a substudy the way the agency requests. Such a compromise helps avoid a complete disaster in case either party is wrong. As discussed earlier, monolithic approaches are best avoided.

Require the evaluators to draw up a list of possible unintended program consequences, both helpful and counterproductive ones. Insist that indicators be devised for these and that, through indicators and other methods, they be examined in the evaluation. Also require that the evaluation summarize the literature on the results of comparable and analogous programs. Although no two programs or evaluations are identical, crucial similarities do exist. A research summary should sharpen and sophisticate the initial and later analyses of the evaluators. For this reason, the research review usually should be completed and submitted by the evaluators before they begin their data collection and analyses.

Require also that, before the data are gathered, the evaluators have a statistician look at the analyses they propose to make, to ensure that the proposed analyses are appropriate to the data. A standard procedure for serious researchers in any field, this is often honored in the breach in evaluation. The danger is that data may be gathered of a sort or in a way that makes the study results uninterpretable.

A process evaluation, which examines the program as an ongoing social system, should be included in the research design. The administrator should require that a part of the design carry the formal title of process evaluation. This part should include a formal statement of how this process evaluation will explain the causes of any program failures that are observed. Outcome data that show that the program failed but provide no idea at all why it failed are insufficient. Part of the process evaluation should include a chapter in the final evaluation report that consists of systematically selected verbatim statements from program recipients and program staff (analyzed and set forth separately) about the inadequacies and achievements of the program and their suggestions for improving it. Requiring a formal chapter ensures that recipients and staff get a hearing, that their insights, which are likely to be substantial, are not lost, transmogrified, or otherwise confused by the evaluators. Moreover it gives the administrator a more vivid and personal feeling of the realities of the program.

Examples of such verbatim presentations include Terkel's *Working* (1975) and *American Dreams* (1980), books justly respected by social scientists for the freshness and clarity with which they present social data. Terkel relies on carefully selected but minimally edited transcripts of his sensitive interviews with informants. The administrator might well require a chapter based primarily on such verbatim reports. A process evaluation should also include observational data by the evaluators, carefully analyzed case studies, clinical or historical analyses, and interpretations of documents and archival materials.

Early Feedback and Program Revision

The next phase of guidance is conceptually and programmatically difficult. An administrator may wish for early and regular feedback of evaluation results to the agency—to himself or herself and to the field staff. This request raises a number of fascinating questions. For one, there is a possibility that the evaluators might be coerced or co-opted by the close relationship that is likely to grow between them and the administrator or by the administrator's reaction to the early results. The administrator must take extreme care that evaluators are not co-opted or discouraged from pursuing any lines of inquiry.

With the field staff the problem may be even more severe, since their jobs may depend on the continuation of the program. If the evaluation gives early indications that it will be adverse to the program, staff may attempt to undermine the study by co-opting the evaluators, withholding data, fudging or fabricating data, or mobilizing political forces against the evaluation. For these reasons, evaluators have often been reluctant to disclose preliminary data to field staff. These possibilities must be balanced against the risk of failing to obtain the insights of the program staff if the evaluators do not work closely with them. There is a chance of alienating staff if the evaluation is a protracted one, done in the field, with no feedback of results during the study (see, for example, Weiss and Rein, 1969, 1970). All things considered, it is less risky for the evaluators to give early feedback of data to the administrator than to operating field staff whose careers are more directly tied to the program.

A result of early feedback is that an administrator may be tempted to revise the program, or recommend its revision, during the evaluation. If this revision takes place, the subject of the evaluation, namely the program, will have changed importantly during the evaluation as a result of the evaluation. This situation is an example of reactive measurement, or more broadly, reactive research, in which the act of carrying out the research changes the phenomenon being studied. Researchers ordinarily try to avoid reactivity on the grounds that if it occurs, what is studied is not the program as it ordinarily operates but rather the program as it interacts with the research process, which is not typical of other instances of the program.

However, a set of interesting arguments can be made for changing a program during the evaluation. If such changes are forbidden, the evaluation, which is only one part of an agency's endeavors, is being permitted to constrict and rigidify the core of the agency's efforts, namely the program. Some evaluators argue that evaluators should be like barking dogs, protecting the program from changes of any kind during the research, even from changes not induced by the evaluation. This protection entails sacrifices by the agency, but an analogy can be made to medical research in which some patients are given a placebo because of the overriding need to find out whether the treatment works. This research raises ethical questions in cases where treatments widely presumed effective are withheld from sick patients. Operations people sometimes feel, by analogy, that their responsibility to their clientele is to make improvements as soon as it becomes evident that improvements are needed.

In classic experimental design, the program is considered as the independent variable and is studied at one time only. The researcher strives to prevent the program from changing autonomously, because any changes will render it difficult to know whether the observed outcomes are attributable to the program as it existed at the beginning of the study, or at the end of the study. But anger and resistance from field staff often result if the evaluator tries to prevent the agency from autonomously improving the program during the evaluation for reasons other than those of the evaluation. Paradoxically, this position also entails a reactive research arrangement, a measurement-induced interference with the phenomenon being studied, since the researcher attempts artificially to keep the program constant when forces inherent in the program would tend to modify it. Whether an administrator should attempt to prevent a program from changing during the evaluation is therefore a difficult question.

The decision is a bit easier for a small local agency that has only a small program, in one site. Since there is only one, or at most a few instances of the program and there are no other instances of the program to which one wants to generalize, little is lost by permitting early feedback to modify the program. The evaluation improves the program, which is the primary purpose of evaluation, and changes do not invalidate the scientific status of the evaluation since there is no intent to generalize beyond the actual instance(s) of the program being evaluated. Consequently, administrators in small agencies probably should ask for early feedback, unless they wish to generalize the evaluation results to similar programs in other agencies.

For a large program, the case is likely to be different. There are many sites or program instances, and only some of them may be sampled for the evaluation. If the evaluators report early data to these sites, the field staff in these sites will make appropriate changes to remedy the shortcomings discerned by the evaluators. Similar changes will not occur in the other sites, since they have no contact with the evaluators. The reactivity produced by the data feedback may well be sufficient to render the instances studied atypical of the program as a whole, so that in fact the program as a whole has not been evaluated. Therefore, the administrator of a large program, one with many sites only some of which are being studied, should probably not ask for early feedback.

The issue is easier when an agency, large or small, makes modifications during the evaluation that apply as matters of policy to all instances of the program whether as a result of early feedback or not. Since all instances are affected equally, the sites selected for evaluation still constitute a representative sample of the program, and the evaluation results can be generalized to the whole program.

To compensate for the organizational stresses that restrictions on early feedback produce, the administrator should encourage the evaluators to set a specific schedule, known to the field staff, for feedback sessions with field staff at the conclusion of the evaluation.

Guiding the Final Report

Our next set of recommendations do not pose such painful policy issues. The administrator should insist that the final report be signed by and attributed to the individuals who did the evaluation and who wrote the report. Consulting firms often obscure individual authorship, omit it entirely, or mention it only in a preface, in order that any benefit from the report accrue to the firm and not to the individual authors. The firms are concerned lest a potential client be reluctant to contract with them for similar work if those individuals are no longer with the firm or are unavailable for that project. But the administrator's self-interest is that the authors be identified so that it is in their career interests to do a good job.

A more radical suggestion is that the administrator ask that the report be structured so that evaluation team members who disagree with part of the report or with its main conclusions be encouraged to write dissenting opinions to be appended to the report. A consulting firm is likely to resist such dissension, but if the administrator can prevail, the dissenting opinions are likely to prove valuable.

The administrator should require the evaluation team to hire an editor to review their report for clarity, correctness, and coherency. Very large consulting firms often have staff editors for this purpose, but the administrator should require such a service from any evaluator not known to be a good writer.

If the report has complex statistical analyses and appears likely to influence agency decisions, it is often worthwhile for the administrator to have an outside statistician write comments on the statistical analyses in the evaluation. Such comments should address the degree of credence to be given the statistical parts of the evaluation. These comments may be circulated with the report. Because statistics can obfuscate or mystify, they are a favorite target for attack by agency skeptics. An informed, outside opinion on these matters strengthens the credibility of the findings and reduces unwarranted skepticism.

Once the evaluation report is final, the administrator

should give program staff, centrally and in the field, an opportunity to reply in writing to the evaluation. If these rejoinders are lengthy and meaty, they can be appended to the evaluation and circulated within the agency. This recommendation, like the suggestion about dissenting opinions by members of the evaluation team, reflects the fact that something important can be learned from dissenting opinions, a fact confirmed by legal history, where dissenting opinions sometimes become the basis for the law in the future. Similarly the administrator may, in some instances, find the dissents and rejoinders more persuasive than the evaluation, or find in them insights not found in the evaluation. In giving the operating staff the opportunity to write rejoinders, an administrator also improves morale by making staff members feel less disenfranchised by the evaluation.

Oral Presentations. Research reports have a way of seeming lifeless. Readers may be unsure of how much to trust the interpretations of the evaluators until they have a chance to confront them, ask questions, and obtain clarification or elaboration. For this reason, the administrator should require that, after the report is final, the evaluators make a series of oral presentations of their findings to the agency, in the central office and in the field. To ensure a workmanlike presentation, the administrator should require that money be specifically allotted in the budget of the evaluation contract for these presentations. The presentations should take place only after the evaluation report is final, lest they become a forum for intimidating or co-opting the evaluators and thus procuring changes in the final report.

Reading an Evaluation. For the administrator who is not an expert researcher, and sometimes even for one who is, evaluation reports can be difficult to interpret, owing to their length, complexity, or use of new statistical and analytical procedures. An administrator has the right to demand that evaluation research reports be clear and readable. A research administrator's reputation depends on the usefulness and intelligibility of research reports; a program administrator's success depends on the value of an evaluative report. Therefore, if a report is incomprehensible, send it back to the researchers for a rewrite. Do not tell the researchers what changes to make—lest they feel co-opted—but do tell them they must make their report under-standable. Do not be intimidated by the technicalities in an evaluation report. Have the evaluators rewrite their report in clear language. But do not request any substantive changes, for those are in the realm of sanitization.

For ease of interpretation, insist on the one- and three-page summaries described in Chapter Three, and do not accept the report without them. These summaries are needed for circu-lation within the agency, and writing them forces the evaluators to take responsibility for their recommendations.

Using an Evaluation

In the new social science jargon, putting an evaluation re-port before an audience is called *dissemination* and acting on the findings is called *utilization*. This awkward language makes these matters sound technical, requiring technical solutions. But the problems of ensuring that an evaluation is used are in part ones of conflict among factions within the agency, and cultural and value differences between the evaluators and the operations staff. They cannot be solved by conflict-avoidance techniques. It is better to air the conflicts and try to resolve them than to try to deny them by treating the effect of the evaluation report on the organization as a matter of technique. Written comments by the staff and oral presentations by evaluators are important in airing and resolving conflicts. Similarly, if a report is to be used, it must be understood and judgments formed about its probative value. Free discussion, even if controversy-ridden, is essential to dissemination and utilization.

After the evaluators submit their final written report, have them present an oral report to the research administration staff. The purpose of this presentation is to familiarize the eval-uators with the kinds of questions that may be asked at the later presentation for the operating staff. The chief administra-tor of a small agency should ask the evaluators to make an oral presentation to him or her before they make one to the operat-ing staff. Do not to try to influence the evaluators' substantive conclusions, merely the organization of their presentation and their responsiveness to questions. Schedule another presentation for the agency operations staff. If the agency has many program sites and the importance of the program and the evaluation conclusions warrant, schedule further presentations at field or regional sites.

Write a critique of the evaluation. Include a statement of those things learned that were contrary to the agency's expectations. Compare the report's conclusions to the lists of predictions made before the beginning of the evaluation. This comparison, in most cases, dispels the idea that the evaluation revealed only what was already known. To the extent that it did, recognize the importance of the certainty afforded by the corroboration of an outside source.

Compose a list of inferences about policy based on the evaluation. Include a list of any pending agency decisions that may properly be affected by the evaluation; these decisions are not necessarily foreclosed because other evidence or political reasons may motivate a decision contrary to the implications of the evaluation. List the probable dates of such decisions. Also state the strengths and weaknesses of the evaluation, and the degree of credibility the report and recommendations deserve. Condense all this material to about three pages, and circulate this commentary with the evaluators' three-page and one-page summaries to operations people. Give these papers and the complete evaluation report with the staff comments and rejoinders to key administrators.

After this information has been circulated, the agency staff and administrators should meet to discuss the policy inferences and policy decisions, if any, to be made on the basis of the evaluation. It may also be helpful to meet with operations people at some of the field locations, to report the results of the evaluation to them and to obtain their comments.

Through a series of structured meetings that allow free discussion of the conclusions and implications of the evaluation report, complemented by written responses, all opinions within the agency are heard, and some resolution about the use of the evaluation can be obtained. The fact that the evaluation used some of the indicators suggested by the operations people and explored some of the realms of data deemed credible by them should foster its acceptance and use.

5

Coping with the Federal System for Evaluation Research

In this chapter, we discuss some salient aspects of the federal system for funding evaluation research. First, we consider some perplexing realities about the way federal requests for proposals are drawn up. Next we discuss some ways to become a favored bidder and how a bidder, whether preferred or not, should respond to a federal request for proposals. We suggest how to improve one's future chances if one is not awarded the contract and how to resolve unforeseen difficulties once one is awarded a contract. Finally, we look at current trends in federal evaluation contracting. Many of our remarks apply also to state and local evaluation funding systems, which often imitate the federal structure, but we shall not consider these separately here.

Requests for Proposals

It is important for the evaluator to know that the project directors who draw up requests for proposals are sometimes not properly trained to do so. In a study of the Department of Health, Education, and Welfare, Saxe (personal communication) reports that fewer than 20 percent of the project officers writing requests for proposals (RFPs) were themselves competent to do evaluation. For example, some RFPs ask for a survey to be designed, conducted, and reported upon in four weeks. Such requests reflect no comprehension of sample survey methods.

Even though a majority of project officers are not trained evaluators, many RFPs specify a design, often one that is quixotic, unfeasible, or ill advised. Even if the project officer is competent and the design is appropriate and feasible, as noted in Chapter Four, the practice of specifying the research design in detail in RFP is a poor one because it constrains the evaluator's judgment.

The Law Enforcement Assistance Administration (LEAA) has found that project officers often cannot express in the RFP exactly what they want to know about the project, because only the operations people may really know what is at issue. LEAA is therefore considering allowing evaluators to provide early feedback to the operations staff, so that the evaluators can be sure they are addressing the most important questions. Although some LEAA staff fear that such feedback will invalidate the research design, LEAA has found that imposing a design in advance can cause difficulties.

The project officer's wish to dictate the design of an evaluation may derive from larger political pressures or restrictions. The Department of Housing and Urban Development has found that sometimes Congress dictates the sample, by specifying the number of cities to be studied, with the result that the RFP is very specific. Other political factors that control RFPs include judgments about methods presumed offensive to certain constituencies.

Practically every federal agency is, of course, a potential source of grants and contracts. Two newer sources are the Office of Management and Budget (OMB), part of the executive arm, and the General Accounting Office (GAO), which is part of Congress. Although they request a smaller number of evaluations than many agencies, these two are particularly interesting since they conduct research on evaluation itself, including studies of evaluations that have been conducted by other agencies, as well as carrying out their own evaluations. By doing evaluation work for OMB and GAO, the researcher can gain a general view of the field.

The evaluator must bear in mind that while the research administrator, or the project officer in some agencies, controls the intellectual substance of any work to be contracted for, or for which a grant is to be issued, another official, the contracts officer, controls the legal procedure by which the contract is let or the grant awarded. Contracts officers have no programmatic responsibility, and their interpretation of their job and career interest often precludes them from taking the risks necessary to foster research.

Locating RFPs would seem to be a simple matter. Agency research people recommend checking the *Commerce Business Daily* and the *Federal Register*. Also the *Federal Research Report*, published by a private firm in Arlington, Virginia, reports on all federal research RFPs. But checking these sources is inadequate and time consuming. Some university research contracting offices circulate to the faculty lists of the most interesting RFPs as they receive them, saving the individual university evaluator the trouble of sifting the published reports. But although it takes about fourteen months for an agency to create an RFP, many federal RFPs have a very short reply time. Thus university evaluators should write to the agencies and ask to be put on the mailing list for their RFPs, so that the RFP does not get stalled in the university grants office and get to the researcher with only a week or two left until the proposal is due. Some agencies, however, will not compose different mailing lists for each RFP. Evaluators should try to develop personal contacts who know their interests and will alert them to the upcoming issuance of a relevant RFP. Since the *Commerce Business Daily* and the *Federal Register* often get the word out too late, the evaluator needs an advance warning that an RFP will be issued.

Personal Contacts. Universities and consulting firms in the Washington, D.C. area have a sizable advantage in bidding, in learning of and replying to RFPs, and in drafting unsolicited proposals. Researchers in that area can visit and chat with a project officer and so learn informally and in depth about the agency's problems. Moreover, evaluators in that area have an advantage at the formal bidders' oral presentations; a distant university or firm can usually afford to send only one person, while local bidders can easily send three or four. Universities in the Washington area have the additional advantage of inviting the agency people to hear the faculty present their work. This can also be done by more distant universities, since the federal government pays the costs for research administrators' travel, and it should be done more often. Federal research administrators can give general orientation talks to a large audience and then meet with individuals or small groups who wish to present their work in detail.

It is vital that the prospective evaluator have personal contact with the Washington project officer so that trust and mutual understanding can be established. The establishment of personal trust is the crucial step toward becoming a favored bidder and receiving contract or grant awards. Personal meetings are the best way to establish trust. Personal contact also permits the research administrator to listen to the evaluator think aloud and to judge the quality of the evaluator's mind and the direction of his or her attitudes. Similarly, the evaluator gains a much deeper understanding of the agency's problems and needs. Rather than hiring a university staff person in Washington, universities should fund travel to Washington for serious researchers (Lyall, 1978).

Personal interaction can also result in an unsolicited procurement, that is, a proposal sent in by the evaluator not in response to an RFP, and therefore not subject to competitive bidding. Ideas for such proposals often arise in the mind of the evaluator from discussions with the administrator. The evaluator can gauge the administrator's informal reactions to such ideas, and if the reaction is encouraging, an unsolicited proposal based on these ideas has a much better chance of success than a reply to an RFP.

Wiring. Wiring refers to a situation in which an RFP is issued, and bids received, and yet a preexisting special relationship between one bidder and the agency virtually assures that that bidder is awarded the contract. Sometimes there appears to be an explicit agreement that the bidder shall have the contract, but an RFP is sent out to avoid legal difficulties with agency contracts officers. At other times, there appears to be no explicit agreement, but both agency and the wired-in bidder know that the bidder will get the award. A contrasting situation exists when a bidder submits an unsolicited proposal, but the agency, owing to regulations mandating competitive proposals or for other reasons, designs an RFP from it, yet denies the original proposer the contract. This happens often. To prevent it, the proposer should copyright the unsolicited proposal and state that the information in it is proprietary.

Advance knowledge, if detailed enough and transmitted informally by the agency to a favored bidder but withheld from others, can be a very effective form of wiring. If the deadline for receipt of proposals is short, only those who know ahead of time that the RFP will be released will have enough time to write a successful proposal (Saxe, personal communication). Short deadlines result partly from administrative inefficiency in the agency and partly from naivete about the time required for a bidder to formulate a sound evaluation design for a complex program.

Another type of wiring arises from the role in the selection process played by the experience of the bidder (Saxe, personal communication). In evaluating proposals, many agencies give some weight to the experience of the bidder in similar projects. If this weighting takes into account the quality of the past work produced, the process is fair. Often, however, the mere quantity of such work is weighted. If the RFP is very rigid in its specifications, all proposals will be much alike, and experience is the major factor in selecting the bidders. When experience is measured solely by the number of previous contracts, the selection process is a form of wiring.

Agencies sometimes do take steps to reduce wiring, that is, unjustified favoritism. For example, HUD disqualifies an organization from evaluating a project if that firm won the contract award for designing the project. In the National Institute of Alcoholism and Alcohol Abuse, the person who wrote the RFP cannot sit on the committee that reviews the responses to it (Chatham, 1978).

Responding Wisely to an RFP. The prospective bidder

should try to avoid bidding on a wired request for proposals. RFPs with short turn-around times are best avoided. Rigid, overly detailed RFPs should be eschewed by bidders who have not done a fair amount of previous work for that agency. As Noble (1978) points out, a well-written RFP is less likely to confuse and mislead the prospective bidder, and it offers some small assurances that the project officer may be someone the evaluator would care to have judge his or her proposal. But some well-written RFPs are also wired. If an evaluator suspects the RFP is wired and if he or she knows the research administrator, the evaluator should telephone. After the RFP has gone out, the research administrator legally cannot say anything substantive to one bidder without giving the same information to all other prospective bidders. Nor will an administrator admit that the RFP is wired. But if you ask "Do you think we have a very good chance on this one?", the administrator may say "I don't think your chances are too good on this one" or even, "I don't advise you to bid on this one " (Noble, 1978). This is a special reason for the evaluator to establish a close relationship of trust with the research officer.

Wiring usually represents an administrator's sincere, though misguided, effort to assure that the best bidders get the contract awards. Wiring is thus on the same continuum as the establishment of trust. While wiring approaches collusion (though ordinarily not for the financial profit of the procurement officer), trust is the means whereby frank, open discussions of the agency's needs, or the program's problems, can lead to insightful unsolicited proposals and sophisticated responses to RFPs. Because wiring and trust are related, the advice given here about personal interactions and establishing trust could be extended to foster a wired relationship.

Although we discuss wiring in relation to contracts, similar favoritism sometimes exists in some grant-giving agencies. People who work in federal agencies frequently form close relationships with the researchers to whom they give grants, leading to additional grants to the same people. Reforms have been made within the Alcohol, Drug Abuse, and Mental Health Administration (ADAMHA) to assure that the people who monitor grants do not serve on the panels that award the grants (Ricks, personal communication). But even so, some agencies have a preponderance of academics on their grant panels, and the panel members may favor friends who apply for grants.

The Contracts Office. It is important for the evaluator to understand the role of the contracts officers in federal agencies. Contracts officers are responsible for overseeing the legalities of the process of contracting; their official duties do not concern the substance of the RFP and the proposals. But in many agencies, their power exceeds that of the research administrator (or the project officer or research officer). At the Department of Transportation, for example, contracts officers ask researchers whose proposals are being seriously considered in bidding on an RFP to submit their "best and final bid," that is, to lower the price made on the original bid (Voas, 1979). Such a demand reflects a contracting model appropriate for bidding on military hardware, not social research. At the National Highway and Traffic Safety Administration (NHTSA) in the Department of Transportation, the contracts officials demand that unsolicited proposals meet the sole-source test, which they interpret to mean that the proposer is the only person in the country who could do the research. This test, in effect, precludes any unsolicited proposals at NHTSA (Voas, 1979).

In some agencies, the research officer's influence is greater than or equal to the contracts office's. These research officers are free to specify in the RFP the "level of effort" that is desired, that is, how much funding the contract will carry. In responding to these RFPs, evaluators do not have to guess blindly whether the agency has $30,000 or $2 million available. In general, bidders can expect more difficulties when the contracts people are dominant over the research administrators. Bidders are even more disadvantaged if a military hardware contracting model is used, or the RFP does not state the approximate level of effort desired. In such circumstances, evaluators should be cautious about bidding since the arbitrary and unpredictable components of the situation are so salient.

Speed of Contract Performance. The amount of time given the evaluator to carry out the contracted research has an important bearing on who is willing to bid. Owing to the short time allotted for research, many university researchers are reluctant to bid on RFPs, leaving much of the field to the consulting firms, who are more willing to scale down the quality of the product to suit the time available. But there are differences among universities. Federal research administrators note that the elite universities want to submit the report when they are ready, while other universities are more willing to submit their best efforts by a fixed date. We discussed the merits of "high quality–too late" versus "low quality–soon enough for the wrong decision" in Chapter Three.

Although unrealistic deadlines discourage some of the most expert evaluators from responding to RFPs, the pressure for rapid conclusions is mounting in a number of agencies. In various sections of the Department of Health and Human Services, "rapid feedback evaluations" are receiving new emphasis (Solomon, 1978). At HUD, great pressure for evaluations in response to requests by the Secretaries and Congress militates against two- and three-year grants and contracts (Lyall, 1978). Agencies are, of course, entitled to seek the best advice within the time they think they have available. But if the time is too short for careful work, they should call the report an "opinion" rather than "research," since the systematic scientific safeguards that characterize research are not present.

Preparing an Unsolicited Proposal

The two best legitimate ways to become a favored bidder are the sole-source procurement and the unsolicited proposal. A sole-source procurement requires the researcher to have done unique work, or work that can be represented to contract officers as unique, for this agency or a similar agency, though occasionally (rarely in the social sciences) it turns on possession of a unique technology. In order to have the opportunity to do this exemplary work, an evaluator must first receive a contract. The unsolicited proposal is the best method for securing this first contract.

To write a useful, appealing, unsolicited proposal, the evaluator must become familiar with the agency's problems, ideology, viewpoint, constituencies, and enemies. As discussed before, the best method is to visit the agency in Washington and talk with the research administrator. Do not discuss possible contracts or grants, but rather substantive matters about the agency and its programs, in an informal, free-wheeling way. Many of the researchers most successful in getting unsolicited proposals funded are those who from time to time drop in on the research administrator and discuss matters of substance. These kinds of conversations, however, even though they carefully avoid specific proposals, are not legally permitted after an RFP has been issued. Therefore, one has to speak to administrators before they formulate an RFP on a given subject. But even if an RFP is later sent out, one's familiarity with the agency's problems, based on prior extended conversations, is a sizable advantage.

To become familiar with the agency's problems, one can also attend congressional hearings on the agency's budget, although this can be time consuming (Noble, 1978). Alternatively, one can read transcripts of the budget hearings, available from the offices of members of Congress. Also very helpful is a visit to nearby program sites. Before writing a proposal, talk to the program staff at the site. Unlike the research administrator who writes the RFP, local staff can talk to prospective bidders at any time in the bidding process. Their idea of the program's difficulties can be very helpful, although the central office may not see the problems in the same way as the field staff.

Another way to become familiar with an agency's problems is to become an outside reader of submitted proposals (Lyall, 1978). By reading a number of them for the agency, one obtains considerable insight into the agency's thinking about its problems. To become an outside reader, meet or write the research administrators and ask to be put on the list of outside readers. Outside readers are barred from bidding on the RFP whose proposals they are judging but can bid on other ones.

The Bidding Process

The decision to bid implies that the evaluator has concluded that there are no grants nor unsolicited proposals to be had, and that this particular RFP is not wired. Some suggestions about preparing a proposal may be helpful. Government research officers say that vague, general proposals lose, and that in response to the RFP an agency wants something substantive. Unfortunately, they also say that many winning proposals merely reword and regurgitate the RFP. The bidder faces a special problem if the RFP is seriously flawed or unworkable. One recommended strategy is to confront the issue head-on by writing a proposal that analyzes the flawed RFP and tells how it should be changed and how the evaluation should be done. Another alternative is not to bid on that RFP, although that decision is a difficult one if the topic is central to an evaluator's area of expertise.

Some administrative procedures in the federal competitive bidding process can be helpful to evaluators. For example, if bidders have major questions about the RFP, they cannot talk privately to the research officer after the RFP has gone out, but can request a "pre-bidders conference," which must be granted if requested. The request must be made soon after the RFP is issued. At the conference, bidders can point out problems in an RFP that seems flawed, inane, or unworkable. The pre-bidders conference may delay the procurement by a month or two, and the agency can clarify or change the RFP, which is then sent in revised form to all bidders (Noble, 1978).

Some agencies hold an open conference before the RFP is issued. All prospective bidders are free to attend; all the attendees, and others, are free to bid. A conference with bidders often helps agencies prepare a better RFP than they otherwise would have. Agencies are also free to hire a private consultant to prepare an RFP, but they must get a secrecy agreement from that consultant, and that consultant cannot bid on the resulting RFP (Noble, 1978).

Public documents of value to prospective evaluators include three publications from the Department of Health and Human Services (HHS): the *Evaluation Compendium,* published every year or two, summarizing all HHS evaluation research materials; the *Handbook for Evaluation Contracting*; and the *Project Officer's Handbook.* Other agencies have similar materials, summarizing their procedures for contracting and the findings of recent studies. Usually they are available from the agency's office for research and evaluation (Noble, 1978).

After the contract has been let to a bidder, there are ways for disappointed bidders to find out how the decision was made and perhaps how to be successful next time. One way is to attend the debriefing conference some agencies hold to announce and explain the results of the bidding. A second, more intrusive and more exhaustive way is to exercise one's rights under the Freedom of Information Act. The losing bidders, or anyone else, have the right to see the winning proposal, the comments by outside reviewers, the meeting notes of the award selection committee, and indeed almost all documentation pertaining to the selection of the winning bidder. If one can obtain these files without alarming or antagonizing the agency, the information allows one to infer the actual, as well as the stated, reasons for the selection. Such information is extraordinarily helpful for subsequent proposals to that agency. When writing for reviewers' comments on unsuccessful contract bids (or on unsuccessful grant applications, for that matter), write very promptly, for many agencies destroy such records quickly, both for self-protection and to save space.

Ensuring Time to Think

Midway through an evaluation, a successful bidder often finds that it would have been wiser to have done the evaluation differently. This unpleasant surprise can be avoided if one has sufficient time to think before embarking on a research course that was designed during the frenzied competitive bidding process. The problem is how to get this time to think. One method is to specify in the proposal and the ensuing contract a planning period, perhaps described not as such but as a period of "reviewing the design." It is always a good idea to include some planning time, because more information is always available after the contract is awarded than during the bidding. Unsolicited proposals and grants should also specify planning time, although the problem is not so severe if there is no deadline for submitting proposals.

Of course, the most direct solution is to first obtain a

grant or contract to develop a proposal. But federal agencies refuse to pay people to develop research proposals and usually refuse to support the data gathering that is prerequisite to a truly informed proposal design. Thus evaluators must include planning time in the proposal itself. Although one is restricted to modifications of the design already submitted, even a very major change can be called a modification.

Agencies also have an administrative mechanism to avoid the pitfall that the winning bid is the best of the guesses, by partly informed bidders, about what to do. In HUD it is called an indefinite quantity contract, or a basic ordering agreement. Other agencies, such as the Agency for International Development, also use them. This device is an umbrella contract that covers a wide range of work, most of which is to be specified by the agency in the future by means of task orders, that is, authorizations to do particular studies. The umbrella contract is competitively awarded but the task orders are not; they are given to the recipient of the umbrella contract.

HUD has several basic ordering agreements, each awarded competitively and each giving rise to task orders. These agreements set maximum and minimum amounts of work to be requested by the agency, guaranteeing the recipient a minimum of work a year and yet protecting him from sudden overload. A basic ordering agreement requires the contractor to maintain a standby capacity with the knowledge that perhaps all of it will not be used (Lyall, 1978). A university usually cannot maintain such a contingent capacity by itself, but a consortium of universities can, and indeed one of HUD's basic ordering agreements was awarded to a consortium of universities (Lyall, 1978).

Some task orders under the umbrella contract are for developing proposals to be carried out in subsequent task orders. This umbrella arrangement solves some of the problems of guessing in the semi-dark, and provides time to think after the contract is awarded. Their disadvantage is that the scope of the umbrella contracts is so great that one can think of them as a competitively awarded mechanism for wiring subsequent task orders. The difficulty is that such wiring serves not only the interests of favoritism but also the purpose of picking bidders who are in fact knowledgeable about the agency's problems, for it is partly this knowledge that permits them to become wired in.

Problems During the Evaluation

Most evaluation research runs into unexpected problems in the field. It is tempting for the researcher to try to stagger through somehow, improvising and hoping that things will work out well after all. But it is wise to inform the research administrator of the difficulties. Telephoning him or her allows an easy exchange of views and maintains trust.

Often research officers are quite understanding of and amenable to changes in research design or instrumentation necessitated by exigencies in the field. They are a bit less amenable to changes in the population sampled, since they often tell their superiors more about who is to be studied than how they are to be studied. An agency can adapt to many contingencies, including delays in data collection or even in report submission, if given sufficient advance notice. What administrators fear most is surprise, because they have been surprised often in the past by researchers whose final report was of far lower quality than expected.

The project officer can also often help solve problems that arise in the field. One evaluator discovered that the week before she arrived on the site to study 16,000 Navaho school children, another federal agency had given them a test very similar to the one she planned to give. By talking with the project officer, she received access to the earlier tests and so did not need to retest. As a result, she had better rapport with the schools and children and used the money saved for another aspect of the study (Stefl, personal communication).

Even if nothing much goes wrong during a study, maintain telephone contact with the research administrator. Without contact, the study and its findings may seem less salient to the agency by the time the final report is submitted. Moreover, as we have seen, the relationship established with the administrator during the study can influence an evaluator's career.

If an agency becomes disenchanted with the evaluation during the course of the study, before the final report is prepared, it is free, under the standard provisions of most contracts, to terminate the study "for the convenience of the government." The agency is also free to terminate a contract for reasons of default, that is, nonperformance of the research by the contractor, but this is rare in the evaluation area. Some research administrators do temporarily stop payment if it appears that a researcher is defaulting. But agencies rarely invoke financial penalties for poor research performance. Agencies are reluctant to invoke penalties because they do not want to risk litigation by the contractor and because they do not want to implicitly admit they made a mistake in the selection of the evaluator.

The Fate of the Evaluation Report

In many agencies, progress reports are logged in but not read. Some agencies also do not read final reports, since they assume that professional journals are the forum by which research becomes influential. In some branches of the Department of Health and Human Services, for example, research administrators who wish to call attention to an evaluation distribute reprints of the journal articles rather than the final report. Moreover, the agency and the researcher may quickly run out of copies of the final report and so be forced to meet requests for information with reprints.

If the evaluation produces a book, so much the better for the agency and the researcher, since books often have a wider audience than specialized professional journals. Since journal articles and books are reviewed by other professionals before publication, they arguably deserve more credence than a final project report. The evaluator can expect these publications, not the final report, to generate any long-term influence of the study unless the subject of the evaluation arouses such intense public controversy that the public and the Congress want to examine the final report.

If an agency considers the evaluation a potential threat, it may take measures to control the publication of the report. Even if the evaluation is not considered a threat, many agencies have review procedures to decide whether the quality of the final report warrants publication by the agency and whether they wish the researcher to publish it. Some agencies have different procedures for contracts and for grants. For example, at the National Center for Health Services Research, the recipient of a grant need only send copies of all published work to the grants officer; however, if the research is done under contract, the project officer's permission to publish must be obtained.

Many universities routinely attempt, sometimes successfully, to have clauses restricting publication stricken from a contract. Some universities, such as Harvard and Stanford, simply do not permit restrictions on publication, though they may allow prior review. Other universities discourage faculty from agreeing to restraints on publication and forbid faculty to sign contracts whose restrictions interfere with the research of graduate students and so inhibit their progress toward a degree (Tepe, personal communication).

Among agencies that publish reports, procedures vary. The LEAA has a research utilization committee that meets within six months after the termination of a contract. It decides whether to publish the evaluation (and if so, whether nationally or locally), ask for redrafts, or not publish it. At the Department of Energy, some reports are left forever marked "draft" (Rockhoff, 1978). At the Department of Housing and Urban Development, Lyall (1978) indicates there is a more complex procedure. Two to six external reviewers examine the final report, and on the basis of this review, HUD decides whether to accept the report as fulfilling the contract. If the decision is favorable, then HUD decides whether to publish it. If the external reviewers do not accept the report as fulfilling the contract, the evaluator is asked to make revisions, usually technical ones. The usual problems are poor execution of a technically good design, as for example when the alleged random sample is not random. If the work is still timely, HUD may ask the researchers to redo a part of the study.

If HUD disagrees with the conclusions of the report,

rather than with the quality of the execution of the design, it can ask for sixty days in order to rebut the conclusions before the contractor begins to print the report in quantity and disseminate it. HUD is in no case required to disseminate the report. Thus if a contractor does not disseminate a report that HUD dislikes, and HUD does not disseminate it, the report is buried.

The Department of Health and Human Services occasionally acts to remedy the situation that arises when the agency disagrees with the conclusions of an evaluation. The agency may publish a methodological critique of the report by the agency, and a reply by the contractor, along with the final report (Noble, 1978). The situation feared most by the agency is a press conference held by the contractor before the final report, and consequently before the agency can rebut anything it disagrees with. The worst timing for such a press conference, from the agency's viewpoint, is shortly before the agency's congressional budget hearings (Noble, 1978). By holding such a press conference, a determined evaluator can affect agency policy and compel the agency to publish a report it may wish to suppress.

More frequently, evaluations affect policy not because of intricate dissemination techniques, but because some political constituency is interested in the results. For example, the National Institute for Alcoholism and Alcohol Abuse is changing its policy to permit third-party reimbursement for alcoholism services because of political pressure by labor unions and by providers (Chatham, 1978). Evaluators cannot apply political pressure, but their research can provide a rationale for the government to make a policy change it wishes to make for political reasons.

How can the evaluator influence the thinking and behavior of staff who implement the project that has been evaluated, and influence the design of future versions of the program and related programs? Glaser (1978) recommends that the evaluator treat the project operating staff as consultants during the evaluation. The evaluator can obtain information from the staff, earn their trust, yet remain independent. The evaluator can reject their recommendations, since the staff are in a consulting role, not a managerial role. If the operating staff have no technical knowledge of research, they are unable to help design the research, but they can comment on the research design (Glaser, 1978). Such consultation is appropriate when the program's political ambience is not so adversarial that the evaluators must keep a respectful distance from each of the parties. The evaluator should also encourage the operations people to make suggestions about the substantive issues to be addressed.

One might assume that a self-evaluation by the agency, without the benefit of outsiders, is more likely to be used than one by outside evaluators, because the agency will be less defensive. The Community Mental Health Centers Act, as Windle (1978) notes, requires all centers to evaluate themselves, share the data with the community, and have the community review the results. But studies show that the citizens who review the results are often the center's board members. Both the agency staff and the board resist involvement of citizens who are not board members. Here, self-evaluation becomes self-justification.

Computerized Systems

One of the more interesting ways an agency can use an evaluation is to systematically combine it with the results of other evaluations. Sometimes an individual researcher will do this. Cotton's *Par for the Corps* (1975), for example, summarizes evaluation research funded by the Peace Corps. Most agencies prepare summaries of their evaluation study results for review by the agency director and for congressional budget hearings.

After preparing written summaries, some agencies store the summaries and other evaluation data in computers. The process of storing evaluation reports by means of summaries keypunched into computers is now used even by small agencies. Among the larger agencies, the Agency for International Development (AID) has 500 evaluations on its computerized system. On request, the computer prints out a two-paragraph abstract of any evaluation (Berg, 1978). The agency hopes that project designers will use the system to avoid repeating past mistakes. The AID computer also furnishes bibliographical lists for each evaluation, though such lists are more likely to be used by researchers than project designers. The system obviously depends on the astuteness of the two summary paragraphs. Even if the summaries are accurate, their value, and that of the computerized system, depends on the quality of the studies summarized.

The AID system is being expanded to include audits and end-of-tour reports by returning field staff. The agency plans to augment its evaluation findings by systematically taking outside literature into account. In 1978, AID decided to evaluate all projects in order to find patterns of evaluation findings. The decision was a major one, since AID has so many projects, over ninety on potable water alone (Berg, 1978). One aim of this comprehensive approach is to provide information that cuts across sectors of the economy, such as information on community participation in managing projects. With so many projects, if evaluation funds are at all scarce, it might be better to take stratified random samples of projects, and evaluate each project more thoroughly. There is a tendency in some agencies to adopt a machismo approach of "let's do everything, let's evaluate every project so we know what we are doing." The possibility of computer storage and retrieval fosters this tendency. The shortage of evaluation funds and of outside evaluation resources then result in a computerized evaluation information system in which the project staff evaluate themselves, opening the way to the possibility of apologia and fudged data.

Evaluators of federal programs sometimes find that their studies are used by an agency to claim results not justified by the program. With the development of data banks and information systems, it is harder for an evaluator to control the use made of the final report and to rectify misinterpretations by the agency of the findings, since the findings can readily be combined with those of other studies in unforeseen ways. For example, in 1978 the World Bank released a story that appeared in detail in the *Washington Post* (Feb. 23, 1978, p. D9), in an article saying that 60 out of 70 of its projects had achieved their goals. But there has been a world-wide inflation, and these figures were in inflated dollars, which was not mentioned. In constant dollars, far fewer had achieved their goals.

Recent Trends

Some parts of the federal government are becoming concerned about the low quality of evaluations. The Senate Appropriations Committee, for example, has become angry on learning that about 40 percent of agency-funded evaluations are not published by agencies because the quality is so low, and that many other evaluations are sanitized by the agencies in order to protect themselves. Some branches of the federal government consequently are taking a more sophisticated look at evaluation, and demanding higher quality. The General Accounting Office (GAO), which reports to the Congress, is studying failures of evaluation, especially in the Department of Housing and Urban Development, and in the Law Enforcement Assistance Agency. The GAO is attempting to codify minimum standards of evaluation methodology, although they may be in danger of adopting an excessively rigid approach (Cronbach and associates, 1980). The federal demand for evaluation, combined with the growing sophistication about it, should ultimately compel products funded by federal agencies to be more workmanlike.

But the attempt to raise the methodological standards of evaluation does not entirely resolve the problem. Unfortunately, dishonesty and dissimulation, as well as loose methodology, appear to account for the poor quality of many evaluations. Regulations making sanitization more difficult seem necessary too. It will be easier to raise methodological standards than to prevent agency distortion and sanitization of the reports, since the latter processes involve political issues.

The evaluator can probably expect increasing methodological sophistication to be reflected in the quality of the agencies' RFPs and in their decisions about which proposals to fund. These changes will be a distinct help to the researcher, for the arbitrariness, capriciousness, and naivete of some RFPs are an even greater problem for the prospective evaluator than the prevalence of wiring or other forms of favoritism. One can learn how to become a favored bidder, but it is harder to learn how to cope with capriciousness and naivete.

6

Taking Program Goals into Account: Some Objections to Objectives

~·

Is it possible or desirable to evaluate programs in relation to their goals? Evaluating a program in terms of whether it met its objectives is the classic approach to program evaluation. It is simplistic and usually misleading, yet for some programs it may have value. An understanding of the shortcomings and occasional merits of this approach can help the evaluator avoid some expensive mistakes.

A lucid statement of the goals evaluation approach is given by Suchman (1972): "Thus evaluation represents a measurement of effectiveness in reaching some predetermined goal. The key elements in this definition of evaluation are: (1) an objective or goal which is considered desirable or has some positive value; (2) a planned program of deliberate intervention which one hypothesizes is capable of achieving the desired goal; and (3) a method for determining the degree to which the desired objective is attained *as a result of* the planned program. All three must be present before evaluation can take place. . . . An evaluation study should not be undertaken until an activity or program has had enough time to prove its possible effectiveness. . . . And, unless a program can specify what value its activities are seeking to further, whether this be the amelioration of some specific social problem or the advancement of some broad humanistic goal, evaluation becomes meaningless" (pp. 53-54).

Rossi states (cited by Deutscher, 1976, p. 250) "any program which does not have clearly specified goals cannot be evaluated without specifying some measurable goals. This statement is obvious enough to be a truism." The vast majority of evaluators subscribe to this position and practice it. They would argue that if a program does what it promised to do, it is successful; therefore, a program should be evaluated in terms of whether it has met its goals. But this approach is often too simple. Somehow most programs do not attain their goals, and there is often disagreement about what the goals of the program are, as when the program's adherents say the wrong goals were inadvertently or wrongheadedly chosen by the evaluators.

In point of fact, a program may be well worth evaluating even if the goals are very unclear, or even if there are no discernible goals. Given the difficulties of social programming, and the frequency with which social programs miscarry, discussed in Chapter Two, it is extremely important to search for consequences of programs, including consequences that are intended, unintended, anticipated, unanticipated, positive, or negative. Campbell (1970) argues that some programs are so baffling in structure and so vague or confused in aims as to be unevaluable. While this appraisal expresses the consternation that a careful experimental methodologist feels when confronting some programs, vagueness and confusion should not constitute a defense against evaluation. Programs that are poorly organized, poorly thought out, or chaotic can sometimes have strong effects, often counterproductive ones, that need to be discovered and understood.

It is worth making distinctions between intended and anticipated consequences and between unintended and unanticipated consequences. Certain consequences may not be intended by program planners, but they still may be anticipated or even expected. These consequences may be readily detectable even if the program is chaotic, and so the program in this sense is readily evaluable even if the goals of the program are vague or contradictory. Proposals for assessing evaluability before deciding whether to undertake an evaluation (Wholey, 1977) do not deal adequately with vague or chaotic programs that have strong counterproductive consequences.

The Nature of Goals

The prevalence of unanticipated or unintended consequences counters the belief that a program should be evaluated in terms of its goals and should not be evaluated if it does not have clear goals. Recognizing the problematic quality of goals, some evaluators try to be a bit more sophisticated about goals as the criteria for evaluation. (Throughout this chapter, the terms *goals* and *objectives* are used interchangeably.) Let us examine several discussions of goals.

Riecken (1972) begins with a familiar assertion: "It is essential not only that the major objectives of an action program be clearly defined, but also that they be stated in operational terms—that is, in terms of concrete behavior, specific accomplishments, or states of affairs—in order that an evaluator can devise appropriate measuring instruments" (p. 92). He believes that developing an "operational statement of objectives is usually the most difficult task in conducting an evaluation study" (p. 92). Riecken's premise suggests that the task of goal formulation is part of the evaluation study and, therefore, is in whole or part the responsibility of the evaluator. Riecken further submits that "It is obvious that objectives must be stated in advance of taking action in order to prevent the trivial occurrence that the stated objectives are merely the observed results of the action" (p. 92). This procedure is not always desirable. If a program accomplishes the same things in repeated program cycles, perhaps the staff ought to be entitled to call these achievements their present goals, even if they were not their original goals. Riecken continues that, despite his earlier reservation, it is sometimes possible for the researcher to derive objectives by working in collaboration with the program staff.

Riecken also proposes a distinction between manifest and latent goals: certain objectives are openly stated, while other objectives are latent. But his discussion confuses two meanings of latent. One kind of latent goal is an objective known to the staff of the program that is not acceptable for public statement. For example, a foreign aid program may have the manifest objective of increasing agricultural production and the latent objective of ensuring the political stability of a government friendly to the United States. A different meaning of latent is denoted in Merton's (1957) concept of functional analysis. A pattern of social behavior may serve a manifest (obvious or apparent) function, and also a latent function, which is hidden from awareness—not consciously concealed. For example, the manifest function of an inner city slum may be to provide low-cost housing for the poor, while its latent function may be to provide illegal services, such as prostitution and drugs, for suburban customers. Many people are aware of the latent function, and most of them treat it as an accidental attribute rather than as a valued social function that perpetuates itself because it meets a social need.

It is not clear whether Riecken uses latent to denote goals in the awareness of the program staff but taboo for public discussion, or whether he uses latent in Merton's sense of serving an unacknowledged and unapparent social function. The distinction between manifest and latent goals provides us with an indication that identifying program goals can be a complex, subtle process. Indeed, as we discuss later, program goals may not exist in a simple, reified way, and so cannot be found in the sense that a chair can be found, but rather are in some sense constructed or inferred.

To clarify what is a goal and what is not, Riecken advocates that the researcher operationally define the goals. An operational definition appears to require the evaluator to find indicators of success in meeting each goal, preferably indicators that the staff can agree on, and then proceed to measure success validly and reliably. Although this is a useful suggestion, the difficulty is that goals tend to be formulated so broadly as to set no guidelines for operational definition.

Riecken offers an example: if the goal is the economic rehabilitation of the client, the indicator could be the client's holding a steady job for a year or more. But this goal may be so difficult to accomplish that Riecken introduces the concept of realistic expectations, with the result that the reasonable level of expectation for success for the cases treated may be as low as 5 percent. This concession casts doubt on the reality of economic rehabilitation of the client as a goal, if it is expected to be met almost none of the time. Goals, even when operationally defined, have a worrisome kind of unreality if realistic expectations are set so low. The funding agency should ask if it is being kidded along and whether its disadvantaged clients are being set up for further disappointments.

Deutscher (1976) takes issue with the usual approach of evaluating programs in terms of their goals. He first notes that organizations change their goals over time, so that goals succeed each other in the natural course of things (Merton, 1957; Michels, 1959; Clark, 1956; Bogdan, 1975). Moreover, organizations displace their goals from the original ones to others that superficially resemble the original ones but are easier to attain (Blau, 1955; Blau and Scott, 1961; Bogdan, 1975; Sills, 1957; Thompson and McEwen, 1958). Deutscher then examines the idea that programs cannot be evaluated without specific measurable goals; he calls this assumption the goal trap.

How does the goal trap work? First, the evaluator seeks measurable goals, as recommended by numerous authorities, by asking the program designers to specify their objectives. Consequently, notes Deutscher, if the goals are not immediately obvious, the evaluator "hounds program people: 'Is this a goal? Or this? Or this?'" (p. 253). The program staff are thus intimidated into agreeing that certain statements are goals. The evaluator now has goals and measures of goals to which no one is committed, goals that have been imposed by the evaluation process.

One result of the goal trap is that, after the evaluation is completed, the program staff claim that the goals measured were not the program's real goals. Evaluators complain about this situation, but fail to see it as a consequence of the fact that the measures and even the goals were imposed on the program. A more sombre result, as Becker (1970), Campbell (see Salasin, 1973), and Deutscher (1976) all note, is that the measures imposed on the program become ends in themselves and distort the program. The worst case is the body count measure of success in the Vietnam War, which, as we noted in Chapter Three, became a goal in itself.

Why are goals imposed by the evaluator? Why do evaluators reject the goals stated in the program document as the real goals? Deutscher notes that "to get funding, the program staff must lie to the funding agency in order to meet the criteria for the proposal to be funded" (p. 252). That is, staff must identify clear goals and specify measurable consequences, whether or not the nature of the program, social knowledge, and social theory permit. Naturally, the actual program bears little resemblance to the funding proposal. Moreover, as Weiss (1973) notes, operations people usually disregard evaluation results if the evaluation is based on the official goals, that is, on the official lies told to the funding agency. To be credible to the operations staff, the evaluation must be based on other goals.

Deutscher suggests ways to sidestep the goal trap. One is to analyze the program in terms of social process, rather than using the classical comparison of input and output. Evaluation in terms of social process is elaborated by R. Weiss and Rein (1969, 1970), and the rationale for this kind of analysis is traceable to Blumer (1956). Deutscher argues that, contrary to Campbell (1970), social process can even be studied experimentally, and cites the work of Weber (1947) as an example. Deutscher also suggests that evaluators be attentive to both unintended (unwanted) and unanticipated (unforeseen) consequences. The formulation of the legal profession—a person is held to have intended the reasonably foreseeable consequences of his actions—also deserves consideration.

Deutscher's third recommendation is to negotiate—not intimidate or manipulate—with the program staff to specify the goals of the program. In many areas, as the social interactionists note (Blumer, 1956), reality is defined by a process of negotiation. Social scientists have studied this process of negotiating the definition of what is taken to be real, as found in medical diagnoses, plea bargaining, and all official statistics. In evaluation, the evaluator and program staff can also negotiate which data are relevant to which program decisions, as advocated in Chapter Four. Deutscher suggests that the evaluator who watches what the program staff do and listens to them talk about doing it has a better chance of understanding their intentions, and these should be taken to be the program goals.

Deutscher advocates drawing up alternative goal formulations, with different measuring instruments and different decision consequences, and negotiating these with the program staff until agreement is reached. But some reservations about the goal negotiating process are in order. Not only the goals and measures but also the research methods, designs, and data for the evaluation should be open for discussion with the program staff. A difficulty is that negotiation implies that the evaluators have a bargaining position, that is, something of value they can offer or withhold. The nature of this bargaining position should be analyzed, not assumed. A final problem is that negotiation assumes that goals are a useful construct in understanding programs. Several researchers have questioned even this premise, and their views merit consideration.

Are Goals Important in Evaluation?

Bogdan (1975) makes a careful case that goals are not of major significance in understanding or evaluating programs. In the job training program for the hard-core unemployed that he studied, the numerical measures of success had so many variants that the success rate of the program varied between 0 percent and 100 percent, depending on the method of computation. These computations depended on more or less arbitrary assumptions about the success of the program clientele (in this case, in finding and holding jobs) had there been no program. Success rates also depended on how certain types of cases were classified, for example, as dropouts, completers, those who accepted a job and appeared for work at least once, those who held a job for a specified period, and so forth. As Bogdan notes, even though many of the assumptions were arbitrary, similar programs or similar instances of the same program could have been compared had the program staff at the various sites agreed on a method of classification and computation, but they did not.

As a result of arbitrariness and lack of consensus, Bogdan concludes that "success measures lose their significance when looked at carefully" (p. 214). Bogdan's point is a good one, since measures of success based on computations applied to indicators are easily manipulated, as the author's own experience in trying to decipher the Peace Corps' measures of volunteer dropout attests. FBI crime rates, federal statistics on unemployment rates, and inflation rates are notoriously manipulated by the agencies involved. But some measures of success are clear; for example, the number of children inoculated against tuberculosis by Peace Corps volunteers in Bolivia. Whether a measure of success has a clear meaning depends on the measure, the program, and the social context.

Bogdan states that some measures of success merely represent people's desire to have measures of achievement. What underlies people's need for such measures even if they are clearly arbitrary? One basis, he believes, is the widespread belief that people form and maintain organizations in order to achieve goals. Goals give organizations a pragmatic, rational, common sense justification for their existence. More often, Bogdan believes, organizations actually serve expressive purposes, that is, they offer "an excuse to get together" (p. 217). Measures of success disguise this fact, legitimize the existence of the organization, and "[become] synonymous with and can replace achieving success" (p. 217). Goals are also "a symbol of the desire of conflicting groups to get together, rather than an agreement of purpose" (p. 217). Goals form "an arena in which organizational activity is fought" (p. 218); that is, goals focus the conflict among subgroups within the organization.

Another purpose of organizational goals, according to Bogdan, is to protect the organization from its environment, that is, to serve as "purposeful misrepresentations of the organization's intent . . . a means of arriving at purposes other than those stated . . . a front to protect the organization from assault" from the outside and a way to "hide its true purposes" (p. 218). But this last formulation shows that Bogdan, who believes goals are misleading, uses "true purposes" to mean "real goals," so that in effect he is unable to jettison the concept of goals as having an instrumental reality. Bogdan asserts the goals of businesses that wanted the training program for the unemployed: to improve community relations, meet federal regulations against discrimination, and receive federal subsidies for training and hiring the hard-core unemployed. Social agencies view goals as prerequisites to funding, and measures of success are valued by the agencies primarily for their usefulness in obtaining more funds. Goals also foster morale among organization members, serving as abstract ideals the members believe they are serving. Measures of success in serving these goals further increase morale.

Bogdan's position does not appear to address organizations that have significant success in reaching or approaching instrumental goals. He believes that many organizations are not "rational coordinated instruments for attaining goals" (p. 220), but rather primarily serve expressive functions, despite their protestations to the contrary. This view appears to resemble an anthropological position that regards the supposedly instrumental activities of the tribe as largely magical in significance.

Moreover, Bogdan appears to refute the view of organizations set forth by Weber (1947), the idea that most modern organizations are bureaucracies, organized in a rational-legal way to achieve their ends most efficiently. The issue is: To what extent does Weber's model of bureaucracy, suitably modified by Blau (1955), Gouldner (1955), Merton (1957), and Bennis (1970) apply, and to what extent does Bogdan's model of a bureaucracy as an expressive organization in disguise apply? The evaluator is wise to keep an open mind while studying the particular organization whose program is to be evaluated. Often, an organization's instrumental goals are real and even overriding, but its announced goals may somewhat mislead the public or serve mythic needs for the members.

The Goal Model and the System Model

Another critic of the practice of analyzing programs in terms of their objectives is Etzioni (1969). He describes two models for assessing organizational effectiveness. In the goal model, the assessment of effectiveness is derived from organizational goals. Findings from studies using the goal model are "stereotyped as well as dependent on the model's assumptions" (p. 101). Such studies usually show that the organization does not reach its goals, or that its goals are not the ones it claims to have.

One reason for these difficulties is that goals are norms or sets of expectations and are, therefore, cultural entities; organizations, however, are social systems. Cultural systems, since they are ideal systems, are more consistent than social systems. The latter do not have the resources to completely attain cultural expectations. Moreover, social systems, such as organizations and programs, have multiple functions: in addition to pursuing goals they must also try to meet system maintenance needs, recruitment needs, and socialization needs.

Etzioni notes that it is an error to compare entities on different levels of analysis, that is, "the present state of an organization, a real state, [should not be] compared with an ideal state, namely a goal, as though the goal were also a real state" (p. 102). If one uses as the criterion the ideal state represented by the goal, most programs are not very effective. Etzioni recommends instead that programs with similar goals be compared in level of effectiveness. This approach is similar to Bogdan's proposal to use the same goal attainment measures across similar programs.

Another error in the goal model, Etzioni believes, is evaluating the program against its public goals (those it claims to follow) rather than against its private goals (those it actually follows). This is an error because public goals are not intended to be attained. Public goals are meant to recruit support (members, funds, legitimation) for the organization, so that it can pursue its private goals, which may be unknown to many of the members. If the public goals were met, Etzioni argues, the organization would lose its power to recruit resources.

Etzioni recommends an alternative model, the system model, for program evaluation. It takes as the criterion not the goal itself but "a working model of a social unit which is capable of achieving a goal" (p. 103). Such a social system must devote some of its energies to system maintenance, such as recruitment of resources and members, social integration (maintaining cohesion), and maintenance of the physical resources of the system. In evaluation, one does not study the effectiveness of the organization in achieving the goal since total dedication to the goal is a short-sighted policy that may endanger the survival of the organization. Instead, the evaluator examines how closely the allocation of resources by the organization approaches what is considered an optimum distribution.

Etzioni examines the case of state mental hospitals and prisons. He states that the actual goals of these institutions are largely custodial and they meet these goals effectively. But these institutions do not have sufficient professional staff to meet their announced therapeutic goals, and they have to meet stringent external demands (from, for example, the surrounding communities) that they be custodial. Thus it is not surprising that state mental hospitals and prisons largely fail to meet their announced, public goal of being therapeutic. Etzioni's analysis prompts the evaluator to ask: Have the institutions organized themselves and allocated their resources so as to be as therapeutic as possible, given the other system needs they must meet?

Etzioni also describes the paradox of ineffectiveness: The system model indicates that sometimes an organization can become more effective by allocating fewer resources to pursuing its goals and more to other activities. If too many resources are devoted to goal activities, the neglect of other activities essential to organizational survival hampers goal attainment.

There are two kinds of system models, a survival model, which specifies the requirements necessary for the system to exist, and an effectiveness model, which specifies the one pattern of interrelationships among the elements of the system that makes the system most effective in pursuing a given goal. This distinction implies that the effectiveness model ought to be used in evaluation studies when a specific goal for the organization can be identified. Etzioni's analysis does not reject goals as a useful analytical construct, but places them within a context of a system model that indicates their proper role.

Etzioni complains about researcher bias in the goal model as compared to the system model. For example, the evaluators may project their own goals on to the organization. Such attribution is especially misleading if the organization's public goals are the same as the evaluator's, but its private goals are not. The fact that it might be beneficial for the society if a program met a given goal does not imply that it is actually a goal of the organization. The researcher whose evaluation uses the organization's goals as the primary criterion may become a critic rather than one who seeks to understand, and thus will lose objectivity. It is not rare to find an evaluator who is angry with an organization for not meeting the program goals.

The goal model, Etzioni asserts, may have a politically liberal bias in that there may be the implicit expectations that societies should move toward progress, a bias that leads to unrealistic, utopian expectations. But the opposite bias, a conservative one, is often alleged about the system model, on the grounds that it is too adept at pointing out how difficult it is to change an established system. Many system models, such as Parsons' theory (1951), assume that systems return naturally to equilibrium, and so these models have difficulty accounting for change. One may view social systems as in a dynamic equilibrium, as in a static equilibrium, or even as moving toward entropy or gradual disequilibrium. Yet most system models appear static, always tending to return to an earlier stable state. Exceptions are models that incorporate multiple exponential feedback loops, such as the Club of Rome models (discussed in Chapter Two) that permit the system to move toward disequilibrium.

In demonstrating another source of bias, Etzioni notes that managers are committed by their role to multiple functions of the organization, such as system maintenance, system integration, as well as to goal achievement. However, evaluators tend to stress the importance of goal orientation and miss the importance of other functions the organization must serve. Etzioni finds the system model less biased in this respect. The overall purport of his analysis is that the program must be evaluated as a social system, not as a mere set of goal-directed activities.

Etzioni's contribution is important and is consistent with the view of programs as complex, ill-understood systems presented in Chapter Two, and with the work of major systems theorists. Churchman (1968), for example, suggests that an alleged goal is an actual goal if the system will knowingly sacrifice other alleged goals in order to attain that goal; to apply this test requires a study of the program itself as a system.

Goal-Free Evaluation

Our analysis thus far suggests that some programs can and should be evaluated in terms of their consequences even if they do not have goals or if their goals cannot be readily inferred. Evaluators should not attribute goals, indicators, or measures of goal achievement to the program without realizing that these attributions entail inferences and the formulation of constructs. Nor should evaluators intimidate program staff into accepting goals and measures of goal attainment. The formulation of what are to be taken to be the program's goals and what are appropriate measures of these goals is in part a matter of negotiation between evaluator and program staff. The evaluator should also consider the program's announced goals, its expressive purposes, and the organizational functions necessary for the program's survival. Some analyses, however, reject goals entirely as an analytical construct, and to these views we now turn.

Scriven (1978) proposes that "Goal-free evaluation is the conduct of evaluation of outcomes without the evaluator being exposed to, or contaminated by, knowledge of the purposes or goals" (quoted by Harrington and Sanders, 1979, p. 3). The basic aim of goal-free evaluation is to examine the total effect of a treatment, not just the main effect at which the program was aimed. This effort is in accord with the recommendations made in Chapter Two about seeking unintended and anticipated program consequences.

The difficulty is that the goal-free method attempts to attain this open-minded, broadly exploratory approach by keeping the evaluator ignorant of the program's goals. The method of goal-free evaluation consists of the effort to reduce the chance of social and ideological bias by reducing interaction between program staff and evaluators. "Ideological bias is abrogated by the central precept of goal-free evaluation: the evaluators have no prior knowledge of the goals or objectives of the project" (Harrington and Sanders, 1979, p. 4). However, the sociology of knowledge holds that no view is without bias. Each perspective or viewpoint contains some truth and some distortion, and both the truth and the distortion are congruent with the life situation of the thinker and his or her social group (Mannheim, 1936). Therefore, a research method cannot abrogate or remove bias, although it can limit, control, estimate, or measure bias. Interaction with program staff may be conducive to certain biases in the evaluator, but lack of contact with the program staff is conducive to other biases. Consequently, the claim that the goal-free evaluation method abrogates bias must be rejected.

Another aim of the goal-free technique is to avoid the goal trap. In one sense, the method does this by avoiding the program itself, but in doing so creates new and more dangerous snares for the evaluator. Another purpose is to detect unintended consequences. Goal-free evaluation posits that evaluators' ignorance of goals renders them open to noticing consequences not specified in the goal statements. This may be so, to a small extent, but having a theory about the nature of possible unintended consequences is far more important than maintaining an ignorance of official goal statements.

A basic difficulty with the goal-free approach is that goals are a social fact about the program, perhaps a misleading formulation or one concocted in order to get funding or public support, yet a fact whose content is in a complex way important to understanding the program. It is doubtless naive and literal to evaluate programs solely in terms of their goals, without considering how those goals function as part of the complex cultural and social system that comprises the program. But it is simplistic to evaluate the program as though it did not have goals, as though the program staff did not have complex ideas about their work. After all, some of the participants may actually be trying to achieve the goals.

The adherents of goal-free evaluation advocate it as a supplement to, rather than a replacement for, other methods of evaluation (Scriven, 1978; Harrington and Sanders, 1979), but their description of it suggests that it is the central technique, if used. Harrington and Sanders note that "after initial contact with the client, the evaluator should avoid any questions that would lead to disclosure of the goals or objectives of the projects. . . . Note also that questions about the project budget, and so on, can produce potentially strong biases, hence they are avoided" (pp. 7-8). The evaluation staff consists of a goal-free evaluator, an evaluation research project manager, and several observers. Only the observers collect the data. Although the goal-free evaluator undertakes the first contact with the client, this contact is sharply delimited to avoid disclosing any information about the goals of the program. The goal-free evaluator formulates the evaluation design, hires staff, develops instruments, analyzes the data, and writes the report. The project manager acts as intermediary between the program staff and the evaluation staff. The observers are also unaware of the goals; the project manager edits out of any program documents any information about goals. Since the project manager may know about the program goals, the manager cannot be permitted to formulate instruments or the evaluation design, lest bias related to goals be introduced. Since the observers must be ignorant of the program goals, too, they cannot interact with the program staff. They function exclusively as observers or raters.

The usual research design involves the collection of baseline data, or comparison group data, which are then compared with data collected during the program. From these data the evaluators formulate hypotheses about possible changes that are due to the program (Harrington and Sanders, 1979). Since these hypotheses are based on data from the program itself, it is hard to understand how more data from the same instance of the same program could be used to confirm them, unless a strong cross-validation design is used; otherwise the researchers would seem to be capitalizing on chance.

The technique is claimed to be a consumer-oriented rather than a management-oriented approach to evaluation. The effort is to force serious needs assessment, since the program's performance is compared to the needs of the target population, rather than to the announced goals of the program. The difficulty here is that a need is a construct rather than a given; a target population may be conceived to have an infinite variety of needs. Needs assessment presupposes some theory on the part of the evaluator concerning what questions to ask the target group in order to identify their needs. Thus the goal-free technique may in effect assess the program against the evaluator's goals rather than those of the program designers or program staff.

The final phase of goal-free evaluation requires a return to goal-based evaluation. After the goal-free report is written, the evaluators learn of the program goals. They use the information about the goals not to revise the report but to add sections to it. This step, however, does not remedy the major difficulties of goal-free evaluation. There remains the danger of misunderstanding the project through ignorance of the program staff's intentions or their professed intentions. Even if the program goals as announced are unreal or unrealistic, they may offer important clues about the program. Further, the evaluator's ignorance of the staff's goals negatively affects rapport with the program staff. Harrington and Sanders (1979) acknowledge that goal-free evaluation can lead to "unusual or unacceptable project staff discomfort and low goal-free staff credibility" (p. 19). Indeed, ignorance of program goals is very likely to lead to drastic difficulties in both rapport and cooperation, and may cripple the evaluation. Weiss and Rein's (1970) analysis shows the dangers of a distant and guarded relationship with program staff.

Because of the likelihood of misunderstanding the program and alienating the staff, goal-free evaluation must be rejected as infeasible in most instances. Apparently very few goal-free evaluations have actually been carried out. Original though it is, the method must also be rejected on logical grounds as being founded on a confusion about the nature of bias that leads to the claim that it is a bias-free method. Actually, the bias inherent in knowing the claimed goals of the program is replaced by the greater bias inherent in being ignorant of a major component of the program context.

Moreover, Harrington and Sanders note that "An intelligent goal-free evaluator can infer intended project outcomes from the editing (for example, holes in cut-up documents) done by the project manager. Other clues to the goals come from the verbal slips of the project staff, paraphrased goals in project materials, and project management plans" (p. 18). In fact, the idea that one could look at a program without readily perceiving its goal is itself unrealistic; the content of the program and the choice of pre- and postmeasures certainly reveal information about goals. It is to be doubted, then, whether goal-free evaluation is a sound way of avoiding the issues posed by program goals.

7

A New Approach to Field Experimentation

~~~~~~

Even if the evaluator and the client have a fine awareness of many of the substantive social-systems issues involved in evaluation, such as the degree of credence to be accorded program goals, they are still faced with methodological issues. Precisely because programs are such complex social systems, the methodologies for studying them can be subtle and complex. Because so many programs resist evaluation, new methodologies or new applications of old methodologies are especially needed. Less intrusive or disruptive or highly cumbersome methods are likely to arouse less opposition from program administrators and staff. Some types of field experimentation have these advantages. In this chapter, we propose a particular kind of field experimentation that merits wider application.

Field Experiments Distinguished from Other Methods

Field experiments must first be distinguished from true experiments, quasi-experiments, fieldwork, and surveys. First, let us define a true experiment. The classic definition involves (1) random assignment of cases to treatments, (2) control of all relevant extraneous variables, and (3) manipulation of the inde-

127

pendent variable by the experimenter in order to observe systematically its effect on the dependent variable. A true experiment ordinarily permits, or at least encourages, what are called strong inferences, which may be cynically defined as inferences that the researcher finds very plausible and that appear to have some kind of clear logical, syllogistic structure.

A quasi-experiment, sometimes called a quasi-experimental method, is an attempt to approximate the strong inferences possible for true experiments through the use of research arrangements or statistical analyses that parallel or approximate the logic involved in interpreting an experiment. Some quasi-experiments do not involve intervention by the experimenter but instead are ingenious statistical analyses of data collected by the program staff for various purposes. Quasi-experimental methods are almost always quantitative.

A survey involves asking a defined sample of people structured questions in a systematic, repeatable way that is amenable to coding, quantification, and statistical analysis. Fieldwork involves participant or nonparticipant observation, or in-depth, unstructured interviews with people who are treated as "informants" in the anthropological sense. The safeguards to valid inference in fieldwork lie in the richness of the data obtained.

Another major social research method is the field experiment. A field experiment can be defined as a study having all of the following characteristics:

1. It takes place in a natural situation. That is, the subjects are usually unaware they are being studied and they have not gone there for the purpose of being studied.
2. There is an intervention that manipulates (alters) or introduces a variable or a new behavior such as a program, which is considered the treatment.
3. There are *systematic* observation and measurement of the results of the intervention, especially with respect to its presumed effect on some dependent variables. Often this effect is hypothesized in advance. This definition involves thinking in terms of the effect of one or more independent variables on the dependent variables.

The three characteristics just noted are all consistent with the definition of a true experiment. However, there are several conditions of a true experiment that a field experiment need not meet. For example, a comparison condition with no manipulation or a different manipulation of the independent variable is not required for a field experiment. Random assignment of cases to treatments is also unnecessary. One element of a true experiment is control, that is, all extraneous variables that cannot be made equal for different groups by randomization are kept constant by the experimenter. The criterion of control is not often met in field experiments. The natural environment, a social system not dedicated to the purposes of experimentation, usually resists efforts by the researcher to exert control.

Clearly field experiments can be true experiments but need not be. What is the merit of using a broader definition for field experiments than for true experiments? Why use the term *experiment* even though some of the criteria for a true experiment are not met? To use this terminology is to recognize the crucial role played in an experiment by an intervention, especially an intervention based on some expectation about what is to happen as a result. Hence, our choice of terms stresses the systematic observation or measurement that enables a researcher to detect the predicted consequences. To make an intervention, along with a hypothesis about what is expected to ensue, is to subject a theory to the possibility of disconfirmation, which is what makes a theory scientific, as opposed to magical or supernatural. For example, astronomy is a scientific field because its theories are susceptible to disconfirmation: Astronomers can specify what would constitute an instance of disconfirmation of one of their theories. Astrology, however, is a magical or supernatural field since a prediction that appears disconfirmed will be reinterpreted by the astrologer as a confirmation; the theory is endlessly plastic and ambiguous.

It is true that many kinds of research are scientific, in that a theory is subjected to the possibility of disconfirmation on the basis of specified data. The research efforts of historians and anthropologists can be scientific in this sense. But the elegance and the persuasive power of an experiment are derived from experimental arrangements that yield a strong chain of logic in the disconfirmation or in the failure to disconfirm; the latter is interpreted as support for the theory since the original hypothesis remains plausible. A key element of these arrangements is the intervention, which permits predictions and disconfirmation.

Also crucial is the systematic nature of the observations, which permits different observers to agree on what they see and also allows the observations to be replicated. Systematic observation permits quantification, which provides both an estimate of the magnitude of what is observed and a way to estimate the degree of errors in the observations. Control, which equates as many variables as possible between the various treatments, and randomization, which attempts to equate all remaining variables, are also important aspects of true experiments. Some of these advantages are retained in field experimentation.

The field experiment's setting gives it additional probative value. In the field, variables need not be redefined, or in some cases parodied, as in the laboratory of the social psycholgist, but can be studied in situ. A researcher need not induce distrust or altruism or authoritarianism in experimental subjects; these phenomena can be studied as they naturally occur in society. Realism is a strength of any study conducted in the field; combined with the experimental method, it gives field experiments their peculiar power.

Another aspect of the increased strength of inference of field experiments is contextual. Variables and relationships can be considered in context. Thus, a field experiment about trust and distrust that examines whether housewives let people into their homes to use their telephones in an emergency examines distrust not as a single variable, but in a particular context, life in a small town. Because the variable is still embedded in its context, the extent of generalizability of the study results can be more aptly gauged.

It is helpful to propose a distinction among field experiments done for evaluation: the usual type of evaluative field experiment, in which the intervention is the program itself, and the field experiment in which the intervention is made by the researcher. In the latter type of field experimentation, the independent variable, the one manipulated by the experimenter, is not the program itself. This kind of field experiment has rarely been used for evaluation. Yet to choose an independent variable other than the program greatly increases the scope and flexibility of field experimentation. The kind of field experiment in which a specific intervention by the researcher constitutes the independent variable can be termed an *analytic experiment,* since it examines the effects of a discrete intervention on the rest of the program and makes inferences about the program based on those effects. The standard evaluative field experiment, in which the program itself constitutes the independent variable, can be termed *program experimentation.*

Let us first consider some important field experiments of the analytic type and examine their methodological characteristics. Then we will discuss some analytic experiments that have clear implications for evaluation. These reviews will yield a set of recommendations for applying analytic experiments to evaluation. We need not discuss the more classic type of field experiment, in which the program is considered the independent variable and versions of a program, or a program and no program, are compared. Such experiments are amply treated in standard texts (Cook and Campbell, 1979; Riecken and Boruch, 1974).

Analytic Experiments

Most of the classic field experiments are of the analytic type. Zimbardo's (1973a, 1973b) famous auto vandalism study offers the reader a sense of the probative value of the analytic type of field experiment. Zimbardo bought an old car, left it on a street in the Bronx across from the uptown campus of New York University, and kept it under continuous hidden surveillance for the next sixty-four hours. At the same time, a similar car was left on a street in Palo Alto, California across the street from the Stanford University campus. At the beginning of the study, Zimbardo and his colleagues opened the hoods of both cars and removed the license plates. In the Bronx, the car was totally stripped, mostly by middle-class whites, within twenty-six hours, and completely destroyed after sixty-four hours.

Most of these activities were carried out in broad daylight, and theft by adults preceded smashing and tire-slashing by teenagers and children. In contrast, the car in Palo Alto was left undisturbed for an entire week. When it began to rain, a passer-by lowered the hood to keep the battery and ignition dry. The experiment dramatically shows very different norms about vandalism and respect for property among middle-class people in two social environments.

The study has obvious persuasive power: In a sense the measure of vandalism, the destruction of the automobile, is the criterion itself, that is, it *is* vandalism (or an instance of vandalism) rather than merely a measure of vandalism. In field experiments, the dependent variable is often a sample of the criterion, not a surrogate or proxy variable. This kind of experiment has also the power to surprise: We are startled that a street across from the uptown campus of New York University is so different from the environs of Stanford. The identity of the auto strippers and vandals in the Bronx is unexpected: all the adults were "well-dressed, clean-cut whites who would under other circumstances be mistaken for mature, responsible citizens demanding more law and order" (1973b, p. 223). Thus a field experiment of the analytic type, that is, one in which a discrete intervention by the researcher is the independent variable, may be both compelling in its realism and surprising in its results.

From a methodological standpoint, we note that there was no random assignment of cases to treatments: that is, passers-by could not be assigned at random to the car in Palo Alto or the car in the Bronx. The two cars were almost identical but were not randomly assigned to Palo Alto or the Bronx. Since the two conditions were run at about the same time, differences between them could not be attributed to different historical events intervening between iterations of the experiment.

Of course, neither the particular streets nor the towns nor the campuses were randomly chosen. Rather, these were all judgment samples, chosen by the investigator on the basis of certain criteria, open to charges of experimenter bias in the choice of the criteria used. Since the two samples are each of size one, one cannot estimate sampling variability. In other terms, the environmental variables are *block-booked* (Rosenberg, 1968); that is, they are intertwined so that the Bronx site is in the East, in a large city, near an urban university, while the Palo Alto site is in the West, in a small town, near an exurban university, and so forth. As a result, one could attribute the difference in outcome to any of a number of variables.

One could answer these objections by replicating the study in other environments, which would make it a bit easier to distinguish which clusters of variables seem most conducive to automobile vandalism among the middle class. Undoubtedly replications in different natural settings and other methodological improvements, such as variations in the stimulus (type and age of car, whether the hood was raised and the license plates removed), would make it possible to understand the phenomena more precisely.

Yet even in its original implementation, in only two settings, the experiment is very convincing, despite the lack of randomization and the inability to hold all other variables constant, because the outcome behavior, the dependent variable, is a criterion sample. The problems of generalizing the results to the natural environment are reduced since the experiment was conducted in that environment. However the experiment is scientific in that it presents an intervention whose consequences were predicted in advance, permitting possible disconfirmation of a theory. Finally, systematic observation offers some assurance that independent observers would agree on the actual outcome.

A second example of analytic experimentation is a series of studies by Feldman (1968) about the willingness of people to assist a compatriot or a foreigner who asked for help in an urban setting. These studies cast important light on the nature of field experiments. A series of five experiments was conducted in each of three cities, Paris, Athens, and Boston, by a variety of sets of natives and foreigners. In the first study, a native couple and a foreign couple each stopped people in the street to ask for directions. To avoid experimenter bias in sample selection, passers-by were selected by choosing the fourth person coming down the sidewalk. The dependent variables were whether directions were given and whether the directions were accurate. The researchers also rated the passers-by who were asked for directions as well dressed, moderately dressed, or poorly dressed. Dress was used as an indicator of socioeconomic status, and interrater reliability on this rating was very high.

This design is worthy of comment. The ratings on dress made it possible to assess the influence of socioeconomic status on helpfulness, even though this was not the variable (responses to natives or foreigners) manipulated by the experimenter. The design demonstrates that contextual variables can be studied in the analytic experiment even though they are not manipulated. Feldman found different results in the three cities, in willingness to help (as compared to not helping or actively impeding) compatriots versus foreigners. Overall, compatriots were treated better in Paris and Boston, and foreigners were treated better in Athens. This result shows that systematic variation of the site of a field experiment can yield useful information, as Zimbardo also discovered in this comparison of the Bronx and Palo Alto. But multiple sites are not a requisite for a useful analytic experiment: Zimbardo's study would have been valuable even if done only in the Bronx, particularly since he coded the race and socioeconomic status of the vandals (some of the pillagers carried briefcases). He, too, was able to study contextual variables he did not manipulate.

Feldman's study is actually a series of experiments, related in conception, whose findings complement each other. In addition to the asking for directions, four other experiments were conducted, by a variety of compatriots and foreigners. One study involved asking a favor from a stranger (the mailing of a letter). In another, a stranger was approached with a small denomination bill and asked whether he had dropped it. A third experiment consisted of slightly overpaying a cashier and seeing whether the cashier returned the money. Finally, a compatriot and a foreigner each hailed a cab and observed whether they were overcharged.

Additional methodological insights about analytic experiments can be gleaned from Feldman's work. One point is that there can be many replications of each experiment. For example, sixty taxicab rides were taken in Paris, forty-two in Athens, and forty-four in Boston. Consequently, analytic experiments, that is, field experiments in which a discrete intervention is the independent variable, can have the robustness that comes from sampling over a number of instances in each site. Since in many cases the same cab driver was hailed in succession by the compatriot and the foreigner, it was possible in some cases to hold this variable, the identity of the driver, constant, for certain pairs of rides. Many cab drivers were hailed in each city, so that there is sampling across the cab drivers. This experimental arrangement illustrates that there can be a breadth and variety of sampling in an analytic field experiment even where there is not mathematically random selection (of cab drivers, or cabs). Further, some subjects can be used as their own control. Note, too, since five experimental interventions were used to measure willingness to help a foreigner versus a compatriot, there can be multiple measurement of the construct under study.

The insights about analytic experimentation yielded by Feldman's study include the observation that the dependent variables can be reliably coded and analyzed through inferential statistics. Analytic experiments can have systematic variation of sites, replications within each site, the use of the subject as his own control, and a systematic study of contextual variables, including dependent and independent variables that are not manipulated by the experimenter.

We also should note that many different kinds of interventions by the experimenter can be used as indicators of the same construct. This multiplicity lends far greater construct validity to the research than is possessed by the frequent experimental procedure in which a given measure is an indicator of the construct because the experimenter says it is. (For example, an alcoholic rat is a rat who is taught to prefer alcohol to water. Generalizations from the rat to a business executive, suburban housewife, or a skid row denizen are a bit dubious.) There can be robustness of the stimulus itself, in that different experimenters can intervene in different replications of the same experiment in the same city. There can be some control over experimenter-induced sampling bias by use of a numerical criterion for choosing subjects, as for example, choosing every fourth passer-by; this procedure constitutes systematic random sampling. (In some of Feldman's experiments, it would have been even better if the experimenters were unaware of the hypotheses of the study.) This is an impressive list of methodological advantages despite the limitations on randomization and on the ability to hold extraneous variables constant.

A study by Altman and others (Milgram, 1970) illustrates two additional methodological strengths of analytic field experiments. They studied the willingness of householders to allow strangers to enter their home to use the telephone. The experimenters rang doorbells, asking to use the telephone to locate the address of a friend nearby. Responses for a middle-income housing development in Manhattan were compared with those in six small towns in Rockland County, outside New York City. Respondents were far more helpful in the towns than in the urban housing developments, and women had somewhat greater ease in getting assistance. It is significant that the same construct that Feldman studied, helpfulness to strangers, could be studied by someone else in another experiment in a different situation, with results that are theoretically meaningful in terms of Feldman's results. That is, cognate analytic field experiments can form a tradition of investigation that is theoretically meaningful, for example, in terms of anomie as conceptualized by Durkheim (1951) and Srole (1956) and urbanism as formulated by Wirth (1938) and Milgram (1970). Field experiments by different investigators can build on previous work and test important theories.

A second issue is that Altman's study design could have used (but apparently did not) random selection of cases (as in sample surveys) and could then if necessary have randomly assigned cases to treatments (male versus female applicants for help). Here, therefore, is an instance of a design for an analytic field experiment that permits both random sampling of persons and random assignment of cases to treatments. Because the subjects are fixed in location and identifiable in advance (from house numbers and doorbell listings), a sampling frame can be drawn up for random sampling of subjects, and the various treatments can be assigned to subjects at random.

One aspect of Feldman's and Altman's studies is problematic. As our descriptions make clear, many field experiments involve deception. Deception in the taxicab rides does not pose an ethical problem since the service is paid for and is routine and nonaversive for the drivers; the deception consists only in the purpose of the rides. In the cashier study, the service is also routine, paid for, and nonaversive, since the cashier is free to keep the extra money. Little ethical difficulty is posed by trivial deceptions that put the respondents to no trouble, are not aversive, do not invade their private lives, and have no enduring consequences for them.

Against the disadvantages of deception (it is, after all, better to tell the truth) must be balanced the great social benefit that can result from research on the crucial social issues of our time. For example, many of the studies of alienation in the city and willingness to help strangers were initiated in response to the murder of Kitty Genovese in 1964 (Milgram, 1970). This young woman was stabbed to death on a street in Queens, New York, while none of the thirty-eight neighbors who heard her scream for half an hour came to her assistance or even bothered to call the police from the locked bastions of their own apartments. A similar incident took place inside the same apartment complex, in 1976, involving some of the same neighbors, with the same result. In the application of analytic field experiments to evaluation, the same moral justification exists for the deceptions sometimes involved, if they are minor, nonaversive, and have no enduring consequences for the subjects, as will become evident from the instances we shall now examine.

Analytic Experimentation for Evaluation

To extend analytic experimentation to evaluative research, one need merely move from studies of how citizens react or help to studies of how program service staff help or otherwise react. Although studies of social service staff are not specifically intended to be program evaluations, they cast light on a systematic pattern of action by government officials. Such an organized pattern of activity by government staff constitutes a social program.

One important study of government service staff is Heussenstamm's experiment, "Bumper Stickers and the Cops" (1971), conducted during a time of violence between the Black Panther Party and the police in California. Student members of that party complained that they were being harassed by the police and that all had received many unfair traffic citations. Discussion revealed that all of these students had Black Panther Party stickers glued to their bumpers. Heussenstamm decided to subject these claims of harassment to experimental test.

Three groups of five students each—three males and two females—were formed. One group was black, one was white, and one was of Mexican descent. The fifteen were selected from a larger group of forty-five, such that each of the fifteen had exemplary driving records, with no moving citations within the past twelve months, as attested by a sworn statement. They promised to continue driving as carefully as before and to do nothing to attract the attention of the police, sheriff's deputies, or highway patrolmen. They also averred that their cars, a variety of American makes and models, had no defective equipment. The researchers inspected the lights, horns, brakes, and tires to verify this. The appearance of the fifteen students varied from straight to hippie styles, with some ethnic styles also. The students recognized the seriousness of receiving moving violations in California, where four of these within twelve months automatically leads to a review of driving records, usually resulting in a year of probation or suspension of license.

All the students were commuters at California State College in Los Angeles. To the rear bumper of each student's car was attached a "bumper sticker in lurid, day-glo, orange and black, depicting a menacing panther with large BLACK PANTHER lettering" (p. 32). The first student to receive a ticket received it on the way home from school with the sticker on his car for the first time. Five students were cited for moving violations the second day, three the third day, and so on. Violations included "incorrect lane change," "following too closely," "failing to yield the right of way," "driving too slowly in the high speed lane of the freeway," "failure to make a proper signal before turning right at an intersection," "failure to observe proper safety of pedestrians using a crosswalk," "excessive speed," "making unsafe lane changes," and "driving erratically" (p. 33).

The study was ended after seventeen days, when the fund of $500 from a private source to pay for the violations was exhausted. One student had to drop out of the study on the fourth day because he had received three citations, the number previously agreed on with the researchers as the maximum feasible. Three others reached that limit within the first week. All told, the participants received thirty-three citations in seventeen days. One student received his second ticket on his way to pay the fine for his first one. Citations did not vary with students' race, sex, or appearance. In only one instance, that of a beautiful blonde woman who was a member of a campus sorority, did the police comment on the bumper stickers. After a few days, the students started to show a "sober, demoralized air of futility" (p. 33). Five cars and their drivers were thoroughly searched.

The quantitative nature of the dependent measure, traffic citations, gives the study a compelling persuasive power. Substantively, the study indicates the Los Angeles police systematically harassed Black Panthers and people suspected of being sympathetic to them. Considered in isolation, this conclusion might seem puzzling. But knowledge of the social context, namely that police officers had been killed in clashes with the Panthers, makes these results comprehensible. Knowledge of the social context of an analytic experiment is often vital in interpreting the results. This is also true for program experiments, but in a different sense, because the context that must be understood is in considerable part included in the intervention itself, the program.

To examine the probative value of Heussenstamm's analytic experiment, one can note that the Black Panthers had often alleged harassment by the police in the form of traffic citations. Indeed, during the trial of a Black Panther leader for a traffic violation, in Denver, Colorado, in 1969, he claimed such harassment. The trial was broadcast in full on national television. The court found for the defendant, in effect agreeing with the charges of harassment. But many television viewers were unsure that the court had reached the correct decision. Heussenstamm's experiment, with its larger numbers, non-Black Panther subjects, its hypotheses specified in advance, and its quantification, adds convincing substantiation.

Earlier we discussed the ethical problems raised by any deception in field experimentation. In Heussenstamm's study, the police were implicitly misled as to the party membership or political sympathy of the drivers. But this minor deception, if deception it was, appears far outweighed in this case by the social importance of the findings. The findings indicate prejudice and abuse of power by the police, who are the law enforcement authorities.

The methodology of Heussenstamm's experiment is instructive, although the design of the experiment could have been improved. The experiment used a "before and after" design, that is, observations of driving tickets before and after the placing of stickers on the cars, which intervention is the independent variable. However, it could have had a control group, a sample chosen from the same pool of 45, or from the same student body, who would not have received bumper stickers and whose citations over the same period would have been measured. Without a control group, one cannot dismiss "history" as a variable (Cook and Campbell, 1979); that is, one cannot rule out the possibility that during the seventeen days, there was a sudden traffic enforcement effort by the police aimed at everyone. But data outside the experiment indicate that such an interpretation is false.

One might also wonder about the threat of selection effects to the validity of the study: the possibility that the student volunteers were different in some way from the rest of the student body and so drive differently and worse. But their previous flawless driving records make this possibility unlikely. Statistical regression of scores on number of traffic citations toward the mean is another danger to valid inference, but this is unlikely since Heussenstamm reports that the number of citations (zero) had been stable over the whole previous year.

Another danger might be the interaction of selection and treatment; that is, whether those who volunteered for the study, reacted differently to the treatment (the bumper stickers) than other students would have. For example, even though their previous driving records were exemplary, they might have driven erratically because of anxiety about the bumper stickers, or because of a wish to be defiant, or a wish to discredit the Los Angeles police. This appears unlikely in view of the severe penalties for multiple violations and in view of their observed dismay at receiving the citations.

More likely, however, is the possibility that the fifteen knew the hypotheses of the study and that this affected their driving. Cook and Campbell (1979) classify this kind of phenomenon as a *reactive arrangement,* which Orne (1959) conceptualizes as "the demand characteristics of the experimental situation," a form of experimenter bias in which the researcher produces the results sought by unconsciously communicating the research hypotheses to the subjects, through cues in the research situation. Whether this happened can best be determined by systematically interviewing the subjects after the study, that is, by conducting a post-experimental inquiry. In Heussenstamm's study, the subjects appear to have tried conscientiously to drive in the same careful way as usual.

Heussenstamm suggests that, if the study were to be redesigned, one could improve it by putting the drivers in the cars, attaching right-wing and left-wing stickers to their bumpers at random, and having them drive set courses at random, "after the drivers were seated in their assigned vehicles and the doors sealed" (p. 33). This method is evidently an attempt to avoid communicating the research hypotheses to the subjects. But this suggestion misses the point. By creating an artificial setting, it removes the experiment from the field and constructs an outdoor laboratory in which the subjects would be acutely aware that they were being studied. This would likely increase the reactivity of the experimental procedures rather than decrease them. The essence of the field experiment as proposed in this chapter is to maintain as well as possible the field situation by having the experimenter's intervention be as nonobvious as possible. Other modifications proposed by Heussenstamm consist of having observers observe the drivers' behavior, and having tape recorders in each car to record conversations with police officers. These efforts to obtain objective observation and re-cording without constraining the participants seem commend-able improvements.

As our review of Heussenstamm's study indicates, ana-lytic field experiments can be used to study how personnel treat their clientele or the general citizenry. The evaluator can use this method to study how program staff treat their clientele or to study any bureaucracy, whether involved in a systematic pro-gram or not. This method can also be used to assess the effec-tiveness of training programs for social agency personnel.

For example, consider an analytic experiment reported in the national press in which researchers turned in allegedly lost wallets to fifty New York City police officers. Only about 40 percent of the wallets were turned in by the police to their dis-trict precinct station; the rest presumably were kept by the offi-cers. The police department raised a great complaint against the ethics of this study, seeing it as a form of entrapment. Yet a simple experiment of this sort seems a most persuasive means of assessing the honesty of a police force.

The evaluative implications of the study are that effects of the police training program were negated by the subsequent socialization pressures on the job. If the study is not used to damage the careers of individual officers, but merely to assess the responsibility and honesty of the force and the efficacy of their training, the deception seems ethically justifiable as an essential means of protecting the citizenry.

Analytic experiments can similarly be used to study other social service operations. As a paradigm, consider a study by Dorris (1972) of the reactions of coin dealers to various kinds of hard-luck stories from students (confederates of the experi-menter) trying to sell allegedly inherited coins. Dorris found that the stories and the students' claim that the money was needed for textbooks markedly influenced the price offered for the coins by many dealers.

Dorris' approach could be used to study how social serv-ice agencies, such as welfare departments, food stamp bureaus, and family service agencies, treat different classes of clientele who use different pleas or present themselves as having different social attitudes. The experimental model implicit in Dorris' study is also related to the model implicit in Hussenstamm's study, where the students' social attitudes—support of the Black Panther party—influenced police reactions.

Other relevant studies include Rosenhan's study (1973) of how mental hospital staff react to perfectly normal persons who have gained admission to the hospital, and Griffin's *Black Like Me* (1961), the story of Griffin's having dyed his skin black and touring the South. This was in effect an experimental study of the influence of race and class on attitudes. Among his melancholy discoveries was the "hate stare" used by some southern whites against blacks. A related model is provided by Lefkowitz, Blake, and Mouton's (1955) field experiment in which a confederate of the experimenter jaywalked against a traffic signal under two experimental conditions: in one, he was affluently dressed; in the second, poorly dressed. The research-ers noted the number of pedestrians who followed his lead in jaywalking, and it was considerably higher for the well-dressed condition. Parallel experiments could be devised to assess the re-action of social program staff to various social classes, races, and ethnic groups, among potential program recipients. Like the wallet study, these analytic experiments are peculiarly compel-ling, since they deviate so little from field conditions, with the intervention being at the same time so theoretically fruitful.

Another model for program evaluation is Peters and Ceci's (1980) study of the editorial review practices of profes-sional journals. One can consider these as constituting a pro-gram, since they are an ordered and planned sequence of social actions allegedly directed toward a goal. The researchers took one article, published from eighteen to thirty-two months ear-lier, from each of the ten most prestigious journals in psychol-ogy. They retyped the articles, changing only the names of the authors, the institutional affiliation of the authors, the title, ab-stract, and introductory sentences, and submitted each for pub-lication to the original journal.

In only three cases of ten were the bogus articles detected by the editors or reviewers. The other seven received a normal journal review, and six were rejected on grounds of methodological flaws, substantive weakness, or lack of appropriateness for the journal. Additional data from a study of three more journals (Peters and Ceci, 1981) yielded three more rejections. In total, therefore, nine of ten undetected resubmissions were rejected by journals that had previously published them. In this study, the review process is the program, the submission of previously published articles is the intervention by the experimenter, and rejection is the dependent variable from which inferences can be made about the review process.

The Logic and Scope of Analytic Experiments

Having considered a number of examples, some of them in detail, we want to examine the logic and the scope of analytic experimentation. The logic is perhaps easier to set forth: the experimental intervention, the treatment, need not be the program, but instead can be an intervention designed by the experimenter for the purpose of finding out about the program. This method provides a solution to one of the difficulties in evaluating broad-aim programs, noted by Weiss and Rein (1969, 1970): Owing to the difficulty of defining a broad-aim program, it is difficult to devise variants on the programs to use as experimental conditions.

Analytic field experimentation allows a researcher to study how a program functions and some of its effects, without having to sharply define the program and its key components in order to run different combinations of program components as experimental conditions. Analytic experiments can yield valuable findings for programs that are not well understood or not well formulated. Of course, the evaluator must have some theory about the program in order to decide how to intervene as the experimenter. For example, one need not know exactly how an agency functions, but one needs some theory—that discrimination against minorities or retaliation for injuries to policemen may be key issues in the urban police force—in order to design the experiment. Although the agency may have no clear theory of the program, the evaluator must be able to formulate a theoretical question about the program that will be answered by the proposed intervention.

The question of the scope of analytic field experimentation is at once more practical and more puzzling. The approach is clearly helpful for evaluation of delivery of services. Analytic field experiments enable the evaluator to specify how services are delivered, a matter of considerable ambiguity in many programs. Even commercial services can be studied; for example, management can study the operations of its sales force, through analytic experiments. Moreover, in programs where high-quality or by-the-book delivery of services can be considered the program goal, analytic experimentation can examine whether the program is effective.

The estimation of program effectiveness from the evaluation of service delivery is a major contribution of analytic experimentation to evaluation. If, for example, the goal of the program is transportation of the indigent to general hospital outpatient clinics, then an experimenter posing as a needy person using the system can discover whether the delivery of services takes place as planned and, consequently, whether the program is effective. For services already known to be valuable, such as inoculating children or transporting the elderly to clinics, an analytic experiment that shows that the service is being delivered with reasonable quality also shows that the program is effective.

For most programs, the value of the service is debatable, thus the consequences of the service that is delivered must be carefully examined. In these instances, even if the service is delivered as planned, the question remains whether it is effective. In such cases, analytic experimentation can reveal exactly what is delivered, and it permits inferences about the process by which the program takes place. For example, analytic experimentation can show staff to be conscientious, or dishonest, or prejudiced, and can highlight the process of interaction between program staff and clients. Since many programs as enacted differ markedly from what was planned, such findings are important and may result in inferences about the effectiveness of the program.

Another central aspect of program delivery that the analytic experiment can examine is whether the target population was reached, and in a nondiscriminatory manner. The evaluator can discover whether all segments of the intended clientele were served or whether the program administered only to the best-off of the poor, who already had the most resources and so were most likely to be able to benefit from it, a situation Miller and others (1970) term *creaming.*

In a different application of analytic experimentation, the researcher intervenes with the program recipients rather than with the staff. Through such intervention, the reactions of the clients can be examined, and from these reactions, inferences can be made about the program. If the program is consumer education, for example, a confederate of the researcher could act as a door-to-door salesperson and call on a random sample of clients and members of a control group. If the program is agricultural extension education, one could observe how a random sample of farmers participating in the program react to the researcher's real offer of some proposed new seed and compare their reactions to those of a control group.

To evaluate a high school new math curriculum that is supposed to create a heightened interest in mathematics, one could compare how students in the program and a control group respond to an offer of a free Saturday morning math workshop. To evaluate a police community relations program, one could see how the community reacts to a police car left unattended for twelve hours, or to a police officer's request to use a telephone or a request for certain kinds of information about the neighborhood. By the analytic experimental method, program effectiveness can therefore be directly estimated from the clients' reactions to the researcher's interventions.

Advantages of Analytic Experimentation

Let us consider the special advantages of analytic field experimentation over other methods. Because a variable is manipulated and the consequences observed, analytic experiments often allow stronger causal inferences than fieldwork, which we defined earlier as a method involving participant or nonparticipant observation, or in-depth interviews with people who are treated as informants. Because predictions and systematic preplanned observations are made, and because analytic experimentation is susceptible to quantitative treatment of the results, disconfirmation of hypotheses is easier than with fieldwork.

A major advantage of analytic experimentation as compared with program experimentation (in which the program itself is the independent variable) is that the researcher does not have to control the program, unlike Fairweather's (1968) method of experimental social innovation, a form of program experimentation. Consequently, analytic experimentation is usually less intrusive and less obtrusive than program experimentation; the investigator does not have to create systematically varied program enactments in order to draw evaluative inferences. Moreover, the researcher need not attempt to prevent the program from changing or adapting to its environment in order to maintain the integrity of the experimental design. Such an attempt antagonizes the program staff and may lead them to undermine the evaluation, as Weiss and Rein (1969, 1970) note in their autopsy of a failed evaluation effort.

Compared with ethnographic studies, and field studies generally, analytic field experimentation is far less labor-intensive. The logic of the field study is that the lack of crispness of experimental design, in terms of quantitative hypotheses stated in advance, is compensated by the richness of the data, that is by the volume, variety, redundancy and multiple perspectives of the data. Field studies attempt to be exhaustive in their description of the social phenomena under study and are therefore labor-intensive, as practitioners of that method note (Johnson, 1975; Wax, 1975; Weiss and Rein, 1970). By contrast, analytic experimentation lends itself more to elegance of design and cleverness of intervention, judging by the studies of Dorris (1972), Feldman (1968), Heussenstamm (1971), and Zimbardo (1973a, 1973b).

Another important advantage over fieldwork is that analytic experiments have much less need for the investigator to become socialized into the culture being studied, whether it be that of the program staff or that of the recipients. Some socialization into the culture is always important, and all researchers need some firsthand acquaintance with the culture to be studied.

But analytic field experimentation requires less direct personal involvement in the study. Zimbardo did not talk with the trashers of the car, and Heussenstamm did not talk with the police. Unlike fieldwork, the systematic observations needed for this method often can be made by research assistants or collaborators, rather than by the principal investigator. This advantage, however, can become a limitation if the principal researcher becomes too far removed from the phenomena under study.

A further advantage over fieldwork is that the systematic observations used in analytic experimentation make possible higher reliability. The analytic experiment trades some richness of data for added reliability of data. Like fieldwork and to some extent like program experiments unless the researcher has severely constrained the program, analytic experimentation precludes the question of whether the findings apply outside the laboratory, because the study is done outside the laboratory.

Often an analytic experiment can be carried out in a much shorter time than a program experiment, since the experimental intervention is not the program itself but rather a lesser intervention by the researcher that permits inferences about the program. For example, Heussenstamm's study was completed within a matter of a few weeks. Elegance has its rewards.

To the extent that subjects are unaware of being observed, as in Feldman's study of the fares charged by taxi drivers to compatriots and foreigners, far less cooperation of subjects is necessary than in most program experiments and in fieldwork. In analytic experiments, one can make elegant inferences about how people think and feel by observing their actions in response to the experimenter's intervention.

Conversely, however, in fieldwork the subjects can act as informants and describe their thoughts and feelings or interpret their actions. Such information can be enormously useful. Nothing, however, prevents a postexperimental inquiry (Orne, 1969) in an analytic experiment. During this inquiry, subjects, or a random sample of them, are asked to account for their behavior during the experiment. This procedure should probably be standard in both analytic and program experiments, as well as in social psychological laboratory experiments.

Let us consider another suggestion. There is no conclusive reason that the site or sites for fieldwork could not be chosen on the basis of a random sample. For example, Tally's Corner, the site of Liebow's (1967) study of unemployed black men who hang out on a street corner, could have been chosen as the result of such a sample. The suggestion seems almost preposterous, because the sample-to-sample variability with a sample size of one, is so great. In addition, practitioners of fieldwork (Wax, 1975) say that they are frequently rejected by the culture or group they are trying to study, so one must infer that it is often not feasible to have a random sampling procedure dictate the site of the study.

The logic of fieldwork is that the richness of the data is supposed to compensate for the peculiarities of a particular site. Strictly speaking, analytic experiments cannot be claimed to be superior to field studies on the basis of sampling considerations; yet the logic of sampling is both more helpful and more necessary in such experiments. Since crispness, inventiveness, elegance, and economy of time are the advantages of analytic experiments, and such experiments do not offer the unusual richness of data provided by fieldwork, the site may be more important than in fieldwork. Sampling is important since any richness of data cannot put into perspective the peculiarities of an ill-chosen study site. Consequently, multiple sites are often necessary in analytic experiments. Multiple sites enable evaluators to sample all forms of the program and all clients, which is very desirable for evaluation purposes. Such sampling makes it possible to estimate the extent or prevalence of the phenomena elicited in response to the researcher's intervention.

In addition, attention to randomization is likely to be helpful. Random assignment of cases to treatments is often impossible in these experiments, since the cases are usually people and it is necessary to avoid communicating to them that they are being studied. However, sometimes this kind of randomization is possible, as in Feldman's study, in which every fourth passer-by was asked for directions. Even if cases cannot be randomly assigned to treatments, often the researcher's intervention can be randomly assigned to situations, times, and places.

For example, an analytic experiment concerning delivery of services at welfare offices could select these on a stratified random basis and also choose a stratified sample of times of day.

By the random sampling of situations, times, and places for the experimental intervention, evaluators are likely to obtain much the same result as by random assignment of cases to treatments. One might consider the combination of situation, time, and place as a case and assign it randomly to the intervention. This perspective has some implications for statistical analysis—for example, the number of cases is not the number of individuals—but the experimental rigor and the strength of inference are much the same.

To give program experimentation its due, we acknowledge that random assignment of cases to treatments and sampling are logically more straightforward and unambiguous with program experiments than with analytic ones. However, the administrative difficulties in sampling are likely to be far greater in program experiments unless the program staff and clientele are unusually cooperative.

Overall, analytic experimentation offers certain advantages over fieldwork and over program experiments. It does not offer the richness of data of the field study nor the elaborate insights provided by in-depth interviews with informants. Nor does it have the forceful logic of the program experiment in which alternative versions of the same program can be compared. Yet the elegance, persuasiveness, incisiveness, and economy of analytic experimentation are often important. Analytic experiments sometimes involve deception, but program experiments are sometimes coercive, and fieldwork can be a co-optive and reactive method. In the next two chapters, we present a more detailed examination of the virtues and applications of a variety of methodological approaches to evaluation.

8

Making Sense of Quantitative and Qualitative Methods

~·

Beyond the debate about the special merits of any particular evaluation method, a major controversy in evaluation has emerged about quantitative and qualitative methods. The issues are important for evaluators to consider in deciding among methods. Moreover, many clients take strong positions about the correct way to do evaluation, some demanding hard quantitative measures, and others saying that certain things cannot be measured and so demanding qualitative studies. It is perhaps surprising to hear a client espousing a particular methodological stance, but such beliefs draw on feelings about one's field of specialization, about how scientific one believes oneself to be, and about one's commitment to values. Discussions of method are often both intellectual and emotional because many administrators have training in the social sciences.

Owing to the importance of the controversy among evaluators and the saliency of the issue in the minds of the users of evaluation, it is worthwhile to clarify matters. Our explication will help the client and the evaluator make a more informed

151

decision on what methodological approach to take for a particular program, a matter of some importance given the conflicting claims of the adherents of each approach. In this chapter, we argue that the matter can be more accurately characterized as a distinction between qualitative and quantitative data, rather than methods, and that both kinds of data can easily be used in the same study.

Qualitative and Quantitative

It is helpful to begin by clarifying the meaning of *qualitative*. In evaluation and elsewhere in the social sciences, at least four usages have emerged. The first usage is "having to do with qualities," in the sense of properties or attributes. This use of qualitative should be rejected as too inclusive and as blurring the more precise uses. A second usage is "having to do with 'goodness' of some sort," as in the phrase, "quality of life." This confusing usage interferes with the attempt to distinguish qualitative and quantitative, since many properties having to do with goodness can be measured, that is, quantified.

A third usage of "qualitative" is "not quantifiable," which takes us into stormy methodological waters, since many methodologists would reject the idea of a property or attribute that is not quantifiable in principle. This usage can be dismissed, as it is neither necessary nor helpful to make such a broad and profound assertion about qualitative data. A fourth usage is the one recommended here, "descriptive but not yet quantified." This usage takes no position on whether the attribute or property can in practice or in principle be quantified.

Quantification here is taken to mean "the assignment of numbers to objects according to rules." Even this simple definition, though it glides over profound issues, suffices to clarify much of the quantitative-versus-qualitative controversy. To say that qualitative data are descriptive but not yet quantified means that instances are placed in categories, such as Protestant and Catholic, and that a distinction of degree is not drawn between the categories. This usage does not imply that it is in principle or in practice impossible to draw distinctions of degree *between* the categories (a form of quantification) such as "less favorable to the use of religious icons" versus "more favorable to the use of religious icons," or "less inclined to acknowledge the authority of the Pope" versus "more inclined to acknowledge the authority of the Pope." Nor does the usage imply that one cannot draw distinctions of degree *within* categories (a form of quantification), such as, for Protestants, "simplicity of the liturgy," or for Catholics, "amount of scope accorded to Papal infallibility." The use of qualitative to mean descriptive but not yet quantified is widely accepted in the social sciences and is preferable to the confused alternative usages in the evaluation literature.

Since quantification is usefully defined as the assignment of numbers to objects according to rules, the realm of quantification is not coterminous with what is mathematical, since some fields of mathematics, notably topology, are nonquantitative. This is one among many misunderstandings in the evaluation literature. That literature describes qualitative methods as holistic, contextual, subjective, and empathic, while quantitative methods are described as particularistic, experimental, objective, and obtrusive. (See, for example, Cook and Reichardt, 1979; Filstead, 1979.) Quantitative and qualitative methods are treated in the controversy as opposite poles.

Indeed, Filstead (1979) describes the competition between qualitative and quantitative methods as a clash of paradigms, in the sense meant by Kuhn (1962), who speaks of a paradigm as a body of assumptions and perspectives underlying an entire scientific world view. At certain crucial epochs, scientific paradigms clash, as with the clash between Ptolemaic and Copernican paradigms. Rist (1977), Patton (1978), Reichardt and Cook (1979), and Filstead (1979) all endorse the application of the idea of a paradigm to this controversy in evaluation, although Reichardt and Cook doubt that the conflict of the quantitative and the qualitative paradigms in evaluation must determine research strategies or prevent elements of quantitative and qualitative research methods from sometimes being used together. But the entire controversy is overblown. Evaluation research is much too young, small, and intellectually feeble an investigative effort to constitute a paradigm or engender a paradigm clash; controversies in the field are not on the same intellectual footing as clashes between Ptolemaic and Copernican perspectives or between Newtonian and Einsteinian perspectives. There is no question of paradigms here, for fundamental assumptions about the nature of reality are not at issue, merely preferences for ways of doing evaluation.

Perhaps the controversy has become so inflated because as resources for social research decline and the demand for evaluation research increases professionals are competing for scarce resources. (See Chapter Three.) This competition results in a loss of perspective, as each profession claims to have something of transcendant importance to contribute to evaluation. Another determinant of this controversy is the difficulty in identifying the contributions of research methods drawn from a variety of specialties in the social sciences. As a result, evaluative research presents an interlocking set of misclassifications of methods and false bifurcations between methods. In this chapter, we seek to clarify matters and correct some of the more egregious errors, so that the evaluator and client can think more clearly about which evaluation methods to use in a given case.

To imagine a polarity between qualitative and quantitative methods is a considerable oversimplification. Some qualitative studies use quantification, and this fact suggests that the two methods are not mutually exclusive. Indeed, some evaluators urge that qualitative and quantitative methods be used together in evaluation to produce a methodological triangulation (Denzin, 1970) in which the shortcomings of each method are compensated for by the advantages of the others; they argue that findings arrived at by a multiplicity of methods are more likely to be valid. There is no doubt that multiple methods allow identification of some of the variance attributable to method in a study (Campbell and Fiske, 1959). A multiple-method approach to evaluation, provided the client can afford it, is perfectly reasonable.

Caparaso (1973) discusses the problem of integrating the findings of multiple-method studies. The work of Hovland (1959) on attitudes, and of Sheuch (1966), Galtung (1967), and others in factorial ecology suggests that a position of methodological complementary operationism is more realistic than one of convergent operationism. The issue is that findings from different methods cannot completely converge, since different methods do not measure exactly the same phenomena and cannot yield identical findings. They can, however, yield findings that are supportive or disconfirming of each other, in the sense of being logically consistent or inconsistent with each other. In evaluation research, the findings of qualitative and quantitative methods cannot be expected to converge completely but rather to complement each other in a complex way. At the least, the two sets of findings usually involve different concepts.

Methodological Misclassifications

Only a minority of researchers assert that quantitative methods are equivalent to experimental ones. They believe that experiments are the only valid, reliable (as opposed to largely suppositional and speculative) quantitative methods. Advances in methodology, such as multiple regression and factor analysis, have rendered this view archaic even within experimental psychology.

A more widespread misconception is that experimental and quasi-experimental methods are the only quantitative methods useful for evaluation. (Quasi-experimental methods are modes of analysis of quantitative data that attempt to duplicate or closely imitate the patterns of inference that are possible with experimental data. These methods include cross-lagged panel analysis, time-series analysis, and path analysis.) But the set of quantitative methods useful for evaluation is much larger than this. Survey research is one example of a quantitative method that is neither experimental or quasi-experimental in its logic. Survey research is highly quantitative; even if the data are gathered at one time, elaboration enables the discovery of lawful relationships among the data, and even the drawing of causal inferences. Elaboration, an analytic process devised by Stouffer (see Stouffer, 1949) and Lazarsfeld (see Kendall and Lazarsfeld, 1950), involves successive cross-tabulations, each designed to confirm or refute various plausible relationships among the data.

Survey research is preeminently a method of sociologists and political scientists. Other professions use other quantitative, nonexperimental methods that do not fall under the quasi-experimental rubric of Campbell and Stanley (1966) and Cook and Campbell (1979). Among the quantitative methods useful in evaluation that do not attempt to re-create the logic of experimental design in a quasi-experimental setting are econometric models, operations research, simulation models, decision theory, cost-benefit analysis, input-output studies (of the type pioneered by Vassily Leontief), information theory, social area analysis, factorial social ecology, and multiattribute utility analyses. Some of these methods have their origins in economics or sociology, rather than in psychology, the field that has thus far dominated evaluation.

Even within psychology quantitative methods in evaluation are not equivalent to experimental or quasi-experimental methods. The use of unobtrusive measures (Webb and others, 1972), for example in the evaluation of the attractiveness of museum exhibits by measuring the wear in the floors in front of the exhibits, falls more naturally into the realm of nonparticipant observation than quasi-experimentation. This is not to deny that unobtrusive measures can be used as dependent or independent variables in an experimental or quasi-experimental design.

Another distortion inherent in the bifurcation of qualitative and quantitative is that too much has been made of the analogy between experimental and quasi-experimental methods in evaluation. Many other kinds of methods make possible strong inferences, if we define these as inferences on which one would be willing to act or wager. Consequently it is erroneous to group together experimental and quasi-experimental methods on the grounds that only they permit strong inferences. Moreover some of the methods usually described as quasi-experimental, such as the time-series and the multiple time-series designs, the nonequivalent control groups designs, and the "patched-up" designs bear as much resemblance to field research and to clinical-historical case studies, as to true (that is, randomized) experiments. Other methods usually considered quasi-experimental, such as rotation experiments, replacement designs, and panel designs, bear decidedly more resemblance to historical studies, economic analyses, and field studies than they do to true experiments. The analogy between these methods and experiments, implicit in the term quasi-experimental, has thus been greatly oversold.

Contextual Approaches

Another misconception is that qualitative methods are identical with contextual approaches to evaluation (see, for example, Britan, 1978). A contextual study is one that seeks to take into account a very wide variety of relevant factors. In point of fact, as recommended by Weiss and Rein (1970), quantitative archival data can be used in a contextual study as part of the interpretative background for understanding a social and cultural phenomenon such as a program. Cook and Campbell (1979) use archival data to examine the plausibility of many of the threats to the validity of the quasi-experimental evaluation designs they have devised; so also do Caparaso and Roos (1973).

The use of quantitative data to provide contextual understanding might be unusual for some field researchers in the tradition of the Chicago school of sociology (such as Elliot Liebow, Herbert Gans, and Erving Goffman), not because they would view quantitative data as irrelevant, but because they might believe that qualitative data are sufficient or more relevant for investigations of the sort they are doing. Yet in *The Urban Villagers,* an ethnographic study of the West End neighborhood in Boston, Gans (1962) cites a few social ecological statistics to give a more precise idea of the ethnic composition of the area. And Zuckerman (1977), a sociologist who studies medical elites, also uses quantitative data to provide context. Goffman does not use statistics, but his followers have carried out quantitative studies based on his ideas; for example, measuring the interpersonal distance people allow in public, such as at beaches, in public libraries, and on buses.

While the use of quantitative data in an intensive way to provide context is still unusual in studies in the tradition of the Chicago school of sociological and ethnographic fieldwork in advanced societies, it is far from unknown. In contrast, many historians use quantitative data in such varied areas as social, political, intellectual, and military history. Consequently the view that only qualitative data can provide context must be rejected.

A related misconception is that an experiment is noncontextual. Britan (1978), an anthropologist, has advanced the proposition that evaluation methods are best grouped into two separate categories, the experimental and the contextual. His argument is that the use of control in experiments makes them noncontextual. (*Control* is the holding of all variables but one in a situation constant, and the systematic introduction of change in that one variable, to ascertain its results on the dependent variable.) This is an appealing argument, but not a valid one. As discussed in Chapter Seven, many field experiments do not require or even permit that the context be held constant. Moreover, a sampling of sites and settings can also permit generalizability, and in fact the results can be cross-tabulated by the characteristics of the site and context (large city, small town; near the campus of an urban university, near the campus of a suburban university). This cross-tabulation permits an understanding of how the context influences the results of the experiment; such comprehension is often essential to the interpretation of an experiment.

There are other flaws in the argument that experiments are a noncontextual method and that the contrast between experimental and contextual is a helpful way to choose evaluation methodologies. The argument is erroneous even where the experiment does hold all variables constant except the independent variable. In the social sciences, research by means of experiments is always sequential and incremental. There is rarely or never a critical experiment in the social sciences, unlike physics, where the Michelson-Moreley experiment on the speed of light resolved the problem of ether. Even landmark studies, like Asch's (1951) experiment on adherence to a false group consensus and Milgram's (1974) work on obedience to authority, involved a very long series of experiments that varied in formulation and design as the data accumulated over a period of years. Experimental investigation is not a one-shot affair in which the context is held constant by experimental control; rather, it is a continuing enterprise whose strategy gradually shifts as results accumulate and insights occur.

These shifts in experimental strategy involve a shifting series of contexts whose nature is crucial to the interpretation of the experimental results. The iterations, and the systematic, heuristic, and even serendipitous variations in context make experimentation an intrinsically contextual process, not a context-free method. At the end of a series of experiments, the results are arrayed systematically according to context, so that the experimenter is able to conclude that certain conditions yield one result, other conditions yield a second result, and so forth. The varying experimental conditions constitute the contexts of the experimentation.

An experiment can be contextual in still another sense, that of an intervention by researchers in a situation that they are studying by an ethnographic method. Ethnographers can intervene in the setting they are studying to ascertain an effect on the rest of the situation. Since the results are intended to be specific to the situation, such a single intervention might not appear to constitute experimentation. Yet, the loose constructionists of the theory of scientific method, including philosophers of science like Kaplan (1964), define experimentation as "prodding nature with a stick to see what will happen" (LaPonce, 1977, quoted by Caparaso, 1973, p. 7), and thus a context-specific intervention clearly qualifies as an experiment.

Quasi-experimental methods also are contextual. For example, consider path analysis, which attempts to derive causal sequences from the pattern of intercorrelations of a set of variables, and rotation designs and replacement designs, which are methods of studying organizations to examine the effects of promotions, shifts in roles, or replacement of some people in a given role by new role incumbents (Caparaso and Roos, 1973). Rotation and replacement designs can be formulated and interpreted only by close examination of the relevant contexts.

One other misconception with respect to context is

worthy of clarification. Many of the adherents of the Chicago tradition believe that sample surveys of the type pioneered by Lazarsfeld are not contextual because they resolve phenomena into quantified variables. For example, Wax (1975) argues that surveys do not describe the context of a phenomenon, so that ethnographic methods must be used to understand context. Lazarsfeld and Menzel (1964) brilliantly refute this objection. Their argument merits a brief review.

The distinctions they formulate regarding the unit of analysis are of crucial importance for evaluation. Many evaluators use individuals as the unit of analysis even though a collective of some sort, such as a community, is the actual focus of the program. The use of an improper level of analysis contributed to the failure of the evaluation effort analyzed by Weiss and Rein (1969, 1970). Manis (1968) notes that such errors are frequent in studies of the effects of community mental health programs. Haney (1980) and Bidwell and Kasarda (1980) also point out the importance of issues of context, aggregation, and level of analyses in evaluation.

Lazarsfeld and Menzel argue that from data about elements or members (such as individuals) researchers can construct variables about the collectives (such as groups, organizations, unions or towns) and hence describe the context of which they are a part. From data about these collectives researchers can also construct variables that characterize and describe the individuals. Several kinds of variables about individuals may be used to characterize collectives, and several types of variables about collectives may be used to describe individuals. With care, researchers can move back and forth repeatedly from level to level, gaining a deeper comprehension of the collective from an understanding of the members and a deeper appreciation of the members from an understanding of the collective.

A collective (like a town, a local labor union, or a university) can itself be a member, an element, of a larger system, such as a state, a national union, or an association of universities, and so collectives themselves can be studied contextually. Thus each element can be investigated in the context of the various collectives to which it belongs, and each collective can be examined contextually, both through variables constructed about its members and through variables constructed about the larger collectives to which it belongs.

For example, a town can be described by variables such as having a town swimming pool or library, which is a global characteristic applying to the whole town. The town, as a collective, can also be characterized by aggregate variables constructed from the variables that describe the individual residents, such as a high socioeconomic status town, a town with a majority of whites, or a town that is predominantly Protestant. Similarly, the town may be described contextually by constructing variables about the town derived from variables about the collectives to which it belongs. The town might be characterized as located in a rural county, in a Republican state.

Thus the claim that quantitative survey methods are noncontextual must be rejected. In fact "characteristics that can be predicated of a unit only by drawing upon data from higher levels of aggregation" are explicitly termed contextual characteristics by Lazarsfeld and Barton (1951, p. 190) and Lazarsfeld and Menzel (1964). An anthropologist involved in evaluation might reply to this analysis, however, by arguing that context is not merely social context but rather the complex of abstract symbol systems called culture. We examine the interpretation of symbol systems in evaluation in Chapter Nine.

Some participants in the debate about qualitative and quantitative methods in evaluation erroneously assume that survey research is entirely quantitative. A competent survey of a little-explored area must be preceded by qualitative work that characterizes the phenomena in sufficient detail to allow researchers to formulate questions that are codable and hence amenable to quantitative analysis. This work consists of exploratory interviews, and may also involve field observations. Such preliminary investigations, often extensive, must be followed by pilot testing of the questions as formulated, so that they can be revised into comprehensible, codable questions.

The Relationship of the Quantitative to the Qualitative

Thus any proposed dichotomy between qualitative and quantitative breaks down on close examination. Quantification is the systematic assignment of numbers to attributes identified by qualitative work, the descriptive classification of phenomena. Quantification rests on a foundation of qualitative work and is a later step that is often not necessary. Some experiments usually considered exclusively quantitative are, in fact, primarily qualitative: those experiments whose results may turn on whether a phenomenon is observed rather than on the degree to which it is manifested.

Investigators cannot understand quantitative variables unless the research is founded on qualitative analysis of the meaning of those variables. For example, a World Bank study of urban development programs in Latin America probably would have benefited much from a qualitative study of the social meaning of attrition, that is, the disappearance from the sample of some people who received a low-cost housing program. Such attrition could have meant, for example, upward social mobility into better housing, downward mobility into worse housing, or failure of the program to reach a specific subgroup of the target population.

Qualitative studies also may provide a necessary background for true experiments and quasi-experiments in evaluation, since qualitative studies enable evaluators to gauge the plausibility of various threats to valid inference. Caparaso and Roos (1973) discuss this issue for quasi-experimental designs such as replacement, rotation, and panel designs. History (intervening or simultaneous historical events), maturation (autonomous internal changes in the subjects), and selection (prior differences between those who received the program and those who did not) are among the threats to validity whose seriousness can often be assessed by collateral qualitative research. Cook and Campbell's (1979) discussion of the many threats to validity also implies the need for qualitative understanding of variables in order to interpret quantitative data.

Qualitative and quantitative studies are not so much complementary or convergent as inseparable. Quantitative methods often cannot be fruitful unless qualitative data are used to inform the interpretation of the design and the variables. The converse is also true: Quantification is often useful in ethnographic studies, studies in which the researcher lives in the culture studied, participates in it in order to observe and understand it, and conducts interviews with informants (see Pelto and Pelto, 1978). Ethnographic studies may, and often do, also code interviews, use rating scales in making observations, employ attitude scales administered in interviews, or analyze quantitative archival data.

Unfortunately, some able ethnographers appear to believe that quantification hampers qualitative studies by substituting the perspective of the investigator for the viewpoint of the respondent, or by interfering with participant observation or the use of informants (see Wax, 1975). Fieldwork does attempt to understand programs from the perspective of the respondents (the program recipients and staff) not that of the researcher. But if quantification is used to better comprehend the respondents' viewpoint (for example, discovering by use of structured questions whether respondents feel they have much control over their destiny; see Inkeles and Smith, 1974), then quantification becomes more a matter of precision of instrumentation, rather than imposing an alien perspective. In some cases, however, the intrusion of the perspective of a third party may be a necessary part of a socially responsible evaluation; for example, including the taxpayer's perspective by measuring the absenteeism of CETA employees. But if not done carefully, such intrusions can disrupt the evaluator's rapport with the program recipients, thus impeding an understanding of the recipients' attitude toward the program.

Bias and Reliability

Bias can be defined as a distortion in the findings produced by a given perspective. Users of evaluations often worry that qualitative methods are more biased than quantitative methods. In one sense, bias is not addressed very directly by quantification, which merely adds precision, permits comparability to other studies, and facilitates statistical inference by making it possible to estimate the probability that the results are owing to the nature of the particular sample. Administrators frequently fear that ethnographic fieldwork produces more biased results than an experiment. But, as we have seen, an experiment need not be quantitative and an ethnographic study may be partly quantitative.

An experiment proceeds from a sharply delineated design involving measures, hypotheses, and experimental manipulations specified in advance; it uses subjects selected from a larger population by specified procedures and treatments assigned to cases by randomization (if possible); hence any one experiment is far more fixed in advance than is an ethnography. The ethnographic study attempts to adapt to exigencies discovered in the field by varying the selection of sites for the study, the choice and use of informants, the kinds of questions addressed, the amount and kinds of data sought, the composition of the research team, and the length of the study. Although a single experiment, by contrast, is fixed, good experimentation usually involves a series of studies allowing flexibility of approach and shifting strategy. The attempt to carry out a conclusive experimental evaluation is like trying for a critical experiment, and is just as apt to be unsuccessful. It is far more desirable in evaluation to conduct a series of smaller experiments.

The difference in flexibility between a one-shot experiment, the usual kind in evaluation, and the ethnographic study has consequences for bias. It is hard to add new bias during the course of an experiment since the procedures of the experiment are fixed; by the same token, it is hard to remove bias during an experiment, or to take account of discovered misconceptions by adjusting the procedures, without devising an additional experiment. Moreover, since the experiment's design assumes knowledge of which variables are important to investigate and what constitutes proper operationalization of variables, the researcher may fail to recognize the biases. Thus, while limiting and specifying bias, an experiment also freezes it and may mask it. For this reason, too, the one-shot experiment is a poor evaluation strategy compared to a series of experiments.

During an ethnographic study, however, the researcher can often modify procedures in order to moderate biases found to be present. Furthermore, the qualitative researcher is more likely to discover the bias, because he or she can discuss the study with the participants during the study itself, since they are not subjects but informants whose task is to help conceptualize the issues. However, in an ethnographic study, new biases can be introduced at any point, owing to the flexibility in the procedures, and not all biases initially present can be removed. The evaluator may be stuck with an unfortunate initial choice of informants, of study sites, or of research team composition.

Orne (1959, 1962, 1969) argues eloquently that experimental subjects should be interviewed at the end of the study by a second experimenter to identify the biases inherent in the procedures. But only a minority of investigators do this, and then usually superficially and without using a second experimenter. A postexperimental inquiry is threatening to the investigator since it might disclose that the experimental results are misleading. Thus although inquiries of experimental subjects could be used to save a series of studies from some biases, or to disclose their presence in a single experiment, such inquiries are rarely done.

We can clarify the relation of bias to qualitative and quantitative methods by discussing the kinds of bias that may be present in any study. One kind of bias results from the selection of an inappropriate method, sample, site, or locale. Even if the method is appropriate and the sample or site is suitable, bias may assert itself in the choice of measures (such as scales or experimental operationalizations) or of descriptive categories. Another kind of bias arises in the analysis of data, and yet another in the report of the findings. Thus any stage of the study can contain bias even though the others are free of it. Bias does not depend on whether qualitative or quantitative data or methods are used. As our earlier discussion shows, it is more correct to talk in terms of qualitative and quantitative data rather than qualitative and quantitative methods, since each method uses, or should use, data of both sorts. This is a major conclusion of this chapter, and should serve to clarify the way evaluators and clients think about evaluation.

Since bias has been defined as a limited, partial, or distorted perspective, bias asserts itself in the choice of what to study. Choosing to study social underdogs rather than social overlords (Gouldner, 1968) represents a kind of bias. Choosing to evaluate an income maintenance program in terms of its effect on the propensity to work or seek a paying job (as in the New Jersey Negative Income Tax Experiment, Kershaw and Skidmore, 1974) rather than its impact on the physical health of the families, similarly represents a kind of bias, as would the opposite choice. Bias, therefore, can be entirely independent of the details of a study, even though bias frequently manifests itself in the choice of measures, respondents, or sites.

Bias is usually not directly addressed by quantification, since quantification makes matters more precise rather than more balanced or comprehensive. However, in one sense quantification does remove one form of bias, idiosyncratic variation between persons conducting observations. Quantified variables permit a measurement of interobserver reliability that enables the designer to rework the observational procedures to lessen variation in results among observers.

Qualitative descriptions can be made reliable if sufficient care is taken with the criteria for classification. Reliable classification can be achieved, for example, for the answers to open-ended questions in an interview survey by grouping them into categories, a process called coding. In coding, the range of answers obtained to a given question from a subsample of respondents is used to establish categories, which are applied to the answers of the other respondents; once the categories are revised and refined to permit relatively unambiguous categorization, the coders are trained to use them precisely.

Since qualitative data can be made reliable, reliability is not a valid dimension on which to draw a distinction between qualitative and quantitative data. Qualitative data are not fundamentally different from quantitative data, as shown by the fact that reliably coded qualitative data can often be made quantitative by scaling or index construction. Quantification is a refinement that can be applied to qualitative data, a refinement not always necessary nor easy to accomplish. Both kinds of data can be used in the same evaluation since a clash of paradigms is not involved.

Campbell (1979) suggests a method for making ethnographic studies more reliable and valid by correcting for the biases of ethnographers. As he notes, ethnographers studying a culture or evaluating a program contribute at least two sources of bias in the findings, their own perspective as individuals and their bias as members of a specific culture. Campbell suggests that two ethnographers from different cultures, A and B, each do ethnographies of two cultures, C and D. Common elements found in C by both ethnographers and not found in D by either could be taken to be objectively known, that is, a product of the culture studied. Attributes in the ethnographies of cultures C and D that occur only in the work of the ethnographer from culture A could be attributed to bias from culture A or from the individual bias of that ethnographer.

Similarly, two or more ethnographers from each culture could perform the studies, so the idiosyncratic bias of each ethnographer could be separated from the bias of all ethnographers from that culture. The influence of idiosyncratic bias is illustrated by comparing Redfield's (1930, 1955) and Lewis' (1951) studies of the same town in the Yucatan; their descriptions of the town are quite different. The application of Campbell's suggestions to the evaluation of domestic programs need not be prohibitively expensive. Ethnographers of different traditions and ethnic backgrounds could cast a great deal of light on program functioning by performing multiple ethnographies. Chicano, Anglo, Black, and Appalachian evaluators could all do ethnographies of programs aimed at each group.

Drawing the distinction between qualitative and quantitative data, rather than methods, suggests that some bias in ethnographic evaluations can be removed by quantification, in the form of previously validated scales or reliably coded categories. "Culture-free" intelligence tests, and scorable projectives, such as the Rorschach and the Thematic Apperception Test (TAT), have been used by ethnographers. Researchers must recognize, however, that not all tests that seem at first to be appropriate for use in other cultures are in fact so; the Draw-a-Person projective test fails miserably with North African children because of the Islamic prohibition against making images. Yet a considerable range of phenomena have been scaled or can be coded reliably in a way that is usable in many cultures. There is, for example, Inkeles and Smith's (1974) measure of overall individual modernity, an attitude measure that has been used in many developing nations and in Appalachia in the United States.

Coding and quantification of behavior and of artifacts in an ethnography is also possible. For example, a measure of social class designed for use throughout the United States derives a social class score for a family from detailed observations of the family's living room. Reliably coded or quantified data remove the bias of the individual scorer but not the perspective of the culture that created the measure. The nature and extent of this cultural bias can be assessed through knowledge of how that measure or coding scheme behaves when used in other contexts. This way of assessing and removing bias has advantages over that proposed by Campbell in being less expensive and permitting an easier comparability of findings from one ethnography to another. Neither we nor Campbell recommend, however, that ethnographies place primary reliance on coded or quantified data instead of participant observation and use of informants.

Clearly the benefits of Campbell's suggestions for controlling bias are considerable, but we must make one important modification to them. Bias, as a partial, or limited, and sometimes distorted perspective, also contains information. Thus the particular cultural perspective that an investigator brings to an evaluation, which we can consider a form of bias, can sometimes be helpful because of the information that it permits the investigator to discover. To choose an example from the study of kinship, an Iroquois investigator would probably understand Crow-Omaha kinship systems more quickly than an European investigator because Iroquois kinship, though not Crow, is more like it than European kinship. Similar insights develop from particular cross-cultural perspectives in program evaluation.

Data Reduction in Evaluation

Most discussions of the perils of qualitative data in evaluation focus on bias and unreliability. However, the literature on fieldwork suggests that the major difficulty is not reliability but data reduction, the effort to summarize qualitative data. Wax (1975) remarks on the enormous mass of field notes that result even from a short study and says that it is realistic to allow as long a period for analyzing and summarizing the field notes as was spent in the field itself. Riesman (personal communication) believes that a group of more than ten interviews is extraordinarily difficult to analyze without the use of categorization; the mass of information is too great to be retained in the mind of the researcher without data reduction. It is commonplace for field workers to grossly underestimate the time required for data reduction.

Published accounts of ethnographic evaluation (for example, Trend, 1979) disclose that the time required to analyze field notes poses serious logistical problems. Anthropologists working as evaluators say informally that their clients simply cannot understand the amount of time required to write up fieldwork notes, or why it is so difficult for the anthropologist living on the program site to send to the home office simple monthly summaries of findings. The issue of data reduction is usually more difficult than the question of whether the results are reliable and valid. The data are so rich that reliability and validity can often be judged from internal evidence in the ethnographic report.

Categorization and quantification of data are highly systematic methods of data reduction. The economies of time and effort made possible by scales or coding systems may be more important than are the precision, reliability, assessment of sampling variability, and comparability with norms also provided by quantification. In addition to scales or coding systems, which may not always suit the preferences of the ethnographic evaluator, we offer a suggestion drawn from the experience of historians, for whom data reduction is a vast problem. Both Samuel Eliot Morison and Henry Steele Commager, two eminent historians, regularly advised their graduate students to begin writing the historical report as soon as they began gathering the data, and to have the writing proceed with the data gathering throughout the study (see Morison, 1948, 1954).

Evaluators may fear that starting to write the report at the beginning of the study creates a response set that colors the interpretation of subsequent data. Yet perhaps a response set occurs anyway early in the evaluation, even if one does no writing; writing may enable the evaluator to identify a response set and to modify it in the light of subsequent disconfirming or discordant data. Of course, this supposition could be experimentally investigated.

Having repudiated the conventional distinctions between qualitative and quantitative methods and having proposed that researchers speak instead of qualitative and quantitative data, we now examine the advantages of qualitative data in evaluation.

9

The Special Role and Use of Qualitative Data

~·

To discuss the special contribution of qualitative data to evaluation we must define data and distinguish two kinds of qualitative data. A datum can be defined as the result of a category (classification) being applied to an instance. The rules for assignment of instances define the category. Qualitative data are instances that have been placed in categories but not yet quantified. Occurrences, events, or impressions that have not been placed in categories of any sort we would call phenomena but not data.

We distinguish two types of qualitative data, systematic and descriptive. For systematic qualitative data, the rules for assignment, that is, the decision rules as to what constitutes an instance of the category, have been elaborately and precisely defined; with descriptive data, the rules have not been so precisely defined. Thus *tyrant* is a descriptive category that could be applied to instances to generate descriptive data. By certain methods of qualitative data analysis, the descriptive category tyrant can be sharpened, refined, and more precisely defined to be-

171

come a systematic category that, when applied to instances, creates systematic data. Not everyone defines data in this way. For example, some people would consider only systematic data to be data.

To accomplish the transition from a descriptive category to a systematic one, the rules for assignment to the category have to be specified precisely and in detail. This process, by which descriptive categories are refined into systematic categories, is called the analysis of qualitative data, and we shall examine it later in this chapter. The formulation of more precise assignment rules is carried out in considerable part through the examination of instances. By examining the range of discovered possible instances, the researcher defines the category more precisely by deciding which instances are to be included and which excluded.

The concept of *fuzzy sets,* as used in logic and linguistics, is helpful in understanding the nature and usefulness of descriptive categories. A fuzzy set is a set whose boundaries are not sharply defined; its boundaries gradually shade off (Kintsch, 1977). Many linguistic terms fit this definition. For example, table and chair in our current society, given the advent of modern furniture design, gradually shade off into each other. Other examples of terms that shade into each other are vase, cup, and bowl (Labov, 1973). Brown (1980) and Wiggins (1980) have made important contributions to the analysis of natural categories and fuzzy sets. For the evaluator, the most important characteristic of descriptive categories, which is another term for fuzzy sets, is that they convey information, though not necessarily the same or as much information as systematic categories. In this chapter, we examine the contribution of both kinds of qualitative data, those resulting from the application of descriptive categories (descriptive data) and those resulting from the application of systematic categories (systematic data), to evaluation.

Several related distinctions must be considered here. A *variable* we define as a group of related categories that are exhaustive and mutually exclusive; each instance to be classified will fall into one, and only one, of the categories comprised by the variable. A variable need not be quantitative; for example, race, sex, and religion are variables. But a variable can be quantified by introducing a distinction of degree among the categories. Since the categories comprising a variable are mutually exclusive and exhaustive, they are a fortiori systematic, that is, sharpness of delineation is prerequisite.

We must draw a further distinction concerning qualitative methods, qualitative data, and qualitative analytic techniques. In Chapter Eight, we argued that the concept of a qualitative method of data gathering is logically flawed, since all qualitative methods can be used to gather quantitative data. However, although qualitative methods do not have a justifiable logical status, some methods are used very preponderantly to gather qualitative data. Thus as we consider qualitative data, we shall often examine methods that, while logically not qualitative, are very preponderantly used to gather qualitative data.

But almost any method can be used to gather both qualitative and quantitative data. Ethnographic evaluations, for example, usually gather qualitative data only, although they could also use standardized instruments. Similarly, elite and specialized interviewing, described later in this chapter, can be used to gather quantitative data; for example, an interviewer can ask an economist to offer estimates of specific expected interest rates, inflation rates, unemployment, investment, gross national product, and other economic indicators.

Finally, we must also distinguish between data-gathering methods (such as interviews and ethnographies and so forth), and data analytic techniques, such as coding, analytic induction, the constant comparative method, pattern analysis, functional analysis, and substruction to a typology, discussed later. Some data analytic techniques seem especially suited for qualitative data but could perhaps also be applied to quantitative data. Other analytic techniques, such as factor analysis, presuppose quantitative data.

Qualitative Data and Phenomenology

In Chapter Eight, we replaced the concept of qualitative methods with that of qualitative data. We also argued that, contrary to the position taken by most qualitative evaluators, the distinguishing contribution of qualitative data to evaluation is emphatically not that they are holistic. Are there distinguishing contributions of qualitative data to evaluation? The qualitative researcher usually answers that a special feature of qualitative data is that they are phenomenological. What are the merits of this claim?

Phenomenological data concern a respondent's description of his thoughts; behavioral data concern observations by another person or the respondent's report of his actions. Phenomenological and behavioral data are both important. To some extent they describe different realms and so do not necessarily predict each other. Sometimes it is more important to elicit a person's feelings or reactions to a situation than to know his or her behavior in that situation. In some cases, phenomenological data may predict better to later situations. In other cases, behavior is important, not in itself, but for its value as an indicator of ideas or feelings, that is, of phenomenology.

The idea that behavior is the only important source of data is rejected by most social scientists as a result of analyses by Mannheim (1936), Chomsky (1959), and others. Diaries, private letters, and autobiographies are examples of sources of qualitative phenomenological data. Are only qualitative data phenomenological, as some qualitative researchers insist? No. Diaries, private letters, autobiographies, and unstructured interview transcripts can be coded or content-analyzed enumeratively, and thus they can be quantified. Quantitative phenomenological data can be created from qualitative data.

Can quantitative phenomenological data arise without such transformations? Not if we accept the argument of Chapter Eight that qualitative data are an earlier stage on the route to quantification. But for some data, the transformation occurs as they are collected because the method of collection is based on a structured scheme designed to code or rate the qualitative data and record only the codes or ratings. Examples are attitude scales, adjective checklists, occupational preference tests, and values scales. Intermediate cases are certain projective tests such as the Rorschach and the Thematic Apperception Test; the phenomenological data are recorded, but a coding scheme that permits quantification already exists and one need not be designed for a particular data set, unlike some content analyses of auto-biographical statements. Some projective tests, such as the Blacky Test with its multiple-choice format, record responses in precoded categories so that the quantification of qualitative data takes place immediately and the qualitative data themselves are not recorded.

A related case is survey research. The answers to some questions describe behavior, such as occupation pursued and years of education attained; such questions are usually pre-coded. The answers to other, open-ended questions are recorded in full and are coded later. These questions may describe behavior, feelings, attitudes, perceptions, understandings, motivations, or fantasies. Even questions that are precoded, that is, whose response is categorized immediately, can elicit phenomenological data; for example, a question asking a person whether he or she is feeling very sad, sad, neutral, happy, or very happy. Thus there are at least two kinds of quantitative phenomenological data, those resulting from the immediate quantification of qualitative data and those resulting from the latter quantification of data originally recorded in qualitative form. Clearly, the assertion that only qualitative data are phenomenological must be rejected.

Qualitative Data and Verstehen

A related concept, Verstehen, has led to considerable controversy. It is often asserted that qualitative data have special or unique merit in permitting or providing Verstehen, which denotes a kind of understanding of a person or a culture. The kind of understanding and its epistemological status is in dispute. Some view Verstehen as an empathic understanding. But the term was brought into prominence by Max Weber, who used it to mean a comprehension of the motives of a social actor that takes into account the cultural patterning of the surroundings. A central purpose of Verstehen for Weber was the imputation of motives to an actor. If Verstehen is defined as the understanding of the motivations and feelings of the actors, as it often is, the behaviorists (Abel, 1974) argue that it can serve only to suggest hypotheses, not to validate them.

Many ethnographers disagree, however. Wax (1974), for example, defines Verstehen as the understanding of language, of cultural symbol systems, and of culturally defined behavioral patterns, such as chopping wood, writing at a desk, having an extended kinship system, or having five words to describe snow. For him Verstehen is not a mysterious, intuitive, empathic process but rather an understanding of symbol systems. The latter is the definition we use in this chapter. Rather than argue whether Verstehen is suited to the so-called context of discovery rather than the context of validation, Wax argues that Verstehen is a precondition to research, not an operation to generate knowledge or to validate it.

Is Verstehen, thus defined, provided only by qualitative data? Some anthropologists answer yes and claim, in addition, that a particular method of gathering qualitative data, participant observation, is the primary way to attain Verstehen, although they treat informants as helpful too. If so, and if Verstehen is a unique contribution of qualitative data, then participant observation has unique status as an evaluation method. Let us look more closely at these claims. Participating in the activities of a culture while observing it helps the investigator to understand the activities and the symbol systems of the culture. One such system is language; others are kinship, religious and magical ritual, and the practice of those actions necessary for the economic structure, such as hunting, fishing, gathering, cultivation, herding, and tool making.

By participating in the culture being studied, the researcher is socialized into that culture, a process called secondary socialization, or resocialization (to reflect the fact that the researcher is already a member of his or her own culture and cannot become a full member of another culture). Resocialization can be achieved only through participant observation, which helps account for the importance of participant observation to the anthropologist. Participant observation allows the anthropologist to understand what he or she observes.

Campbell (1974, 1979) espouses a view strikingly close to

that of Wax, arguing that qualitative, common-sense knowledge of phenomena underlies all scientific understanding. He does, however, tend to equate the scientific with the quantitative and the experimental. This gives us additional reason to look at the claim that Verstehen is a special kind of understanding, and that qualitative data and participant observation are necessary to achieve it. Martin (1974) argues against the idea that participant observation is a sufficient, a necessary, or always the most efficient way to understand a culture, noting that Sir James Frazer did not live with the natives, and yet did anthropological work of major importance. In support of Martin's point, Wax (1975) notes that although Boaz and his students emphasized the importance of fieldwork, Boaz's thirteen trips into the field were all of only a few weeks duration. Boaz preferred to use informants, and "There is little evidence in Boaz's letters that he himself did much participant observation or learned any native language well. It is hard to see how he could have done either, given the short duration of his trips" (p. 33). Martin argues that informants, written records, and archeological reconstructions often replace participant observation in giving the kind of cultural understanding denoted by Verstehen. For evaluators, the key point is that the use of informants appears to be a lively alternative to participant observation as a way of gaining the understanding of symbol systems designated by Verstehen.

The tradition of participant observation in ethnographic fieldwork in modern cultures is a strong one, beginning with the work of Beatrice Potter Webb in the late 19th century, and extending to the more recent efforts of Liebow, Gans, and Polsky, who studied the disadvantaged, the ethnic, and the socially marginal.

But some studies attain an understanding similar to Verstehen through informants only. Terkel's (1975, 1980) studies of the working classes in various occupations are a notable example; so is Howe's (1977) study of pink-collar workers, working-class women employed as waitresses and typing-pool clerks. The work of oral historians (Zuckerman, 1977) also uses informants. A number of other methods, such as an analysis of historical documents, may also facilitate the achievement of

Verstehen. Thus participant observation is not the only means of achieving Verstehen. Now we must ask whether, in evaluation, Verstehen is a special contribution of qualitative data.

Empathic Understanding. If Verstehen is viewed as an intuitive empathic understanding, not as the understanding of symbol systems, only qualitative data are likely to provide it. Znaniecki (see Abel, 1974) argues that vicarious experience is a source of sociological data unavailable elsewhere. This kind of insight seems akin to clinical empathy, and it is often stated that a clinician becomes a measuring instrument. Actually, a detection instrument is a more accurate description since the clinician does not quantify what is detected. The clinician asks, "How is this patient making me feel now?" and uses the answer to understand the patient. For example, if the therapist feels criticized, perhaps the patient is angry. Of course, the therapist's vision may be clouded by the feelings the patient is evoking, and a therapist may have idiosyncratic feelings in response to the patient's feelings. Nevertheless, most clinicians believe that empathic understanding is essential to the therapeutic process; only the radical behaviorists try to exclude such feelings from the therapy.

The role of empathic understanding raises more general questions of the value of studying mental phenomena in evaluation and of the contribution of qualitative data to that study. Although some might argue that mental and emotional phenomena do not have the same empirical qualities as external objects, events, and actions, strictly speaking, we can no more prove the former unreal than we can prove the latter real. Thomas, whose study of Polish immigrants (Thomas and Znaniecki, 1927) is based on interviews, observation, informants' letters, and diaries, argues for the importance of "the definition of the situation." He states, "if men define situations as real, they are real in their consequences" (cited by Truzzi, 1974, p. 42; see also Thomas, 1971). Thomas concludes that definitions of the situation, and other mental constructs, are worthy of study.

In sum, Verstehen in the sense used by Wax (1974) is valuable in studies of cultures and programs, to understand not only behavior, but also mental constructs, which are important in themselves. Vicarious experience, as described by Znaniecki, or empathy, as it is used in clinical practice, can also provide important clues to these mental constructs. One may argue that vicarious experience and clinical empathy are merely part of the context of discovery, the formulation of hypotheses, rather than their verification; but creating hypotheses is vital. Moreover, Verstehen defined as the understanding of language, cultural symbol systems, and behavior patterns, is indeed better described as a precondition to research rather than as a part of the context of discovery or validation.

The reader should note that vicarious experience and clinical empathy do not require the investigator to feel sorry for a person's plight in order to understand the person; that kind of empathy is not meant here. Rather, the observer's feelings can be a clue to various mental constructs that are important in themselves and that may presage later behavior.

Empathy and Verstehen in Evaluation. Let us examine the specific applications of Verstehen, vicarious understanding, and empathy in evaluation. To give an example of Verstehen first; if one is looking at a job training program, it is important to understand the characteristics of the putative job the trainee is being trained for, how the trainee and the job counselor each perceive the job, and the sequence of acts that are involved in the training. The evaluator needs to understand the meaning of terms of approval and opprobrium applied to the trainee, and the patterns of interaction between trainee and counselor and among trainees. The evaluator's participation in the program will likely yield such understanding; so may proper use of informants.

The application of empathy to evaluation is illustrated by the following situations. Perhaps during a study the researcher feels confined, constricted, and almost stifled; the researcher examines whether such feelings reflect an authoritarian, suspicious atmosphere that pervades the program. Similarly, if a researcher in a public job training program feels depression or hopelessness, this mood may be that of the trainees, who may have little hope of finding jobs at the conclusion of the program. If the evaluator feels drifting and bemused, he or she may be detecting the tone of a program that is chaotic, disorganized, or unsupervised.

Both Verstehen and empathy depend largely on descriptive qualitative data. Verstehen is an attempt to "crack the code" of the culture, that is, detect the categories into which a culture codes actions and thoughts. (The respondent's awareness of the investigator's preconceptions or expectations, the so-called demand characteristics of the research situation, can be considered a kind of counter-Verstehen.) Empathy in evaluation is the detection of emotions manifested in the program participants and staff, achieved by evaluators' becoming aware of similar or complementary emotions in themselves. Identifying cultural categories and detecting emotional reactions are stages of research that precede quantification, which attempts to give dimensionality to existing categories. Consequently, one special merit of attention to qualitative data in evaluation is that it facilitates Verstehen and empathy.

Benefits and Limitations of Qualitative Data

We must now consider more generally the status in evaluation of qualitative data. The analysis of qualitative data consists of making descriptive data systematic by sharply defining the boundaries of the categories and by formally relating the categories to each other. If one chooses not to formally analyze qualitative data, that is, relate the descriptive categories to each other in a formal way, one's study is an ethnographic description (Guba, 1978) or journalistic investigation (Levine, 1980; Peters, 1968-1981, monthly; Woodward and Bernstein, 1974). It is often alleged that such data are mere opinions or are impressionistic, but let us consider the strengths and weaknesses for evaluation of descriptive data that are not formally analyzed.

As noted in Chapter Eight, administrators and users of evaluation sometimes question the credibility of ethnographic description. Descriptions may be hard to make reliable if not based on systematic formally defined categories. The more the categories are formally stated and the rules for inclusion or ex-

clusion are sharply delineated, the more the data can become reliable. Such data could still have cultural biases, but if the data
are not made reliable, they could have idiosyncratic biases in
addition. If the categories are rich in content but imprecise, the
reliability of the data may be questioned because such data do
not allow easy verification of disconfirming cases; for example,
one cannot disconfirm a posited relationship between two categories, because the imprecision of the categories does not permit one to identify a disconfirming case. As methodologists
have noted, what cannot be false, cannot be true. Validity cannot exceed reliability, and descriptive data may not be reliable
enough to permit assessment of validity.

Researchers using qualitative data often argue that if the
criterion of disconfirming cases cannot be used, the validity of
the inferences drawn by the researcher can be judged by the
client on the basis of the data themselves. They note that the
data are so rich and are presented in such detail and with so few
transformations (such as quantification) that the readers can
judge whether they would draw similar conclusions. Indeed,
many anthropological ethnographers and practitioners of fieldwork, such as Liebow (1967), Gans (1962), Polsky (1969),
Wirth (1969), and Terkel (1975, 1980), present their data at
what may seem inordinate length. The extended presentation of
data permits the liberal use of direct quotations from the informants. These enable the users to form their own judgments of
the merits of the conclusions the investigator has drawn, but
only to conjecture whether the data were chosen in a biased
way.

A related limitation of descriptive data is that neither researchers nor their clients can easily estimate statistical repre-
sentativeness, sampling bias, or sampling variability, since
rarely are random procedures used to select the instances for
study or presentation. This difficulty is obviated in evaluation
in which there exist only one or a few instances of a pilot program, all of which are studied. The generalizability of descriptive data is also difficult to determine. Some qualitative researchers argue that their conclusions are idiographic, that is,
they apply only to the instance studied. But evaluators, con-

cerned with how to improve a program or whether to continue a program, need to be able to generalize their findings.

Historians such as Brinton (1952), historians of science such as Kuhn (1962), and political scientists who study comparative political systems do use qualitative data to draw inferences across varied cultures and historical situations. Such inferences are also part of the standard methodology for sociologists, following the examples of Weber (1947) and Durkheim (1951). If one seeks generalizability across instances using qualitative data without random sampling, cases can be chosen that are representational (Weiss, 1971), that is, that show the range of the phenomenon, even though they are not statistically representative. Random sampling can be used to gather descriptive data, but sometimes it is unfeasible because any sharply defined procedures are considered too intrusive by the program clients or staff.

Avoiding Premature Resolution into Variables

We have noted the richness of qualitative data, and that such data facilitate Verstehen, vicarious experience, and empathy. A further advantage is suggested by Blumer (1956) in his critique of research that is confined to variables: Using qualitative data, researchers can study situations for which stable, sharply defined, mutually exclusive, exhaustive categories (variables) have not been established. Premature resolution of phenomena into variables freezes the terms of analysis and interferes with the understanding of the unfolding of situations. Premature resolution also ignores the social definition of the situation by the actors; the situation is defined by the observer only, not by the way the actors see it, what is important to them, or what factors they believe they take into account in shaping their actions.

The interactive nature of social action is slighted by a premature reliance on variables (an early stage of premature quantification), since the researcher neglects to consider action as in part dependent on the reactions and expected reactions of other actors. Thus the process by which one variable influences another may be excluded from study. Blumer believes that the way in which actors define a social situation constitutes the way in which the situation is real for them. Other exponents of the value of qualitative data have noted, for example, that medical diagnoses are socially defined and even socially negotiated by the actors themselves (Bogdan, 1975).

Blumer's analysis constitutes a defense of the search for Verstehen, in the sense defined by Wax (1974); it is also relevant to the somewhat different use of Verstehen by Weber, and even to the still different use of empathy as an investigative tool by clinicians, since it concerns the social definition of the situation constructed and negotiated by the actors (Berger and Luckmann, 1967). Blumer's critique has another relevance for the evaluator: descriptive categories enable one to study situations for which one has not formulated stable, sharply defined categories. One can shift categories as one encounters new aspects of the phenomena or reconsiders previously encountered aspects.

A similar analytic stance underlies the critique of evaluation methodology by Weiss and Rein (1969, 1970). In their argument, concerning the inapplicability of classic experimental design to broad-aim programs, they state that variables are not always useful in studying programs with extremely broad aims, irrespective of whether experimental or quasi-experimental designs are used. For programs that are extremely vague about their aims, intended effects, and the aspects of the program expected to produce these changes, Weiss and Rein believe that an analysis through the use of variables does not make sense, since neither independent nor dependent variables are specified in the program's conceptualization. Some programs adapt greatly to local conditions, changing markedly and unpredictably over time; others are unclear about who the intended beneficiaries are, who has been exposed to the program, who actually received the program, and what program they received. In a situation of ambiguity, casting a broad net for independent variables may result in some of them being statistically significant by chance. More important, such a program situation is not understood well enough to make resolution into variables possible or helpful.

For evaluations of extremely vague, broad-aim programs, Weiss and Rein suggest that it is crucial to study process, to analyze the sequences of events that constitute the operationalization of the program. These shifting sequences of events, Weiss and Rein assert, can best be understood through the use of qualitative data, describing the forms the program takes and the forces producing these forms. Using this approach, the evaluator considers the program and its environment as a system and seeks to understand how the elements in the system interact.

Weiss and Rein suggest several modes of analysis for broad-aim programs, using a descriptive, systems-oriented approach. Each of these modes uses descriptive categories with the characteristics of fuzzy sets. Clinical-historical case studies give intensive attention to the unfolding of an individual case, as a clinician understands a patient or a historian understands a historical phenomenon. Dramaturgic analysis is the understanding of the process of the program through the interactions of the dramatis personae of the program as a story line unfolds. Thus a program can be analyzed after the manner of a drama. Peattie (1970) evaluates a citizen participation program using a dramaturgic method. Weiss and Rein consider Watkins' (1953) methodological individualism, "a framework that attempts to explain events by analyzing the actions of individuals within situations" (1970, p. 106), to be closely related to dramaturgic analysis, since the latter is the construction of "a story about actors who engage in coalitions and conflicts and whose interactions form plots and subplots moving to a resolution" (p. 106).

Their third suggestion is systems analysis, a mode of thinking that does not always require quantification; consider, for example, Ackoff's (1973) definition of a system, reviewed in Chapter Two. A fourth mode is analysis in terms of political forces, as a political scientist would do. Appropriate for this mode is force field analysis, developed by Lewin (1936) and widely applied as a diagnostic method in the organization development field. Reason analysis is another appropriate method, not mentioned by Weiss and Rein. Zeisel (1968) developed this analytic framework in order to comprehend the reasons people give for their actions; it is broadly applicable but almost unknown in evaluation. It involves framing the questions to the respondents and cross-tabulating them in such a way that different kinds of reasons can be identified, such as proximate causes, motivations, and desired goal states.

Finally, Weiss and Rein suggest functional analysis, as formulated by Merton (1957), which interprets social actions in terms of their manifest and latent functions in the maintenance of some larger system, and pattern analysis, the search for expressions of a common theme in a variety of phenomena. Rosenberg (1968) implies that pattern analysis is especially valuable in the analysis of cultural practices, that is, behaviors and ideas that are parts of a common cultural system or cultural complex. Such behaviors and ideas are symmetrically related, that is, they need not be treated as causing each other but rather as expressions of a common cultural theme. Pattern analysis could be applied to culturally defined practices of program staff and participants.

All these analytic methods can use descriptive rather than systematic qualitative categories. One may revise and sharply define the categories as the study progresses, but it is frequently not necessary to do so; the data are useful if the descriptive categories are formulated with insight. The use of descriptive categories in process evaluation permits the study of rapidly changing programs. As the program shifts, the categories can be revised or new categories can be devised.

Descriptive categories allow the researcher to explore and describe a program that is not well enough understood at the beginning of the study to permit quantification or the formulation of variables or other systematic (sharply defined) categories. Moreover, at later stages of the study, the researcher can reanalyze the phenomena in terms of new categories based on the increased understanding of the program provided by the early stages of the study. This process is analogous to the secondary analysis of quantitative data; reanalysis is just as feasible with qualitative as with quantitative data.

Eliciting the Respondent's Perspective

Qualitative data can make another special contribution, one rarely mentioned in the evaluation literature. They allow the respondent's viewpoint to shape the study, framing the questions as well as the answers. The most definitive account of this matter is Dexter's (1970) discussion of elite and specialized interviewing. In standard interviewing, including much of focused interviewing (Merton, Fiske, and Kendall, 1956), "the investigator defines the question and the problem and seeks answers only within the bounds of his assumptions" (Dexter, 1970, p. 5). In elite interviewing, the interviewer allows the respondent to stress his definition of the situation, encourages him to structure his account of the situation, lets him introduce his ideas of what is important, and has him define the problem. Elite interviewing is not so much a method as a willingness to accept data framed by the respondent. The respondent may also volunteer quantitative data, such as estimates of future employment or interest rates. Other opportunities in which a respondent can choose the descriptive categories to frame the issues include the autobiographical statement.

Permitting the respondent to frame the issues is an appropriate method if the respondent is in a prominent or public position or has expert knowledge of a particular subject, such as a tool and die maker or a returned hostage would have, and the interview concerns that position or that subject. In those cases, the respondent's definition of the situation is crucial. Given the bargaining power provided by position or special information, the prominent or expert person cannot be made to adhere to the interviewer's definition of the situation. For example, the Chairman of the Senate Foreign Relations Committee might not sit still for a highly structured survey on foreign relations, although he or she will mail back a census form that does not concern his or her expertise or prominence. Prominent persons often need to control the interview, for self-protection, and experts are usually unwilling to accept the assumptions or preconceptions of the interviewer and insist on explaining the issues to him or her (Dexter, 1970). The interviewer should not attempt to force the respondent to conform; the respondent's formulation of questions is often more illuminating than any answer to an interviewer's questions.

Cultural differences also contribute to the need for elite

and specialized interviewing. Lerner (1956) points out that some cultural groups object to structured questions and insist on presenting their own definition of the situation; hence the respondent must be allowed to act as the expert and guide the interview. But Lerner (1958) used survey interviews in the Middle East, and Inkeles and Smith (1974) used their own survey questionnaire in many cultures, so there is much cultural variation in this matter.

An elite or specialized interviewee differs from an informant in that an informant devotes much more time to the study and participates almost as a member of the research team in the formulation of issues for the entire study (Dexter, 1970). For elite interviewing, the investigator should have considerable knowledge of the subject under study, supplied by background or experience. Participant observation is important in elite interviewing; it provides the investigator with information needed to interpret the interviewee's responses.

Though Dexter, a political scientist, developed his method to interview politicians, he notes that it applies to the work of insurance investigators, detectives, oral historians, and journalists. His approach is cognate to the method of journalistic investigation (Levine, 1980). Because a shortcoming of such investigation is the validity and reliability of the findings, Dexter suggests how to determine if an elite interviewee is telling the truth. What the respondents say is itself data, representing what they wish to pass on to the interviewer in the particular interviewing situation. Respondents may report their current emotional state, opinions, attitudes, values, or hypothetical reactions if certain situations prevail. All of these may conflict, and these conflicts are also data. The interviewee may have different attitudes and sentiments in different situations; interview data are, therefore, highly dependent on the situation. Such data can be interpreted by considering ulterior motives, bars to spontaneity, desires to please the interviewer or give the socially acceptable response, and idiosyncratic factors that cause only one aspect of the interviewee's viewpoint to be expressed in this situation. One should not assume correspondence between expressed attitudes and behavior; the task is to relate them (Dexter, 1970). The informant's report of what happened on a particular occasion may also be distorted, owing to faulty or selective observation or recollection, or conscious or unconscious distortion in the report to the interviewer. Such distortion can be judged from the plausibility of the account, the investigator's prior knowledge of the reliability and mental set of the informant, and comparisons with other accounts (Dexter, 1970).

In elite interviewing, the respondent sets the framework of the discussion and, consequently, the categories that are used. Respondents, not being researchers themselves, generally do not frame issues in systematic categories, but the loose descriptive categories they use are fuzzy sets that contain valuable information. Dexter's approach to interviewing maximizes the potential for the emergence of the respondent's own categories. In this sense, qualitative data can be phenomenological in a way that quantitative data, more dependent on formulation by the researcher, cannot be.

The unique contribution of qualitative data to evaluation is that they permit the respondent's viewpoint to shape the study. This characteristic, not contextuality or holism, is their distinctive contribution. Blumer (1956) argues that the shared social meanings developed by the social actors are crucial, and Bogdan (1975) extends this argument to evaluation. This understanding of some of the actors' descriptive categories can also arise from participant observation or even from contemplation of archival documents.

Analysis of Qualitative Data

Once descriptive data have been elicited, it is possible, but not always necessary, to make them systematic, that is, to define sharply the boundaries of the sets. If desirable, the data may then be quantified. Methods for quantifying systematic qualitative data, such as scaling and index contruction, have been widely described, but ways of making descriptive data systematic appear less familiar to most evaluators and clients. These are not qualitative methods in the sense of research approaches yielding only qualitative data, but rather they are modes of analyzing qualitative data however they have been gathered. Three methods outlined by Glaser (1965), the constant comparative method, analytic induction, and inspecting for hypotheses, presuppose a detailed firsthand knowledge of the social situation studied. (See also Glaser and Strauss, 1967; and Schatzman and Strauss, 1973.) For the analysis of qualitative data, Blumer (1956) criticizes hypothetico-deductive, variable-oriented research approaches that are not based on such a firsthand understanding. To gain this intimate acquaintance with the social world under study requires exploration and inspection.

Exploratory inquiry uses interviews, group discussion, participant observation, and examination of records to try to construct a comprehensive, accurate picture of the social world under study. Inspection, the second step, Blumer (1972) describes as "an intensive focused examination of the empirical content of whatever analytical elements are used for purposes of analysis and this same kind of examination of the empirical nature of the relations between such elements. . . . By analytical elements I have in mind whatever general or categorical items are employed as the key items in the analysis, such as integration, social mobility. . . . The procedure of inspection is to subject such analytical elements to meticulous examination by careful flexible scrutiny of the empirical instances covered by the analytical element" (pp. 35-36). He notes that exploration and inspection represent respectively depiction and analysis.

Glaser (1965) provides a detailed description of the mode of analysis Blumer calls inspection. It involves the gradual specifying of the boundaries of a category by careful attention to what constitutes an instance. By this means descriptive qualitative data, faithful to the phenomenon itself, yield systematic qualitative categories that more sharply delineate the phenomenon.

In Chapter Eight, we noted that quantitative data are built on a foundation of qualitative data. We believe that the following methods for the analysis of qualitative data, by enabling researchers to more sharply delineate their qualitative data, render such data more susceptible to subsequent quantification, if necessary. In Chapter Eight, we also noted the centrality of the problem of the reduction of qualitative data. The modes of analysis of qualitative data set forth here are, in fact, concerned primarily with data reduction.

The Constant Comparative Method. Glaser's constant comparative method for systematizing qualitative data has four stages. The first stage consists of comparing incidents applicable to each category. The analyst tentatively codes each incident in the data in all possibly relevant categories. While coding an incident for a category, the analyst compares it with all previous incidents coded in the same category; this is the basic procedure for the constant comparative method. Once several instances are coded, the analyst starts to infer the properties of the category and the range of application of the category. Gradually, the analyst determines the boundaries of the descriptive category, and it becomes a systematic category.

In the second stage, the analyst integrates the categories and their properties. The criteria for coding gradually change from comparisons of individual incidents to comparisons of incidents to the properties of the categories that resulted from the initial comparison of incidents. Thus the boundaries of the category become sharper, and the analyst begins to see the various properties of the category as integrated. During the third stage, the analyst delimits the theory. Fewer modifications in the categories based on coding are needed, and the categories are reduced to a smaller set of higher-level concepts that subsume the original categories. These higher-order categories are theoretically saturated, that is, new incidents to which a category applies do not point to a new aspect of the category.

At this point, the fourth step, the analyst writes a theory that relates the categories to one other. The resulting theory is thus grounded in the data (see Glaser and Strauss, 1967). This procedure complies with Blumer's exhortation that the analyst use firsthand acquaintance with the empirical reality to generate the theory, rather than impose a prefabricated theory on the empirical reality.

Analytic Induction. Another mode of analysis of qualitative data, which also transforms descriptive data into systematic, is analytic induction, formulated by Znaniecki (1934) and reviewed by Robinson (1951) and Glaser (1965). Znaniecki argues that analytic induction is the method used by the physical and biological sciences while the social sciences overemphasize enumerative induction, which uses correlations to which there are always exceptions. Analytic induction yields general universal laws of the form "All S are P," conclusions that are exhaustive in that further study of the situation will not reveal new information (Robinson, 1951). Analytic induction seeks to derive and validate "an integrated, limited, precise, universally applicable theory of causes accounting for a *specific* phenomenon, for example, drug addiction or embezzlement. It tests a limited number of hypotheses with *all* available data, which are numbers of clearly defined and carefully selected cases of the phenomena" (Glaser, 1965, p. 438).

The analyst first roughly defines the phenomena, then formulates a hypothetical explanation, and then studies one case in the light of the hypothesis. If the hypothesis does not fit the facts of the case, the analyst revises the hypothesis or redefines the phenomenon to exclude that case. The analyst follows this procedure with several cases. Cressey (1950) observes that "practical certainty may be attained after a small number of cases is examined, but the discovery by the investigator of a single negative case disproves the explanation and requires a reformulation. . . . This procedure is continued until a universal relationship is established" (p. 31).

Robinson demonstrates that analytic induction identifies only the necessary conditions for a phenomenon to occur and not the sufficient conditions. Since noninstances of the phenomenon are not studied, one cannot assume that the necessary conditions identified by analytic induction are always also sufficient to produce it. Enumerative induction, that is, probabilistic statistical analysis, studies all available cases, including some in which the phenomenon does not occur, and so can discern the sufficient conditions.

Most users of analytic induction do in practice study noninstances too, such as cases of nonaddiction, to make sure that the necessary causes are not all also present in some noninstances. Consequently, analytic induction in practice seeks to identify necessary and sufficient conditions. Since analysts also tend to allow for the possibility of future cases that do not conform to the hypothesis, there is no logical difference between analytic induction and probabilistic statistical analyses except that the latter method does not require the analyst to explain the deviant cases.

Stating in another way the fact that analytic induction and the probabilistic method are not logically distinct, Robinson elegantly observes, "We know how to set fiducial limits to an observed zero frequency of exceptions, and we know that the lower limit will be zero and that the upper will be some small fraction" (1951, p. 817). Cook and Campbell (1979; based on Russell, 1913) suggest that the distinction between necessary and sufficient conditions is misleading in analyzing a continuous causal function in terms of two-category, present-absent data. Analytic induction is therefore best summarized simply as a method of very intensive analysis of a small number of cases.

By redefining the phenomenon as new cases are considered, the investigator using analytic induction moves from descriptive categories to systematic categories. Again the special value of descriptive data is apparent: They enable the researcher to analyze the phenomenon without first having developed a complex hypothetico-deductive theory. It is not the case, however, that the use of descriptive categories permits an evaluator to quickly conclude a study, a claim made by some evaluators and clients. The availability of measures of attitudes, values, behavior, social class, and demographic factors, and the use of random sampling, allow instrumented evaluations to be as fast as, or faster than, ones using descriptive categories, if the program staff and clients are receptive.

Inspection for Hypotheses. One of the claims often made for qualitative data is their value in generating hypotheses and theories, or at least generating working hypotheses. Glaser takes this view, and his third method for analysis of qualitative data is the inspection for hypotheses. The analyst studies the data to see what hypotheses they suggest.

Glaser distinguishes this method from the constant comparative method, in which the relation of instances to categories and the definition of categories are exhaustively considered. Glaser also distinguishes the constant comparative method, in turn, from the typical coding procedures used in survey research. In the latter method all relevant data that can be brought to bear on a point are coded. The constant comparative method does not code all available instances, but stops when the properties of the categories have been refined and developed. It therefore cannot be used for statistical tests, since data are not coded systematically enough to provide intercoder reliability. A further problem for statistical analysis is that the decision to stop coding is made in a biased way; that is, based on the results of the coding of the previous data.

Qualitative data do have definite value in generating theory through analytic induction, the constant comparative method, or inspection for hypotheses. But the assertion (Glaser, 1965) that quantitative coding cannot yield new hypotheses or theories, only test existing ones, is false. Analysis of quantitative data frequently generates new hypotheses (Rosenberg, 1968). Moreover, data, the application of categories to instances, are not necessary to generate hypotheses or theories; introspection and thought experiments frequently serve this purpose. The generation of theories and hypotheses cannot be accepted as a special contribution of qualitative data to evaluation.

Substruction to a Typology

The reliable coding of data into categories that have already been made systematic is the next step toward quantification—if the number of instances in each of the categories is counted, these numbers may be compared and analyzed statistically to test a hypothesis. But other methods for the further analysis of qualitative data do not involve quantification.

Barton and Lazarsfeld (1969) argue that a group of related categories constitute a set of types (for example, in the area of political participation, Riesman and Glazer's (1965) involved, inside-dopester, indignant, and indifferent). From consideration of these types, the analyst can deduce the criteria by which an instance is to be placed in one category rather than another. These criteria are attributes that considered together form a multidimensional attribute space. The categories or types themselves are formed by combinations of attributes. In the example from Riesman, the attributes are affect about the political process, and competence in understanding the political process. The involved are high on both affect and competence; the inside-dopesters are high on competence but low on affect; the indignant are high on affect but low on competence; and the indifferent are those who are low on both.

Once the researcher derives the multidimensional attribute space from a consideration of the types he or she has created (the process of substruction), the researcher can see how these types could have been deduced from this attribute space (the process of reduction). Often this process helps the investigator to better understand the resulting typology. By substruction and reduction, the investigator may notice overlooked types that are logically possible; for example, had Riesman forgotten the possibility of indignants, the substruction would have called it to his attention.

It is often theoretically fruitful to create an attribute space by means of substruction, so that the reduction involved in the types can be specified and understood. Barton and Lazarsfeld do not suggest that the researcher begin with an attribute space and try to construct a typology from it. Rather, the investigator should gain close, firsthand acquaintance with the data, impressionistically form the types, and then perform the substruction and reduction to ensure that the types are logically complete.

The operations of substruction and reduction presuppose that the qualitative categories are related, and hence constitute types, but these procedures do not assume that the categories are systematic. Descriptive categories can be used since the purpose is not reliable coding but fruitful theoretical analysis. By this method, the evaluator can analyze qualitatively a set of descriptive categories in a theoretically powerful way.

In sum, the special contributions of qualitative data to

evaluation, namely their ability to express the perspective of the informant and their usefulness in facilitating Verstehen and empathy, need not be at the expense of formal analysis. Formal analytic methods for qualitative data include analytic induction, the constant comparative method, coding to test hypotheses, and the procedures of substruction and reduction of an attribute space based on a typology. Descriptive data make a special contribution to evaluation that stems from their status as natural categories and hence fuzzy sets, and descriptive data can be analyzed formally. Since later analyses and transformations are possible, evaluators need not always begin by collecting quantitative data, or even systematic qualitative data, and clients need not always demand such data.

10

Applying Managerial and Administrative Analyses

⌇⌇⌇⌇⌇⌇⌇⌇⌇⌇⌇⌇⌇⌇⌇⌇⌇⌇⌇⌇⌇⌇⌇⌇

An underlying theme of this book is the social nature of the evaluation enterprise. We have discussed the political and economic aspects of the evaluation profession, and the contracting system, the social nature of program goals, and means of avoiding some of the administrative burdens of classic field experimentation. In the present chapter, we consider managerial and administrative analyses in evaluation, including cost-benefit and cost-effectiveness analysis and zero-base budgeting, and again stress certain social characteristics of evaluation. Many evaluators and clients believe that evaluation research exists primarily to provide data for these techniques, while others use the techniques without adequate data or theory. We discuss managerial and administrative analyses in terms of the social systems aspects of programs and the limitations on quantification imposed by these aspects, including the perplexing conceptual status of program goals and the presence of social and political conflict in our society.

Our approach is that managerial and administrative analyses are useful only if they are faithful to the data. Some of the analytic techniques described in this chapter can, if used incautiously, leave one worse off than planning based on judgment alone. In fact, managers and administrators must rely heavily on their own judgment based on careful consideration of the data. That is why we recommend an approach to evaluation that is based on research, rich data, and full use of relevant social theory, rather than on a single analytic model. Many analytic models for evaluation transform the data excessively; examples are cost-benefit analysis with its rigid metric of dollars, and multiattribute utility analysis, which calculates artificial estimates of social utilities. Such analytic schemes should be used only as secondary methods, and then only to stimulate thought, not to dictate conclusions.

Our discussion of administrative and managerial analytic methods focuses on several major categories of limitations imposed on such analyses by the assumptions of the analytic model, by various logical and conceptual principles, and by uncertainties inherent in any social forecasting.

Cost-benefit analysis, which underlies some of the other techniques, attempts to compare the costs and benefits of a single program by translating each into dollar values and comparing the resulting figures: cost in dollars is compared to benefits in dollars. *Cost-effectiveness analysis,* born of disappointment with the difficulties of cost-benefit analysis, is a more modest but still problematical enterprise that attempts to compare the costs of various programs for attaining a goal known or assumed to be worthwhile.

The *planning-programming-budgeting system* (PPBS), which has recently fallen into some disrepute, is the application of cost-benefit analysis to a set or several sets of programs. For example, all educational programs are arrayed and compared to one another in terms of cost-benefit ratios, and all agricultural programs are compared in the same way, and the general fruitfulness of educational and agricultural programs is compared in terms of relative cost-benefits. Thus instead of requesting funding for the traditional line-item categories (personnel, supplies, maintenance, travel, and consulting), the budgetary formulations are made in terms of entire large programs, such as agricultural subsidies, or even program packages like education, public health, or nuclear defense. This approach focuses on outputs (programs) rather than inputs (line items) in the hope of being more useful for policy decisions. The aim is to have each program or program package compete with every other (Wildavsky, 1974, 1975). In this competition, cost-benefit analysis plays a large role, identifying those programs that have the best ratios.

Zero-base budgeting involves considering the goals the agency wishes to attain and deciding the optimum way of attaining them, under the crucial assumption of a zero base, that is, that there are no existing investments by the agency in buildings, people, contracts, and so forth (see Hammond and Knott, 1980). This process serves to identify the inappropriateness of existing allocations of resources, investments, and staff to the goals the agency would like to meet. But since the agency does have sunk costs (prior investments in plant and people), such as buildings of a certain design in a certain location and contractual salary commitments, it cannot reallocate in accordance with the zero-base analysis except perhaps very incrementally.

Multiattribute utility analysis, discussed only briefly herein, is a method of attempting to use the ratings of involved judges, such as involved decision makers, to quantify the social utility of a given program. Various dimensions of social value, such as "promote child health" (Edwards, Guttentag, and Snapper, 1975), are chosen by the decision makers and program analysts because these dimensions are assumed or known to be relevant to program outcomes. These dimensions are weighted in terms of their comparative social importance, and each program is given a score on each dimension, based on the extent to which it is assumed or known to further that social value. Each score is multiplied by the corresponding weight, and the results summed across the dimensions to give a measure of the overall social utility of the program. If the judges can agree on the relevant value dimensions involved in the programs, the comparative importance of each dimension, and the place each program falls on each dimension, they can compare two programs, such as public housing and CETA, in terms of their overall social utilities.

Limitations of the Private Sector Model

One class of limitations on such managerial and administrative analyses is imposed by the analytic model underlying these analyses, namely, the private sector model. Cost-benefit analysis applies evaluative criteria used by private enterprise (costs, anticipated benefits) to public social programs. Just as a business firm compares costs to anticipated or actual receipts from sales, in order to determine whether it is worth marketing the product or service, or to choose among products, services, or courses of action, the program analyst compares the total costs of the program with its total benefits, to determine whether it makes sense to implement or continue the program. The appeal of applying analyses from the private sector to the public sector is strong, perhaps owing to recent political conservatism in the United States or perhaps owing to the appeal of dollars as a simple common metric. Although cost-benefit analysis has long been used in certain parts of the public sector, such as by the Army Corps of Engineers in analyzing water resource projects, we must ask whether a private enterprise metaphor such as cost-benefit analysis can be applied meaningfully in the public sector.

The defining characteristic of the private sector is that a market mechanism sets prices. A market ideally consists of a number of potential sellers and a number of potential buyers; the price is established by the interplay of competition among the sellers to obtain buyers, and competition among buyers to obtain the goods or services. With government-sponsored programs, however, the services are usually furnished to the clients without dollar cost to them. A program is therefore a free good rather than an economic good as far as clients are concerned, except for opportunities they forgo in order to be in it.

If a similar service or program is provided by several agencies, let us say several community health centers or family service agencies, then clients' preferences in terms of programs patronized can be used as an indicator of the programs' relative appeal to the clients. But, regardless of these preferences, in public social programs there are no market and no prices. Free goods have production costs, but they do not have prices by which their worth to the client can be computed.

Economists have formulated a number of constructs to treat the differences between the private and the public sector, such as the distinctions between private goods, merit goods, and public goods; and the concept of shadow prices. But these constructs are usually not adequate to justify the application of the private sector analogies, such as cost-benefit analysis in dollar terms, to program evaluation. Some programs, however, do have parallels in the private sector, such as private psychotherapeutic treatment, which have a price established by market forces. In such cases, one can estimate prices for publicly provided free services of a similar type. But no such parallels exist for the great majority of publicly funded social programs, such as welfare, CETA, sheltered workshops for the retarded, assistance to the elderly, and so forth. Even when a market price exists or can be estimated, the difficulties of comparing all costs and benefits in terms of dollars remains.

There are, however, some important parallels between the evaluation of social programs and activities of the private sector. Evaluation resembles market research for a firm, in that it attempts to determine whether the product is meeting the needs of the consumers: but since the program is not for sale, consumers cannot register this information with their sales dollars. Evaluation also resembles industrial quality control, since it can involve inspection of samples of the product to note structural or workmanship defects. Evaluation can be compared also to technical service by an industrial producer to industrial customers; experts are sent forth to debug the product and make sure that it is being used properly, just as an evaluator may intervene to remedy program defects (Perloff, 1979). Evaluation can be compared also to industrial research and development conducted for purposes of improving the product. But none of these comparisons of evaluation to the private sector implies that the benefits of the program can be tallied in dollars.

Another set of limitations imposed by the private sector model is apparent from even a cursory examination of how that model functions in the private sector. First, it is not at all clear that the private sector consistently outperforms the public sector. In fact, there is a great deal of evidence to rebut the widely held conception that the private sector consistently manages better than does the public. The shutdowns of American steel mills, throwing tens of thousands out of work, are owing to gross underinvestment in new technology, so that costs are higher for steel produced in America than for Japanese steel even after transoceanic transportation costs are added. The decline of the American auto industry has been a result of management over-concern with the pursuit of short run profits, with consequent underattention to quality control and underinvestment in new technology, particularly industrial robotics. The relationship of management and workers is also a problem. At General Motors, according to the board chairman, worker absenteeism, running from 20 to 23 percent, costs the firm a billion dollars a year (*Cincinnati Post,* January 14, 1981, p. 1). Second, cost-benefit analyses are neither unambiguous nor all-powerful in the private sector. Various accounting conventions yield different estimates of profitability, and profit margin is not the sole motivating force in the private sector.

Katona (1963) notes that the measurement of profits is subjective and variable, depending on accounting conventions and on business decisions about the allocation of costs, about putting some profits into reserves or reinvesting them, and about accruing or deferring expenditures and receipts to reduce taxes, and about the time frame for planning the pursuit of profits. Consequently it is not clear how to maximize profits, or what maximum profit is. The quest for maximum profit is also regulated by laws and constrained by prudence, the firm's need to maintain customer good will, and the reputation of its brand name (Katona, 1963).

Personal motives may also restrict a firm's search for profits; for example, top executives want high salaries and stock options, which reduce the firm's net profit. What Veblen (1918) calls the instinct of workmanship also plays a part; for example, when a West coast firm switched from making missile casings to making aluminum canoes, it had enormous difficulties persuading its engineers that canoes do not have to be manufactured to tolerances of a few ten thousandths of an inch.

Third, many corporate goals compete with the pursuit of

profit. Firms strive for volume of sales and for share of the market; while both of these are conducive to the stability of the firm, they are not the same as profit. Similarly, business strategies intended to avoid losses, decline in profits, or bankruptcy compete with the quest for maximum profits since the latter entails risks. Firms that prefer regular and secure profits to maximum profits seek to reduce risks, to "minimize regrets." In the decision as to which goals to pursue, and therefore which economic calculus to apply, the size and economic viability of the firm are important factors (Katona, 1963). Whether the firm is prosperous or is struggling for survival affects its perspective, and its time frame. There is also a difference in these respects between large and small firms, and between firms in developed and underdeveloped countries, and between old industries like railroads and new ones like microcomputers.

Consequently, the cost-benefit calculus that some analysts apply to social programs is based on a profit-maximization model that applies only in a limited way in the private sector. We must also question the model's assumption that individuals seek to maximize profits or other benefits to themselves, part of the economists' conception of economic man. Cost-benefit analysis, for example, implies that people seek an optimum, with either maximum benefit for a given cost, or minimum cost for a given benefit (both at once are logically impossible). But analyses by Simon (1978) suggest that people neither maximize nor optimize; instead, they *satisfice,* that is, they seek a satisfactory level of result. As Simon demonstrates, the decision processes and the actions resulting from the optimization assumption and the satisficing assumption are quite different.

The Cost Metaphor

Part of the analytic model applied in cost-benefit analysis involves the notion of costs. As used in the public sector, the conception of costs is a metaphor, not an identity. Cost-benefit analysts, however, often treat program costs as though they were purely financial costs in the most literal sense: dollars that are expended on behalf of a program or that will be expended to fulfill contractual obligations and to implement the program. But other kinds of transactions are comprised by the term *costs,* and these are important in evaluating social programs.

Wildavsky (1974), building on the work of Diesing (1962), describes one set of such costs. Wildavsky points out that economic analysis presupposes that economic rationality is the only determinant of the functioning of programs. Wildavsky argues that political rationality is also a factor and that, in addition to economic costs, programs have a set of political costs. These include hostility costs, the cost incurred by an advocate of the program from hostility engendered in the opponents of the program; for example, costs incurred by legislators who support the program in Congress. Similarly, programs have exchange costs, that is, the repayment the supporters of the program must give to those they persuaded to join them in fostering the program. The latter may demand support for a program of their own.

Reputation costs are another kind of political cost. The reputations of the advocates of a program rest on the program, and program defects harm the credibility of its proponents. Like hostility costs, exchange and reputation costs are incurred by legislators, program advocates within an agency, and the agency itself as the advocate for a program with Congress and with the Office of Management and Budget. When programs are implemented, power is redistributed, and further political costs are incurred in that some individuals lose power and some gain it as a result of their involvement in the sponsorship, funding, or implementation of the program (Wildavsky, 1974, 1975). Such political costs cannot adequately be converted into the economic terms cost-benefit analysis demands.

Three other kinds of costs resist conversion to financial costs: undesired consequences (what economists call "secondary costs"), opportunity costs, and passivity costs. As with political costs, to assign a dollar value to them is usually an arbitrary and misleading act. Consider a program of industrialization that is known to entail a considerable increase in pollution and a correlative increase in cancers and emphysema. This increase in disease is a cost of the program of industrialization, and one could tally the predicted cost in terms of days of work lost and hospitalization costs, as cost-benefit analysts have sometimes done. To do so, however, is but to partially measure the cost of cancer and to ignore the serious unpleasant consequences of cancer. To label these consequences as costs is a metaphor, since no dollar metric can measure more than a small part of the undesired effects.

Another example of the arbitrariness involved in comparing consequences and financial costs is the recent Department of Transportation decision that the amount of gasoline that has been saved by newly established traffic laws permitting right turns on red was sufficient to justify a yearly increase of 11,200 accidents nationwide predicted by the department, but not large enough to justify the increase of 20,000 accidents per year that actually resulted ("Study Finds Turns . . . ," 1980).

Cost-benefit analysis also often treats consequences as externalities, that is, as costs imposed on units outside the firm or agency. For example, pollution engendered by a program of industrialization is considered an externality since the polluting firm receives only a small part of it, and the rest goes into the larger atmosphere, or is sent downstream or spills from damaged tank cars onto some other community.

By means of the concept of externalities, cost-benefit analysts often treat negative consequences to units other than the firm or agency as unimportant for policy making. Negative consequences that have many nonfinancial dimensions, such as cancers, are too often dismissed as externalities. By assigning dollar values to negative consequences and by ignoring more important nonfinancial dimensions, or considering them as externalities or intangible costs, program analysts and legislators render an implicit social judgment on the societal value of such consequences.

Opportunity costs are the costs of implementing a program reckoned in terms of alternative uses of the money, time, and other resources involved. Measuring opportunity costs is useful in deciding between alternative programs when an agency can afford to implement only one of them. However, lost opportunities are not always primarily economic and so cannot always be quantified in dollars. Whether one can reasonably measure the cost of an opportunity forgone by assigning it a dollar value depends primarily on the *meaning* of that opportunity to the persons involved and to the society as a whole. Calling lost opportunities costs is often metaphorical.

A third kind of metaphorical cost are passivity costs, that is, the costs incurred by doing nothing. In evaluating a free-lunch program in the public schools, one must compare the cost of the lunches against all the costs that would be incurred if there were no program. These costs include delinquency, crime, and vandalism by embittered youths growing up in deprived homes. In calculating the social costs of inaction, financial terms are insufficient since passivity costs are both financial and nonfinancial. Even inaction involves costs, and free lunches may be much cheaper than no lunches at all.

Social Conflict

Unfortunately cost-benefit analysis very often tends to conceal social conflict rather than analyzing it usefully. It is a myth that program costs and benefits accrue to all people equally. Moreover, the greatest benefit for the greatest number is an analytic impossibility. A major issue is whose ox is gored. Consider, for example, the social costs and benefits of a publicly funded highway through the center of a city. The suburban commuters get the benefit, and the displaced central city residents bear the lion's share of the costs. Similarly, there are political constituencies for many programs, such as the farm program, CETA, protective tariffs, and so forth. Although the program's benefits to the constituencies may exceed the costs to them, costs may exceed benefits for society as a whole. In our political system a program usually needs a constituency to maintain itself, but, in economic terms, to design programs for constituencies to the detriment of the rest of society represents suboptimization, that is, optimizing the condition of one part of a system at the expense of the rest.

Some program analysts deal with the problem of whose ox is gored, by use of the concept of a Paretian optimum, the situation in which some individuals gain from the change and nobody loses. But social conflict arises when someone does lose while another gains. For this situation, some program analysts reason that if a given program produces a net benefit for person A of $10 and a net loss for person B of $5, then if A pays B $5 in compensation, A is ahead $5 and B is no worse off. Such formulations, however, assume that social gains and losses are quantifiable and that society will adequately compensate the losers. But, to return to our example of city highway construction, the persons whose neighborhood is destroyed by a highway project can never be restored to their former status; friendship groups and kinship groups are dispersed (Fried, 1963; Fried and Gleicher, 1961), and if they are renters rather than owners, they are usually not compensated at all.

Cost-benefit analysis must also confront the political constituencies within an agency. Internal constituents have a political stake in particular programs, and so they may distort or fudge the data given to the agency leadership, adjusting estimates of costs and priorities to produce the results they want. If asked about budget cuts, for example, they sometimes suggest cutting those things they know the agency's directors would least like to give up. Thus the data needed for cost-benefit analyses are hard to obtain and, as we will see, some of the needed data cannot exist, since social conflicts of interest render logically impossible the calculations required by the cost-benefit model.

Some of the social conflicts that cannot easily be taken into account in the cost-benefit model involve cross-cultural, subcultural, and interindividual differences in values. These differences in values result in the assignment of different economic values to the costs and benefits of a program. Since programs have no market mechanism, the values attributed to program outcomes and costs are by definition the representation of cultural values (and political ones) in economic terms, but the economic valuations assigned vary with the underlying cultural valuations. Cost-benefit analysis cannot take into account the various individual and cultural value systems that determine a program's costs and benefits.

Anderson's (1974) parody of the cost-benefit analysis of a symphony orchestra implicitly poses these crucial questions of cultural values. As Anderson implies, the quality of the orchestra's music (as a basis for the orchestra's receiving federal support) must be rated by expert judges, not by a deaf management specialist. But even among expert judges, differences in cultural values lead to differences in the assignment of dollar costs and benefits, for a random sample of judges might rate rock music as better than symphonic music. Any judgments about the qualifications of these judges are laden with cultural values about popular and highbrow taste.

A second problem concerns differential resources for kindred programs: Is symphonic music twenty times better than chamber music, which requires only one twentieth the number of musicians? That problem could be addressed by introducing a criterion of diversity of musical forms and presentations as desirable. However, such heterogeneity is itself a cultural value not shared by all subcultures. The underlying issue raised by Anderson's satire is not, as first appears, quantification but rather cultural differences.

Various techniques have been devised to help resolve the cultural and individual differences in the way program costs and benefits are weighed. These methods include multiattribute utility analysis and various systems for the iterative pooling of judgments under conditions of mutual feedback and partial or complete anonymity, such as nominal groups or the Delphi technique (see van de Ven and Delbecq, 1974). These methods can be used to gain consensus among a group about the dollar value of costs and benefits to be assigned. Such methods work most easily when they are used to resolve individual differences within a subculture, such as a corporation. It would be more difficult to produce consensus among Black, Hispanic, Appalachian, Native American, and Oriental raters of the cost and benefits of programs for various minorities.

Furthermore, multiattribute utility scaling, nominal groups, and the Delphi technique can be considered techniques that *impose* consensus as well as elicit it. Intimidation is a dynamic of small groups, as exhibited by Asch's (1955) experiments in false group consensus, in the risky shift in small group behavior (Cartwright, 1971), and in Janis' (1972) work on groupthink in policy making by top government groups. Such dangers may be inherent in techniques meant to broaden the base of experience and expertise of program analysts' judgments. These methods do not fully resolve the cultural value differences inherent in our society as they affect the valuation assigned to program outcomes. Depending on how they are used, these methods can obscure cultural value differences, suppress these differences, or promote free discussion of the differences. It is doubtful, however, whether value differences can be resolved by arithmetical techniques like multiattribute utility scaling.

In the private sector, the market mechanism assigns an economic value to many costs and benefits. The market mechanism is also a culture-bound attribution of value, for a rock star makes far more money than a leading modern composer, symphonic performer, or classical music soloist. However, the populist attribution of a differential value to performances has at least the empirical consequence of differential income to the performers. The attribution by a program analyst of a differential value to program results does not have such direct expression in market transactions. Also the locus of consensus is smaller since an evaluation may be decided by the vote of a few program analysts rather than the large populist vote of the market mechanism. Dollar costs already incurred by the program or reflecting future market transactions, such as supplies and salaries, however, are more grounded in the populist market mechanism than in the restricted or elitist views of the program analyst.

Political and social conflict issues pose even more severe issues for zero-base budgeting than for other managerial analytical techniques. Political constituencies inside and outside the agency can work to block any drastic change, and, of course, internal constituencies usually refuse to provide information that might lead to the termination of their jobs. Consequently, agencies find it difficult or impossible to use zero-base budgeting even as an analytic exercise, much less as a programming tool (see Hammond and Knott, 1980). The power of the relevant constituencies is as important as the agencies' prior investments in imposing these limitations on a zero-based analysis.

Analysts may, however, find it worthwhile to use a method that is like zero-based budgeting in reverse. Instead of trying to deduce how the organization should function from its stated goals, one could try to infer the goals from the existing organization. Specifically, one could infer the actual goals of an organization from observations of what things it is willing to give up in order to get others and what percentages of time are spent in various activities. Such an analysis might serve as a useful adjunct or corrective to zero-base budgeting. Instead of attempting to deduce the ideal or rational allocation of resources from the stated goals, one takes the existing allocation of resources to reflect the real goals, that is, those actually pursued by the organization.

Logical Limitations

Logic imposes another class of limitations on cost-benefit analysis. A major problem, discussed in Chapter One, is that many of the conceptual categories required for the analysis of program costs and benefits are socially unacceptable for discussion or even taboo. Since some of the crucial terms cannot be named, the equation cannot be solved. Some of these taboo concepts include social class, caste, income redistribution, class conflict, triage, the lifeboat concept, irredentism (the fact that a group displaced from its homeland rarely gives up the attempt to return), the unconscious, and the importance of judicial interpretation. To choose the last, for example, if there is a refusal to acknowledge that statutes derive much of their meaning from interpretation by the courts, it is nearly impossible to analyze fully the costs and benefits of a proposed reform such as the Equal Rights Amendment (ERA). Consider the fate of the Fourteenth Amendment, originally intended to protect the rights of freed slaves from abridgment by the states. The courts have interpreted the due process clause in the amendment to apply to corporations as well as individuals, an interpretation unforeseen by its sponsors. What might happen with the ERA? In 1981 a California man appealed his conviction for statutory rape, on the grounds of sex discrimination, since under California law women cannot be convicted for sexual intercourse with a minor. He lost the appeal in the United States Supreme Court. Might passage of the ERA strengthen his case?

To choose a related example, if one refuses to discuss concepts of the unconscious and the Oedipal conflict, one cannot completely analyze the prevalence, only recently coming to light, of child abuse and of incest, and one cannot design programs to reduce the incidence of these practices. Similarly, unless one discusses irredentism one cannot analyze effectively the impact of various policy alternatives in the Middle East.

Wildavsky (1974, 1975) suggests other logical difficulties with both cost-benefit analysis and the planning-programming-budgeting system (PPBS). PPBS failed dismally on the federal level, but is now being used by states and cities. Wildavsky sees two major logical limitations. First, some of the social theory necessary for performing the calculations has not yet been formulated. Particularly inadequate are present causal knowledge and causal theory. Without adequate theories of social causality, one cannot adequately analyze program outcomes in terms of the full range of societal costs and benefits that may ensue. This is an aspect of the problem, analyzed in Chapter Two, that programs in complex systems frequently operate in counterintuitive ways that are not fully understood.

Second, Wildavsky states that the data required to make the calculations do not exist, even were sufficient causal theory available to guide the calculations. To put it baldly, cost-benefit analysis is not sufficiently data-based. As Wildavsky (1975) notes, program categories are "not 'simply out there,' reified, waiting to be found; they must be invented; they are social constructs" (see Berger and Luckmann, 1967). The broad program categories created by agencies in generating program data are frequently meaningless; Wildavsky (1974, p. 203) cites the categories "Communities for Tomorrow" and "Expanding Dimensions for Living," used by the Department of Agriculture, as ones that no one would actually use for decision making. Neologistic program categories transmit little information since they have no generally accepted meaning.

The more traditional categories like health, education, community development, poverty programs, are also arbitrary to a great extent. For example, community mental health programs have an education component, as do health programs and housing programs. Job training programs affect health, housing, and education, and education programs affect jobs, housing, and health. Programs have multiple effects and multiple aspects, not easily separable for cost allocations. PPBS uses large categories such as welfare, education, and housing, but most programs fit several categories.

Some analysts hope that program evaluation can provide the needed data, but the demands of cost-benefit analysis are too great for social theory and social research data to meet in the foreseeable future. By reason of the lack of causal theory and data, Wildavsky concludes that PPBS, using cost-benefit analysis, "has failed everywhere at all times" (1975, p. 363), and his studies of budgeting in the United States and in many other nations support this view. Attempts to make program budgeting comprehensive by comparing all programs either fail outright or produce unrealistic results.

A further logical problem in cost-benefit analysis involves measurement. Cost-benefit analysis, and the methods built on it, like zero-base budgeting and PPBS, require a kind of quantification, since they express program results in numerical terms. But quantification requires a metric, and what metric can relate cancers to rapes or to jobs? One can use dollars as the common metric, and estimate the costs of cancers, emphysema, or chemical poisoning in terms of medical bills, and the dollar value of days lost from work. But such measurement is termed fractional by sociologists (see Etzioni and Lehman, 1967); that is, the dollar figure represents only a fraction of the program consequences. Fractional measurement also results from excessive transformation of the data, through which most of the data's meaning is lost.

These defects can also be understood as issues of construct validity, involving trivialization and indicators insuffi-

ciently related to the construct. The use of an operational definition rather than multiple operationism in the explication of a
construct is also involved. As noted, the difficulty of finding a
common metric is compounded by the fact that consequences
(such as cancer, rapes, and jobs) that emanate from a given program accrue to different people, so that one person's benefit
must be balanced against another's loss. In measurement, such
balancing constitutes a kind of illegitimate aggregation.

In a sense, cost-benefit analysis of some sort is inescapa-
ble, for some consideration of the pros and cons of various
courses of action is a necessary part of planning. However, a
fractional measurement—whether a dollar metric, a body-count,
or a kill-ratio—cannot yield a comprehensive, informed judgment.

The characteristics of social systems pose further logical
problems for cost-benefit analysis. Components of a complex
system affect each other in complex and nonlinear ways that
cannot be expressed well by the simple addition and subtraction
of costs and benefits. Many concepts are used in the social sciences to cope with these issues, but they are little used in cost-
benefit analysis: multiple feedback loops, synergy, catalysis,
gestalts, latent functions, and levels of analysis. These concepts
are essential for understanding complex, open social systems
(see Ackoff, 1973; Forrester, 1971a, 1971b). Some of these systems issues are apparent in Anderson's (1974) parody of the
cost-benefit analysis of a symphony orchestra in which the
needed concepts ignored by the analyst include pattern recognition (one cannot omit a little-used instrument), synergy (the
whole result is greater than the sum of the contributing parts),
catalysis and nonlinear relationships (the conductor makes a
disproportionate contribution), and the social value of variety
and heterogeneity.

Cost-effectiveness analysis, which is used when one already believes the goal is worth pursuing, is more modest in aim
than cost-benefit analysis, since only costs and not benefits are
to be compared. The comparisons are often between closely related programs that are treated as alternative ways of reaching
the same goal. But logical and metrical difficulties arise here,

too. For example, consider a narrow program goal such as high-rise public housing. One can compare the costs of various closely related programs, such as direct federal construction, subsidies to the states, or tax incentives to the private sector, to achieve that result. But the more highly defined the program goal, the less clear it is that the goal is worth pursuing. Newman's (1972) studies have shown that high-rise public housing is often worse than the slum housing it replaces. However, if far broader goals are chosen, such as improved housing for the poor, a large number of very different programs, with very different consequences, and hence different costs and benefits, could address that goal. Consequently, for both the narrowly defined and the broadly defined social goal, cost-effectiveness analysis is likely to prove very difficult.

Excessive Complication

Managerial and administrative analyses are often characterized by excessive complication: The analytic framework is too complex to be understood by program managers and so complex that the managers cannot detect errors or logical flaws. The time and energy required of managers to understand some analytic models is so great that managers have to accept the results on faith. Any attempt to understand them quickly leads to a form of instrument fatigue (Cook and Campbell, 1979) that renders the mind of the manager less able to make the required distinctions.

Complication is not a function of mathematical complexity; complication refers to the number of substantive ad hoc assumptions about social and organizational processes, and the intricate interrelationships of these postulates, required by a model. Mathematical complexity characterizes nonlinear multiple regression, factor analysis, path analysis, and other methods in which the computations are intricate, or mathematical sophistication is required to interpret the computations. Complication describes the interactions of too many ad hoc or idiosyncratic substantive assumptions that are difficult to detect and unsupported by data.

Simulation models and management information systems tend to be high on the dimension of complication. A management information system involves the gathering of data, or numbers, deemed to be useful for the management of a program or organization, and their storage in a computer from which they can be retrieved for use in management decision making. Such systems, designed to facilitate agencywide evaluation analyses, have been installed at the Agency for International Development, for example. Management information systems range from the simple and straightforward (permitting comparisons of programs in terms of staff turnover, for instance) to ones that are highly intricate and highly dependent on hidden ad hoc substantive assumptions.

Simulations are a special kind of analytic model. If a model is defined as the representation of a theory in mathematical terms, a simulation model is a mathematical representation of a theory about a system such that the unfolding of system processes over time can be represented and specified. Simulation models range from the simple to the intricate in the number of substantive assumptions postulated by the model, but usually they are prone to complication.

Brewer (1973) analyzes two major simulation models devised by private consultants for the government of the city and county of San Francisco and the city of Pittsburgh, to aid in community renewal programming. Both models he views as disasters. Brewer's analysis implies that the underlying difficulty is complication: In the absence of the requisite social theory and data, analysts must make an intricate network of questionable substantive assumptions. Many of the postulates for each model appear doubtful and some appear wrong. Equally important, the models present too many assumptions for users to grasp, and many crucial assumptions are not easily identifiable even on close examination of the model. (Recall the problem of assumptions in the models of world systems in Chapter Two.)

For example, the San Francisco simulation model, by Arthur D. Little, Inc., attempted to model changes in housing stock in San Francisco, but entirely omitted the effect of transportation changes, a dubious assumption of stasis since the Bay

Area Rapid Transit system was under construction. More subtly, the categorizations of minority groups in San Francisco, which is ethnically very diverse, with large numbers of Irish-Americans, Hispanics, Chinese, Japanese, and blacks, were far too simple. Furthermore, the spatial analytic unit devised by the consultants, the "fract," did not refer to a geographical unit that could be shown on a map, and so was not understandable to the policy makers. The model, high on complication, could not be used at all, and the computer outputs from the model countered the known facts in their predictions and were incomprehensibly complex.

Some of the hazards of complication can be remedied if system designers identify their ad hoc assumptions, but frequently the designers are unaware of some of the assumptions logically involved in the system. Wildavsky (1973), generalizing Brewer's analysis to information systems of all kinds, proposes ten rules for the potential purchaser of an information system, many of which reflect a recognition of the dangers of complication.

> First, the rule of skepticism: no one knows how to do it. . . . Second: the rule of delay; if it works at all, it won't work soon. Be prepared to give it years. . . . Third, the rule of complexity: nothing complicated works. . . . Fourth, the rule of thumb: if the data are thicker than your thumb (skeptics—see rule 1—may say 'pinky') they are not likely to be comprehensible to anyone. . . . The fifth rule is to be like a child. Ask many questions; be literal in appraising answers. Sixth is the rule of length and width . . . Potential users of information ought to be able to envisage the length of the data flow over time, that is, who will pass what on to whom. . . . The longer the sequence of steps, the wider the band of clientele, the less likely the information is to be of use. Seventh, the rule of anticipated anguish (sometimes known as Murphy's Law): most of the things that can go wrong will. Eighth, the rule of known evil: people get used to

working with what they have, they can estimate
the "fudge" factor in it. . . . Ninth . . . the rule of
the mounting mirage . . . The benefits of better information . . . are readily apparent in the present.
The costs lie in the future. But because the costs
arrive before the benefits, the mirage mounts, as it
were, to encompass an ever finer future that will
compensate for the increasingly miserable present.
Once this relationship is known, however, it becomes possible to discount the difficulties by stating the tenth and final rule: Hypothetical benefits
should outweigh estimated costs by at least ten to
one before everyone concerned starts seeing things
(pp. 1377-1378).

Some consultants in the area of management information
systems are aware of these issues from personal experience and
have formulated a caution against complication, expressed in
the acronym KISS (keep it simple, stupid). This admonition
recognizes that cognitive overload leads to mystification, paraly-
sis, and error. The simpler the management information system,
the less fearful we need be of being befuddled or misled, since
its flaws and their consequences are more readily detectable.
Our general admonition for the use of such systems is to keep
things simple; if the system cannot be kept simple, try to be
skeptical until it has proved its usefulness.

Forecasting

Cost-benefit analyses and related techniques involve forecasting in that the benefits and many of the costs are in the future. Consequently cost-benefit analyses, like other forecasting
techniques, are inherently uncertain in a way that evaluation
methods confined to the study of past outcomes of programs
are not. In theory, cost-benefit analysis is designed to be a prospective technique that estimates future costs and benefits. In
practice, however, it is often used retrospectively to answer the
question, "Given what we now know about the program's outcomes, was this program worth what we spent on it?" But this

use is only truly retrospective if the important outcomes have indeed already taken place.

Cost-effectiveness analysis is even more frequently used retrospectively. For example, suppose that outpatient psychotherapy provided by a community mental health center is found to have cost $120 an hour when all costs are divided by the number of patients seen. If one assumes that the quality of the therapy provided is equal to the best private psychotherapy, then it costs too much. Retrospective analyses are easier to make than are prospective ones, since retrospective analyses do not require forecasting.

The difficulties of forecasting, inherent in many decision analytic methods, are acute in prospective cost-benefit analysis, since future income and future costs are each discounted by an interest rate to account for the fact that a dollar in the future is worth less than a dollar now. Since a dollar invested in the present will produce more than a dollar in the future, analysts estimate an interest rate deemed to hold until the end of the program's benefits. Herein lies the difficulty. The exact amount of the interest rate has a great bearing on the cost-benefit ratio of the project; the lower the interest rate, the more feasible the project. Even a small difference, say a quarter of a percentage point, in the interest rate can, because of compounding, have a great effect on the feasibility of the project as measured in cost-benefit terms (Sherrill, forthcoming). Even in serene times, it is extremely difficult to forecast interest rates with any accuracy.

Other forecasting difficulties for cost-benefit analysis, cost-effectiveness analysis, and related techniques stem from the inherent uncertainty of social systems. In Chapter Two, we describe programs as having counterintuitive consequences, since they are subsystems of highly complex, open social systems that themselves operate counterintuitively. This argument implies the need for skepticism about analysts' ability to predict program consequences with any accuracy. Cost-benefit analysis, which attempts not only to identify all future benefits and costs but also to express them in dollars, is a very uncertain and hazardous procedure.

Ackoff (1973) argues that the unpredictability and intractibility of systems require analysts to make a continuing series of adjustments of various sorts, depending on the current state of the system. Such adjustments are especially important for open systems like programs, that is, systems whose boundaries are relatively permeable. Management by objectives (MBO), the attempt to allocate resources in a way that matches the organization's goals, appears to be more consistent with Ackoff's suggestions than is cost-benefit analysis. MBO can be applied incrementally and does not require wholesale reconstruction of the system. MBO is a conceptual kin to zero-base budgeting in the attempt to reallocate resources according to the organization's aims, but since MBO is incremental it is more feasible.

One variant of MBO takes a more data-oriented and less exhortative approach than traditional MBO in applying evaluation data to managerial and administrative contexts. This variant of MBO suggests that resources, for example, program staff and program plans, be directed toward those endeavors in which the agency or firm is actually successful, not toward those it merely thinks it wants to undertake. This variant uses the agency's experience as feedback to perform reality testing for the agency. The rationale is that experience shows that one does some things well or superlatively, and others poorly or execrably. Consequently, although various activities may serve equally desirable social goals, agencies ought to do the former and not the latter.

There is a danger, however, that an agency or firm may continue to do what it does well, even after that activity is no longer useful. The National Cash Register Company, for example, made the best electromechanical cash register, but almost went out of business because it was so slow to change to electronic cash registers with their many advantages for information storage and retrieval (see Mantel, forthcoming). Like cost-benefit analysis, MBO is a model derived from the business sector, but unlike cost-benefit analysis, it does not presuppose a dollar valuation of outcomes. Therefore, an MBO mode of analysis seems more appropriate to the public sector, in which there is no market mechanism to set prices.

Irrationality and Analytic Models

A major difficulty in managerial and administrative models is that there seems to be an irrational substratum of human behavior that is disguised or denied by analytical schemes such as cost-benefit analysis. This irrational substratum can make the behavior of persons and the outcome of programs difficult to predict. Examples of such behavior include neighbors' reluctance to call the police in the Kitty Genovese case (see Latane and Darley, 1969) and the many instances of emotionally regressed behavior in public places detailed by Zimbardo (1973b). More recently, a crowd of bystanders in Chicago jeered as an old man tried to pull himself onto a subway platform out of the path of an oncoming train, but was unable to because of his crippled arm ("Subway Drama...," 1980). The concepts needed to analyze the crowd's irrational behavior are deindividuation (the loss of individual identity and therefore sense of responsibility in an anonymous situation such as a crowd), taboo, and stigma. For example, the old man was stigmatized as dirty and taboo since he was down and out, bedraggled, and perhaps a tramp or derelict.

Influenced by Latane and Darley's approach of rationally weighing costs and benefits, Piliavin, Rodin, and Piliavin (1969) studied onlookers' willingness to help a fallen man (a confederate of the experimenter) inside a subway car. Differences in onlookers' willingness to help depended on the man's appearance and race. But some of the irrational factors affecting the costs of helping, such as taboo and contamination, were not discussed by the researchers.

As Zimbardo (1973b) points out, if a society or subculture dehumanizes a social group, individuals can treat the dehumanized group with brutality without becoming deindividuated. Programs directed at ethnic and racial minorities and groups such as aftercare patients, prisoners, the handicapped, the retarded, the sexually deviant, the aged in nursing homes, and hospitalized patients must frequently contend with the tendency of the program staff either to dehumanize the program's clients or to become deindividuated themselves. Deindividuation and dehumanization are less likely if the individuals involved retain an identity in their own eyes and in the eyes of each other. Thus hostages know that their captors will treat them better if they think of them as people; hence hostages often tell their captors about their lives, their families, and their children. Similarly, the deliberate effort to present oneself as human, as an individual, may be a necessary strategy for program clientele in dealing with bureaucracies.

Consider, in this context, the Coliseum tragedy of 1979 in Cincinnati, in which fourteen teenagers were trampled to death by a crowd of other teenagers rushing into the hall in order to get better unreserved seats. It might be possible to analyze such a situation in cost-benefit terms, using the methods of linear programming, operations research, and queueing theory, and conclude that the costs of the rush exceed the benefits. But to analyze the event in these terms ignores the dehumanization that made such a stampede possible, and no theoretical construct can provide a simple metric for irrational behavior. We may well suspect that many social programs are also implemented in a deeply irrational way, public housing, law enforcement, and the treatment of prisoners being noteworthy examples.

Another chilling application of the rationalistic weighing of comparative costs and benefits is outlined by Glaser and Strauss (1964) in studying how nurses apply computations of social value and social contribution to the dying in order to rationalize to themselves that a particular patient is dying. The nurses tell themselves that the patient is old, or unemployable, or leaves no family behind. The rationalization involved in such weighing of social costs and benefits, and the irrational substratum that is involved, is little disguised. Chatterjee's (1975) grim parody, in which cost-benefit analysis is used to justify capital punishment by hanging, also underscores the irrational elements that underlie program designs, program implementation, and program analyses.

If we consider irrationality in terms of the sociology of knowledge and apply Mannheim's (1940) distinction, cost-benefit analysis and related administrative and managerial analyses have the potential to be functionally rational but not substantially rational. That is, these analytic methods may be used to analyze how the parts of a program fit together, but they cannot discern whether the program itself makes sense. (Mannheim's illustration is that of a soldier who follows orders and marches where he is told, but has no understanding of the purpose of the war nor how it is progressing.)

Many of the administrative and managerial analytic methods are more concerned with the problem of order than the problem of reasonableness; as a result they are overstructured, overspecified, overquantified, and overcomplicated. These methods focus on the orderly arrangement, coordination, and synchronization of parts of a program or program package; they cannot readily promote an understanding of what the goal actually implies and whether it is a reasonable one. If a program is substantially irrational, that is, if aspects of its implementation are deeply unreasonable, the logic of cost-benefit forecasting is certainly inadequate.

The Proper Scope of Administrative and Managerial Analyses

Let us now briefly assess the overall usefulness of some of the major kinds of managerial and administrative analyses. Zero-base budgeting is a conceptual exercise, not a planning tool. One cannot act on the results, but they can indicate differences between a program's actual functioning and its alleged goals. Cost-benefit analysis may be a useful procedure if the metric is not dollars and if results are viewed skeptically; the metric of dollars is fractional measurement at best and, consequently, is often very misleading. Cost-effectiveness analysis has some of the defects of cost-benefit analysis, unless one is interested only in comparing the financial costs of extremely similar programs. But, it is often hard to know if two programs really are similar in outcome.

Comprehensive program budgeting has all the difficulties of those three methods and others of its own; it has no proper scope. Management information systems must be taken cautiously and in small doses at first. Simulation modeling of program functioning and consequences magnifies the difficulties of management information systems since it models the unfolding of consequences over time.

All these methods would be more feasible if we had much better causal social theory and social data. The task of evaluation research by social scientists, is to help provide the needed social data and generate the needed social theory. But evaluation cannot itself generate all the social theory and data needed; much of that must come from other social scientific research and from experience suitably reflected upon.

Evaluators and managers are consequently urged to adopt a research-based approach to evaluation, making a careful social scientific study of the particular program under consideration, rather than a study based on an analytic model. Whatever substantive social theory is available (usually less than one would wish) should be used to the fullest. The substantive assumptions of models are not substitutes for adequate substantive social theory. Estimates of program outcomes are not substitutes for actual data about the outcomes based on sound social research methods.

Primary reliance on a research-based, theoretically rich approach to evaluation is therefore emphatically recommended in preference to approaches based on administrative and managerial models. No such model should ever be used to replace the administrators' and evaluators' own judgment based on a full consideration of the available data and theory, and their own applicable experience. Managerial and administrative analytic models are, however, sometimes useful in stimulating new thoughts about a program or problem, and in certain circumstances they may have probative value, if the many caveats in this chapter are borne in mind. An adage from an old German folk tale is applicable to the use of such analytic techniques: "Be brave, be brave, but not too brave." Or, as Talleyrand is said to have advised young diplomats, "Above all, not too much zeal."

11

Impending Changes
in Society: Impact
on Evaluation

●~•~•~•~•~•~•~•~•~•~•~•~•~•~•~•~•~•~•~•

In the present chapter, we attempt to anticipate some of the
changes that will occur in evaluation over the next ten or fifteen years. Because evaluation is shaped by the social structure
in which it is embedded, changes in evaluation will be largely a
product of changes in society. Our predictions are based on social changes that have already begun to occur rather than solely
on daring speculations about the future. This makes the predictions less remarkable but probably more accurate.

Hume noted that there is no logical reason to expect the
future to be like the past. Nevertheless, the best single predictor
of an individual's performance is usually that person's past performance in a similar situation. One wonders whether this can
be applied to societies, which undergo convulsive and unexpected changes with some frequency. The variety and complexity of social change in itself can help us in our predictions; the
complex and changing interactions of social systems that make
program functioning and outcomes counterintuitive, as discussed
in Chapter Two, will continue to make it difficult to design so-

cial programs that have the desired effects. As a result, there will be a lively demand for the services of evaluators and the evaluation field should continue to grow. Disorder and uncertainty will foster evaluation, since evaluation attempts to reduce uncertainty.

In this chapter, we consider applications of evaluation broader than those most evaluators are familiar with. In particular, we examine applications of evaluation to the environment, social control, the military, and the private sector. This expansion in the scope of evaluation is a likely result of social changes that will make the social consequences of programs not designed for the amelioration of specific social ills far more important than previously, while the traditional ameliorative social programs may become less important.

This expanded scope of program evaluation is consistent with the definition of program offered in Chapter One, namely, a planned sequence of activities directed toward achieving some goal. Many of these newer types of evaluation, in both the public and the private sectors, such as the study of the effect of pollution on public health or the study of the estimated "cost" (in lives) of not installing a safety device on cars, pose problems that are to some extent new to evaluators. For that reason and because the physical environment as well as the social environment must be considered, it may be difficult initially to get theoretical and methodological leverage on these problems. As a consequence, evaluative studies in those areas may at first be only fairly adequate, not optimal, in methodology, and will also be hampered by lack of enough relevant social theory. Yet the findings of such studies should be an improvement over any judgments that are unsupported by a careful consideration of relevant evaluation research data and available theory. Our message in this chapter, therefore, is that significant social changes will lead to more evaluation, or opportunities for it, and to evaluations in areas other than the traditional social programs.

Social Changes

Specific social changes are not always easy to predict, and naturally an exhaustive list will not be attempted here. We can, however, consider some of the changes impending or under-way that appear to have particular consequences for evalua-tion. At present, one major program that appears likely to miscarry is the development of nuclear reactors. Since the half-lives of radioactive by-products are irreducible, radioactive environmental pollution can be expected to increase. Unless fusion is developed, radioactive by-products and radioactive spent fuel will continue to be produced without any safe means to store or dispose of them. Accidents in nuclear reac-tors will continue to occur, and statistically it is to be expected that some of them, unlike the Three Mile Island accident, and the accidents in France and Japan, may not be minor. Mishaps during shipment of nuclear materials around the nation may also occur, just as they presently occur during shipments of chemicals. As a result of mishaps and undesired outcomes, the need for evaluation of hazards from nuclear programs will in-crease.

Another social change, which is in part responsible for the initial boom in the evaluation field, is the growth of politi-cal conservatism in the United States since 1968. If this trend continues, several consequences appear likely. One is additional large reductions in federal and state social programs, for reasons of perceived ineffectiveness, voter rebellion at tax burdens, and public resentment of the government officials who design and administer the programs. Some of these cutbacks will be made with the aid of evaluation data, since the conservative credo in-cludes a belief in rationality and a businesslike approach.

Thus, as in 1969 at the beginning of the Nixon adminis-tration, as described in Chapter One, the movement toward con-servatism may lead to further reliance on evaluation. Given the conservative viewpoint, those aspects of evaluation that are de-rived from business analyses, those developed by economists ra-ther than sociologists, will be the most acceptable. Such methods include the management information systems and simulations discussed in Chapter Ten, as well as operations research and eco-nomic indicators. Less acceptable to government funding sources may well be methods that stress sociological principles or hu-manistic compassion.

Among the casualties of the cutbacks in federal programs

will probably be social research of most sorts other than evaluation, since such investigations will be considered as liberal, soft-hearted, or impractical by conservatives. Such selective cutbacks have already begun. The Reagan administration's 1981 budget for the remainder of fiscal 1981, and for fiscal 1982 and 1983, selectively cut social research in the National Science Foundation, the National Institute of Mental Health, and many other agencies, far more than other scientific research. An examination of the cuts discloses that psychological and sociological research of all sorts are the targets of these reductions. The impoverishment of social research will work to the disadvantage of evaluation, since the fundamental insights for a substantive understanding of programs depend in part on basic social science research. Program evaluation lives in part off the accumulated capital of the social sciences, and any reduction in the latter will constrict the former.

Budgetary constraints may continue to be accompanied by the ridicule and intimidation of social research, like the efforts of Senator Proxmire. Besides destroying morale, such tactics inhibit funding. We may also expect continued regulation of social research on ethical grounds, on the assumption that the same rules of full disclosure and informed consent should apply there as apply to biomedical research. This assumption, however, is inappropriate in that a large proportion of social research, electroshock experiments and similar stressful situations aside, is basically a form of talking to people or observing people in their everyday activities, and is usually harmless.

Some of the administrative regulations as presently enforced may be unconstitutional, however, as they appear to abridge the freedom of speech and of association. For example, a present regulation states that if a university receives any federal funding from any agency for health-related research, then all research involving human subjects by any faculty member or student of that university, whether that researcher receives federal funding or not, must be approved in writing by a university-wide ethics committee using rules approved by the Department of Health and Human Services.

For a long while reviews by ethics committees even included research involving watching people in a natural environment, such as a public square, or talking with people. Heavy and impractical requirements of informed consent were often imposed for these harmless procedures. But revised guidelines for the protection of human subjects were promulgated by the Department of Health and Human Services in 1981 (U.S. Office of the Federal Register, 1981), and these revisions exempt from review most studies involving only interviews, surveys, observation of public behavior, archival studies in which data are publicly available or subjects cannot be identified, educational tests in which subjects cannot be identified, and research on school curriculums. The remaining restrictions on interviews, surveys, and observational studies concern only protecting the subject from civil or criminal liability from the information that is discovered. This liberalization of the Health and Human Services guidelines is a bright note.

In the present harsh climate, program evaluation will flourish, but the basic social scientific research on which evaluation ultimately depends may founder for lack of funding and from overregulation. Thus most advances in evaluation may be in research design and statistical analysis rather than in the substantive understanding of social programs. But not all research will dwindle under a conservative emphasis in American politics. Practical research that does not raise embarrassing social questions and research that, like evaluation, can be used to trim programs may indeed flourish.

As part of the swing toward conservatism, reductions in many federal and state social programs will be enacted by state tax limitation initiatives, legislation, and executive orders. To the extent that such cuts are made by fiat rather than by reliance on outcome data, the demand for evaluation may lessen in the area of social programs. But new applications of evaluation in the public sector will emerge.

Moreover, needs for evaluation in the private sector—evaluation of management training programs, executive compensation programs, and personnel programs—consequently should increase. For evaluators interested in that sector, opportunities should abound. These evaluators must first translate the terminology of program evaluation into terminology more familiar to the private sector. The literature on marketing services originally designed for the public sector in the private sector indicates that such translation is important. Among the terms that suggest themselves as already familiar to business people are effectiveness measurement, performance measurement, strategy assessment, organizational assessment, management audit, and organizational audit.

Owing to increased conservatism and to efforts to compete with huge military expenditures by the U.S.S.R., the military segment of the U.S. economy will grow. The military segment comprises the Department of Defense and its private suppliers of goods and services. The Department of Defense itself will constitute a major growth area for evaluation, since the military has so many personnel-intensive programs, including training programs of all sorts. Evaluations of man-machine systems will also be an expanding area of activity. In the private part of the military sector, evaluation will also be needed.

A number of other major social changes have begun to occur and appear likely to continue. Among them are the drift of the population to the Southwest of the United States, the increase in the percentage of working women, the emergence of Hispanics as the nation's largest minority, and the increase in the mean age of the population. Programs aimed at these constituencies will take on greater importance. Jobs in evaluation will move slowly westward with the population. Evaluators who are sensitive to cultural and subcultural differences, those who have training in Hispanic culture, women's issues, or aging are likely to find their services in particular demand.

Growth in Technology

The continued growth of technology is likely to produce marked changes affecting evaluation. The effects of technological changes are already becoming apparent in the area of social control and its opposite pole, terrorism (see Parry, 1977). The technology of terrorism has been advancing rapidly with the widespread availability of Uzzi machine guns, plastic bombs, equipment for two-way radio communication between terrorists, small portable rocket launchers, and other sophisticated devices. The social technology of terrorism has been advancing too, with the development of a network of terrorist training camps, in Algeria, Jordan, Lebanon, Cuba, and other places in Africa, the Middle East, and Latin America.

The growth of technology has made society more vulnerable, since it has tied society more closely together in an interdependent net that can be ruptured seriously at any one of a number of points. Accidental disruptions with widespread though short-term effects, such as regional power failures, have already occurred repeatedly. But disruption by intent is also becoming more and more a possibility. Nuclear reactors for example are susceptible to terrorist attack. Social disruption by assassination attempts on major political and religious leaders, diplomats, industrialists, and journalists continues to be a problem. The vulnerability of the society to intentional disruption, made much easier by the growth of sophisticated technology of terrorism and by the increasing technologically based interdependence of society, means that programs for social control, involving the military and the police, will provide a fertile area for evaluation.

The decline of the competitive position of the United States compared to other modern economies, notably Western Europe and Japan, has begun to affect the standard of living of Americans through diminishing industrial productivity and increasing inflation. There are consequently demands for reindustrialization, for greatly increased capital investment and industrial research and development. Attempts to bring about such industrial change will be important in the coming years, for many fear that the U.S. economy will otherwise continue to decline. There are also worries about rapidly increasing foreign ownership of American assets, including business firms and real estate.

The reindustrialization effort to reverse these trends will entail programs to improve productivity on the assembly line, in offices (where diminishing productivity is very marked), and in research and development laboratories. Among the program-

matic efforts to improve productivity, besides higher investment, will probably be participative management, profit sharing, organization development, team building, and efforts to
improve the organizational climate. A great deal of evidence indicates that a major factor in low American productivity is the
antagonism between workers and management. The evaluation
of programs of organizational change to alleviate such antagonism could be an important field of development for evaluation.

The recent increase in the economic interdependence
among nations will most likely continue, as will the political,
economic, and military consolidation of the United States with
Western Europe. Less obvious, but still important, is the U.S.
economic consolidation with Japan; for example, many cars and
television sets marketed under the trade name of American
manufacturers are made in Japan. Closer trade relations with
Taiwan, Korea, and China are to be expected. Through such
economic relations, the perspective of the American people may
become more cosmopolitan, and American culture may gradually become more international. While direct foreign aid programs may decline further, owing to the conservative ethos,
international programs of other types, such as hard loans, cooperative ventures, and military aid, will probably expand under
the pressures of growing international interdependence, and
such programs will require evaluation.

The changing energy situation will continue to have a
profound effect on the U.S. economy, our standard of living,
our rate and mode of economic development, and ultimately on
our social structure. Coal and natural gas are plentiful in the
United States, and greater reliance on natural gas is to be expected. A breakthrough in coal gasification, which may occur in
the next fifteen years, would produce huge quantities of natural
gas at acceptable prices. Sometime in the next two decades, scientists might develop a commercially feasible way to derive
energy from fusion, an energy source that would produce few
radioactive by-products and little pollution except thermal. We
can expect additional progress with solar energy, which could
become an important element in the heating systems of many
new homes and some old ones, and there may be a breakthrough

in battery-operated automobiles. These developments could be of tremendous social consequence. But until they occur, transportation costs for people and goods will continue to increase sharply. To economize on transportation, businesses may rely more on telephone and video communication and on computerized information transmission through telephone lines, becoming less dependent on automobiles and airplanes to bring workers to their offices, conferences, and clients. Evaluators can contribute importantly by making comparative studies of the effectiveness of these various modes of communicating and transmitting information.

With continued technological progress and cost reduction in the microprocessor industry, and in the computer field generally, we will all be linked more completely in an information-processing and communication system. As is happening already, many managers and professionals will be able to work at home using personal computers and home computer terminals. There will doubtless be two-way video communication and accessibility to industrial and governmental data banks from home as well as the workplace. Evaluation of the functioning of these new man-machine systems will become important and will require evaluators who are knowledgeable about computers, information systems, office automation, and communications technology. This increased use of computer systems, in addition to political conservatism, will accelerate the development of quantitative methodology in evaluation.

With reindustrialization, and even without it, environmental evaluation will grow markedly in importance. This field is already developing within anthropology and urban planning. In architecture and urban design, the evaluation of the functioning of the built environment, variously called postconstruction evaluation (see Zube, 1980) and environment-behavior research (see Zeisel, 1981), is the relevant area. Sommer (1969), Appleyard and Lintell (1972), Carr (1973), and Whyte (1980) contribute pioneering work in this area, and the field will develop further.

The need for environmental evaluation of the effects of pollutants will also increase, for continued industrial development will make pollution worse; for example, about 500 new chemical compounds are added to consumer products each year. Political conservatism and short-sighted disregard for the environment will not be able to silence pollution evaluation as the consequences for health become more obvious. For example, rates of several kinds of cancer will rise and water will continue to become scarcer and less drinkable. As scientists and journalists report on the presence of large numbers of unsupervised industrial waste dumps, indiscriminate dumping into rivers and lakes, and the resulting chemical poisonings, popular outcry will increase. As the effects of pollution and other unsound environmental practices become more clearly life-threatening, evaluators trained in biology, urban studies, or natural ecology will find a rapidly growing demand for their talents.

A frequent error of evaluators, and of organizational consultants generally, is to believe that their expertise in particular methodologies is sufficient to do their work well and that substantive expertise in the problems addressed by the program will be provided by the client. But evaluators may soon be forced to take a different stance. It is well known, for example, that attorneys for the plaintiff in automobile accident suits acquire a competent understanding of anatomy; oil and gas regulation lawyers become expert in the technology of oil and gas fields and pipelines. To compete for clients and to evaluate adequately, evaluators will be forced to acquire substantive expertise in several areas. For some evaluators, these areas will be cross-cultural or subcultural. Other evaluators will develop expertise in environmental issues, computers and communication, military matters, energy, and international issues.

Growth in Evaluation

Our account has discussed how some specific predicted social changes are likely to cause a growth of evaluation in several fields. Major social changes are good for evaluation since the field represents an effort to improve programs to cope with such changes. As one might expect from the current social turmoil, the evaluation field is growing steadily (see Chapter One).

A national Directory of Evaluation Consultants (Johnson, 1981) now exists. A step in the growing social recognition of the field, it serves to help clients find the most appropriate evaluation consultants in terms of specialization and location, and it may attain fairly wide use by prospective clients. Unlike many other social scientists, evaluators are deficient neither in entrepreneurship nor in marketing. Thus the profession is likely to prove responsive to changes in the nature of the demand for its services, and errors are likely to be in the direction of overenthusiasm rather than excessive modesty about what can be achieved by evaluation.

Programs are complex entities often functioning counterintuitively and having counterintuitive consequences, and often requiring a cross-disciplinary evaluation research effort. There will emerge perforce a close relationship between evaluation and certain other fields. Closer relationships are being established among the Evaluation Network, oriented to research in education, the Evaluation Research Society, which covers social programming, and the International Association of Applied Social Scientists, which focuses on organizational research and organization development. Evaluation will establish close ties with policy analysis, which sprang from economics, public administration, and political science. As close links are being forged with related fields, the pressure of social changes will force the growth of substantive subspecialties. As a result, many professional schools will hire faculty in evaluation, as has already happened in urban planning. Architecture and urban planning schools will develop specialties and faculty within environmental design evaluation, blending postoccupancy evaluation and environmental impact studies.

We can expect evaluators to turn to many other fields as well. In public health, evaluation will focus on programs of the classic types (such as in epidemiology and health education) and on new programs related to ecology and pollution. Reflecting the growing merger of the public and private sectors, business schools will need evaluators to analyze the public policy implications of business decisions. In fact, policy analysis is now the most lively new field of recruitment by business school faculties.

Although the demand for large new social programs is waning, our society is concerned about the difficulties of creating programs that achieve their intended effects. Through economic, energy, and environmental mishaps and catastrophes, our society is reluctantly becoming aware of the interrelationship of all parts of the social and ecological system. This concern is producing a more systematic and conscientious effort to examine the workings and results of programmatic interventions in the public and private sectors, an effort that will require evaluators to apply their professional art and science to new substantive areas. It is to be hoped that we are up to the job.

References

Abel, T. "The Operation Called Verstehen." In M. Truzzi (Ed.), *Verstehen: Subjective Understanding in the Social Sciences.* Reading, Mass.: Addison-Wesley, 1974.

Ackoff, R. "Beyond Problem Solving." Paper presented at fifth annual meeting of the American Institute for Decision Sciences, Boston, Mass., November 1973.

Alinsky, S. D. *Reveille for Radicals.* New York: Vintage Books, 1969.

Altman, D., and others. Unpublished research, Graduate Center, The City University of New York.

Anderson, H. G. "Science and Management Techniques." *Science,* 1974, *183,* 726-727.

Anderson, S. B., and Ball, S. *The Profession and Practice of Program Evaluation.* San Francisco: Jossey-Bass, 1978.

Appleyard, D., and Lintell, M. "The Environmental Quality of City Streets: The Residents' Viewpoint." *Journal of the American Institute of Planners,* 1972, *38,* 84-101.

Asch, S. E. "Effects of Group Pressure on the Modification and Distortion of Judgments." In A. Guetzkow (Ed.), *Groups, Leadership, and Man.* Pittsburgh: Carnegie Press, 1951.

Asch, S. E. "Opinions and Social Pressure." *Scientific American,* 1955, *193,* 31-35.

Babbie, E. R. *Survey Research Methods.* Belmont, Calif.: Wadsworth, 1973.

235

Barton, A. H., and Lazarsfeld, P. F. "Some Functions of Qualitative Analysis in Social Research." In G. J. McCall and J. L.
Simmons (Eds.), *Issues in Participant Observation: A Text
and Reader*. Reading, Mass.: Addison-Wesley, 1969.

Becker, H. S. *Sociological Work*. Chicago: Aldine, 1970.

Bennis, W. G. "Post-Bureaucratic Leadership." In W. G. Bennis
(Ed.), *American Bureaucracy*. Chicago: Aldine, 1970.

Berg, R. Speech at a Symposium at annual convention of the
Evaluation Research Society, Washington, D.C., November
1978.

Berger, P. L., and Luckmann, T. *The Social Construction of
Reality: A Treatise in the Sociology of Knowledge*. Garden
City, N.Y.: Anchor Books, 1967.

Bernstein, E., and Freeman, H. *Academic and Entrepreneural
Research*. Beverly Hills, Calif.: Sage, 1975.

Bidwell, C. E., and Kasarda, J. D. "Problems of Multi-Level
Measurement: The Case of School and Schooling." In K. H.
Roberts and L. Burstein (Eds.), *New Directions for Methodology of Social and Behavioral Science: Issues in Aggregation*,
no. 6. San Francisco: Jossey-Bass, 1980.

Blalock, H. M., Jr. *Causal Inferences in Non-Experimental Research*. New York: Norton, 1972.

Blau, P. *The Dynamics of Bureaucracy*. Chicago: University of
Chicago Press, 1955.

Blau, P., and Scott, W. R. *Formal Organizations*. San Francisco:
Chandler, 1961.

Blumer, H. "Sociological Analysis and the Variable." *American
Sociological Review*, 1956, *21*, 683-690.

Blumer, H. "Methodological Principles of Empirical Science."
In N. K. Denzin (Ed.), *Sociological Methods: A Sourcebook*.
Chicago: Aldine-Atherton, 1972.

Blumer, H. "Social Problems as Collective Behavior." *Social
Problems*, 1972, *18*, 298-306.

Bogdan, R. "Working Out Failure: Measuring Success in a Poverty Program." In R. Bogdan and S. J. Taylor (Eds.), *Introduction to Qualitative Research Methods: A Phenomenological Approach*. New York: Wiley, 1975.

Brewer, G. D. *Politicians, Bureaucrats, and the Consultant*. New
York: Basic Books, 1973.

Brinton, C. *The Anatomy of a Revolution.* (Rev. ed.) Englewood Cliffs, N.J.: Prentice-Hall, 1952.

Britan, G. M. "Experimental and Contextual Models of Program Evaluation." *Evaluation and Program Planning,* 1978, *1,* 229-234.

Bross, I. D. J. "The Role of the Statistician: Scientist or Shoe Clerk?" *The American Statistician,* 1974, *28,* 126-127.

Brown, L. R. *The Twenty-Ninth Day.* New York: Norton, 1978.

Brown, R. "Natural Categories and Basic Objects in the Domain of Persons." The Katz-Newcomb Lecture, University of Michigan, Ann Arbor, 1980.

Campbell, D. T. "Administrative Experimentation, Institutional Records, and Non-Reactive Measures." In J. C. Stanley (Ed.), *Improving Experimental Design and Statistical Analysis.* Chicago: Rand McNally, 1967.

Campbell, D. T. "Reforms as Experiments." *American Psychologist,* 1969, *24,* 409-429.

Campbell, D. T. "Considering the Case Against Experimental Evaluations of Social Innovations." *Administrative Science Quarterly,* 1970, *15,* 110-113.

Campbell, D. T. "Methods for the Experimenting Society." Paper presented before the American Psychological Association, Washington, D.C., Sept. 5, 1971a.

Campbell, D. T. "Administrative Experiments, Institutional Records, and Non-Reactive Measures." In W. Evans (Ed.), *Organizational Experiments.* New York: Harper & Row, 1971b.

Campbell, D. T. "Qualitative Knowing in Action Research." Kurt Lewin Award Address, Society for the Psychological Study of Social Issues meeting with the annual convention of the American Psychological Association, New Orleans, September 1, 1974.

Campbell, D. T. "Assessing the Impact of Planned Social Change." *Evaluation and Program Planning,* 1979, *2,* 68.

Campbell, D. T. "Degrees of Freedom and the Case Study." In T. D. Cook and C. S. Reichardt (Eds.), *Qualitative and Quantitative Methods in Evaluation Research.* Beverly Hills, Calif.: Sage, 1979.

Campbell, D. T., and Fiske, D. W. "Convergent and Discriminant Validation by the Multitrait-Multimethod Matrix." *Psychological Bulletin*, 1959, *56*, 81-105.

Campbell, D. T., and Stanley, J. C. *Experimental and Quasi-Experimental Designs for Research*. Chicago: Rand McNally, 1966.

Caparaso, J. A. "Quasi-Experimental Approaches to Social Science: Perspectives and Problems." In J. A. Caparaso and L. L. Roos, Jr. (Eds.), *Quasi-Experimental Approaches: Testing Theory and Evaluating Policy*. Evanston, Ill.: Northwestern University Press, 1973.

Caparaso, J. A., and Roos, L. L. (Eds.). *Quasi-Experimental Approaches: Testing Theory and Evaluating Policy*. Evanston, Ill.: Northwestern University Press, 1973.

Carr, S. *City Lights and Signs: A Policy Study*. Cambridge, Mass.: M.I.T. Press, 1973.

Cartwright, D. "Risk-Taking by Individuals and Groups: An Assessment of Research Employing Choice Dilemmas." *Journal of Personality and Social Psychology*, 1971, *20*, 361-378.

Chatham, L. R. "A Federal Manager's Position on Accountability." Paper presented at the annual convention of the Evaluation Research Society, Washington, D.C., November 4, 1978.

Chatterjee, P. "Decision Support System: A Case Study in Evaluative Research." *Journal of Applied Behavioral Sciences*, 1975, *9*, 62-74.

Chomsky, N. "Verbal Behavior." *Language*, 1959, *35*, 26-58.

Churchman, C. W. *The Systems Approach*. New York: Dell, 1968.

Clark, B. "Organizational Adaptation and Precarious Values." *American Sociological Review*, 1956, *21*, 327-336.

Cole, H. S. D., and others. *Models of Doom: A Critique of the Limits of Growth*. New York: Universe Books, 1973.

Commoner, B. *The Closing Circle*. New York: Bantam Books, 1980.

Cook, T. D., and Campbell, D. T. *Quasi-Experimentation: Design and Analysis Issues for Field Settings*. Chicago: Rand McNally, 1979.

Cook, T. D., and Reichardt, C. S. *Qualitative and Quantitative*

Methods in Evaluation Research. Beverly Hills, Calif.: Sage, 1979.

Cotton, J. W. *Par for the Corps: A Review of the Empirical Research on the Selection, Training and Performance of Peace Corps Volunteers.* ERIC Document ED 110-672. Washington, D.C.: Educational Resources Information Center, National Institute of Education, Department of Education, 1975.

Cressey, D. R. "Criminal Violation of Financial Trust." Unpublished doctoral dissertation, Indiana University, 1950.

Cronbach, L. J., and others. *Toward Reform of Program Evaluation: Aims, Methods, and Institutional Arrangements.* San Francisco: Jossey-Bass, 1980.

Denzin, N. K. "Introduction to Part Twelve: Triangulation, A Case for Methodological Evaluation and Combination." In N. K. Denzin (Ed.), *Sociological Methods: A Sourcebook.* Chicago: Aldine, 1970.

Denzin, N. K. "The Logic of Naturalistic Inquiry." *Social Forces,* 1971, *50,* 166-182.

Deutscher, I. "Toward Avoiding the Goal-Trap in Evaluation Research." In C. C. Abt (Ed.), *The Evaluation of Social Programs.* Beverly Hills, Calif.: Sage, 1976.

Dexter, L. A. *Elite and Specialized Interviewing.* Evanston, Ill.: Northwestern University Press, 1970.

Diesing, P. *Reason in Society.* Urbana: University of Illinois Press, 1962.

Dorris, J. W. "Reactions to Unconditional Cooperation: A Field Study Emphasizing Variables Neglected in Laboratory Research." *Journal of Personality and Social Psychology,* 1972, *22,* 387-397.

Dorwart, R. A., and Meyers, W. R. *Citizen Participation in Mental Health: Research and Social Policy.* Springfield, Ill.: Thomas, 1981.

Downs, A. "Some Thoughts on Giving People Economic Advice." In F. Caro (Ed.), *Readings in Evaluation Research.* New York: Russell Sage Foundation, 1971.

Durkheim, E. *Suicide.* New York: Free Press, 1951.

Ellul, J. *The Technological Society.* New York: Knopf, 1965.

Etzioni, A. "Two Approaches to Organizational Analysis: A Critique and A Suggestion." In H. C. Schulberg, A. Sheldon, and F. Baker (Eds.), *Program Evaluation in the Health Fields.* New York: Behavioral Publications, 1969.

Etzioni, A., and Lehman, E. W. "Some Dangers in Valid Social Measurement." *The Annals of the American Academy of Political and Social Science,* 1967, *373,* 1-13.

Fairweather, G. *Methods for Experimental Social Innovation.* New York: Wiley, 1968.

Feldman, R. E. "Response to Compatriot and Foreigner Who Seek Assistance." *Journal of Personality and Social Psychology,* 1968, *10,* 202-214.

Filstead, W. J. "Qualitative Methods: A Needed Perspective in Evaluation Research." In T. D. Cook and C. S. Reichardt (Eds.), *Qualitative and Quantitative Methods in Evaluation Research.* Beverly Hills, Calif.: Sage, 1979.

Forrester, J. *Industrial Dynamics.* Cambridge, Mass.: M.I.T. Press, 1961a.

Forrester, J. *Urban Dynamics.* Cambridge, Mass.: M.I.T. Press, 1961b.

Forrester, J. "Counterintuitive Behavior of Social Systems." *Technology Review,* 1971a, *73,* 53-68.

Forrester, J. *World Dynamics.* Cambridge, Mass.: Wright-Allen Press, 1971b.

Freeman, H. E. "Conceptual Approaches to Assessing Impacts of Large-Scale Intervention Programs." In *Proceedings, American Statistical Association* (Social Statistics Section), 1964, pp. 192-198.

Freeman, H. E., and Sherwood, C. C. "Research in Large-Scale Intervention Programs." *The Journal of Social Issues,* 1965, *21,* 11-28.

Fried, M. "Grieving for a Lost Home." In L. Duhl (Ed.), *The Urban Condition.* New York: Basic Books, 1963.

Fried, M., and Gleicher, P. "Some Sources of Residential Satisfaction in an Urban Slum." *Journal of the American Institute of Planners,* 1961, *27,* 305-315.

Galbraith, J. K. *The New Industrial State.* New York: New American Library, 1972.

Galtung, J. *Theory and Methods of Social Research.* Oslo: Universitetsforloget; London: Allen and Unwin; New York: Columbia University Press, 1967.

Gans, H. J. *The Urban Villagers.* New York: Free Press, 1962.

Glaser, B. G. "The Constant Comparative Method of Qualitative Analysis." *Social Problems,* 1965, *12,* 436-445.

Glaser, B. G., and Strauss, A. "The Social Loss of Dying Patients." *American Journal of Nursing,* 1964, *64,* 119-121.

Glaser, B. G., and Strauss, A. *The Discovery of Grounded Theory: Strategies for Qualitative Research.* Chicago: Aldine, 1967.

Glaser, E. Myrdal Prize Address at annual convention of the Evaluation Research Society. Washington, D.C., November 1978.

Gleser, G. C., Green, B. L., and Winget, C. N. *Prolonged Psychosocial Effects of Disaster: A Study of Buffalo Creek.* New York: Academic Press, 1981.

Gouldner, A. W. "Metaphysical Pathos and the Theory of Bureaucracy." *American Political Science Review,* 1955, *49,* 496-507.

Gouldner, A. W. "The Sociologist as Partisan: Sociology and the Welfare State." *American Sociologist,* 1968, *3,* 103-116.

Greene, W. "Again Triage: Who Shall be Fed? Who Shall Starve?" *New York Times Magazine,* July 5, 1975, p. 11.

Gregg, A. "A Medical Aspect of the Population Problem." *Science,* 1955, *121,* 681.

Griffin, J. H. *Black Like Me.* Boston: Houghton Mifflin, 1961.

Gruenberg, E. "The Failures of Success." *Health and Society,* 1977, *21,* 3-24.

Guba, E. G. *Toward a Methodology of Naturalistic Inquiry in Educational Evolution.* Los Angeles: University of California, Los Angeles, Center for the Study of Evaluation, 1978.

Guttentag, M. (Ed.). *Handbook of Evaluation Research.* Vol. 2. Beverly Hills, Calif.: Sage, 1975.

Haley, J. *The Power Tactics of Jesus Christ and Other Essays.* New York: Avon, 1973.

Hammond, T. H., and Knott, J. H. *A Zero-Based Look at Zero-Base Budgeting.* New Brunswick, N.J.: Transaction, Inc., 1980.

Haney, W. "Units and Levels of Analysis in Large-Scale Evaluation." In K. H. Roberts and L. Burstein (Eds.), *New Directions for Methodology of Social and Behavioral Science: Issues in Aggregation*, no. 6. San Francisco: Jossey-Bass, 1980.

Hardin, G. "The Tragedy of the Commons." *Science*, 1968, *162*, 1243-1248.

Hardin, G. "Nobody Ever Dies of Overpopulation." *Science*, 1971, *171* (3971).

Hardin, G. "We Live on a Spaceship." *Bulletin of the Atomic Scientists*, 1972, *28*, 23.

Hardin, G. "Lifeboat Ethics: The Case Against Helping the Poor." *Psychology Today*, 1974, *8*, 38-42, 123-126.

Harrington, P. J., and Sanders, J. R. "Guidelines for Goal-Free Evaluation." Paper presented at annual convention of the Evaluation Network, Cincinnati, Ohio, October 1979.

Heussenstamm, F. K. "Bumper Stickers and the Cops." *Transaction*, 1971, *8*, 32-33. [Also in P. G. Swingle (Ed.), *Social Psychology in Natural Settings: A Reader in Field Experimentation*. Chicago: Aldine Publishing Company, 1973.]

Horst, P., and others. "Program Management and the Federal Evaluator." *Public Administration Review*, 1974, *34*, 300-307.

Hovland, C. I. "Reconciling Conflicting Results Derived from Experimental and Survey Studies." *American Psychologist*, 1959, *14*, 8-17.

Howe, L. K. *Pink Collar Workers*. New York: Putnam, 1977.

Howe, S. R. "Fear, Danger, and the Use of Public Places: Some Initial Studies and a Theory." Unpublished doctoral dissertation, Psychology Department, University of Cincinnati, 1980.

Hyman, H. H., Wright, C. R., and Hopkins, T. K. *Applications of Methods of Evaluation: Four Studies of the Encampment for Citizenship*. Berkeley and Los Angeles: University of California Press, 1962.

Inkeles, A., and Smith, D. H. *Becoming Modern: Individual Change in Six Developing Countries*. Cambridge, Mass.: Harvard University Press, 1974.

Janis, I. L. *Victims of Groupthink*. Boston: Houghton Mifflin, 1972.

Johnson, J. M. *Doing Field Research.* New York: Free Press, 1975.

Johnson, R. *National Directory of Evaluation Consultants.* New York: Foundation Center, 1981.

Jones, R. P. *The Peace Corps Overseas: Some First Steps Toward Description and Evaluation.* Eugene: Oregon Research Institute, 1969.

Kalish, J. A. "Flim Flam, Double-Talk, and Hustle: The Urban Problems Industry." *The Washington Monthly,* 1969, *10,* 6-16.

Kaplan, A. *The Conduct of Inquiry: Methodology for Behavioral Science.* Scranton, Penn.: Chandler, 1964.

Kaplan, M. Personal interview concerning the firm of Marshall Kaplan, Gans, and Kahn, 1969.

Katona, G. *Psychological Analysis of Economic Behavior.* New York: McGraw-Hill, 1963.

Katzenmeyer, L. Speech at a Symposium of the annual convention of the Evaluation Network, Cincinnati, Ohio, October 1979.

Kendall, P., and Lazarsfeld, P. F. "Problems of Survey Analysis." In R. K. Merton and P. F. Lazarsfeld (Eds.), *Continuities in Social Research: Studies in the Scope and Method of "The American Soldier."* New York: Free Press, 1950.

Kershaw, D. N., and Skidmore, F. *The New Jersey Graduated Work Incentive Experiment.* Princeton, N.J.: Mathematica, 1974.

Kintsch, W. *Memory and Cognition.* New York: Wiley, 1977.

Kuhn, T. S. *The Structure of Scientific Revolutions.* Chicago: University of Chicago Press, 1962.

Labov, W. "The Boundaries of Words and Their Meanings." In C.-J. N. Bailey and R. W. Shuy (Eds.), *New Ways of Analyzing Variation in English.* Vol. 1. Washington, D.C.: Georgetown University Press, 1973.

LaPonce, J. A. "Experimentation and Political Science: A Plea for More Pre-Data Experiments." Paper presented at meeting of International Political Science Association, Vancouver, Canada, 1977.

Lappe, F. M. "Causes of World Hunger Are Social, Not Physical,

References

Institute Head Declares." *Behavior Today,* January 30, 1978, pp. 4-6.

Latane, B., and Darley, J. M. "Bystander Apathy." *American Scientist,* 1969, *57,* 244-268.

Lazarsfeld, P. F., and Barton, A. H. "Qualitative Measurement in the Social Sciences: Classification, Typologies, and Indices." In D. Lerner and H. D. Lasswell (Eds.), *The Policy Sciences: Recent Developments in Scope and Method.* Stanford, Calif.: Stanford University Press, 1951.

Lazarsfeld, P. F., and Menzel, H. "On the Relation Between Individual and Collective Properties." In A. Etzioni (Ed.), *Complex Organizations, A Sociological Reader.* New York: Holt, Rinehart and Winston, 1964.

Lefkowitz, M., Blake, R. R., and Mouton, J. S. "Status of Actors in Pedestrian Violation of Traffic Signals." *Journal of Abnormal and Social Psychology,* 1955, *51,* 704-706.

Lerner, D. "Interviewing Frenchmen." *American Journal of Sociology,* 1956, *62,* 187-194.

Lerner, D. *The Passing of Traditional Society: Modernizing the Middle East.* New York: Free Press, 1958.

Levine, M. "Investigative Reporting as a Research Method: An Analysis of Bernstein and Woodward's *All the President's Men.*" *American Psychologist,* 1980, *35,* 626-638.

Lewin, K. *Principles of Topological Psychology.* New York: McGraw-Hill, 1936.

Lewis, O. *Life In a Mexican Village: Tepoztlan Restudied.* Urbana: University of Illinois Press, 1951.

Liebow, E. *Tally's Corner: A Study of Negro Streetcorner Men.* Boston: Little, Brown, 1967.

London, P. "The Rescuer: Motivational Hypotheses About Christians Who Saved Jews from the Nazis." In J. MacCauley and L. Berkowitz (Eds.), *Altruism and Helping Behavior: Some Psychological Studies of Some Antecedents and Consequences.* New York: Academic Press, 1970.

Lyall, K. C. Speech at a Symposium at annual meeting of the Evaluation Research Society, Washington, D.C., November 1978.

Manis, J. H. "The Sociology of Knowledge and Community

Mental Health Research." *Social Problems,* 1968, *15,* 488-501.

Mannheim, K. *Ideology and Utopia.* New York: Harcourt Brace Jovanovich, 1936.

Mannheim, K. *Man and Society in an Age of Reconstruction.* New York: Harcourt Brace Jovanovich, 1940.

Mantel, S. *What Every Engineer Should Know About Decision Making.* New York: Marcel Dekker, forthcoming.

Martin, M. "Understanding and Participant Observation in Cultural and Social Anthropology." In M. Truzzi (Ed.), *Verstehen: Subjective Understanding in the Social Sciences.* Reading, Mass.: Addison-Wesley, 1974.

Meadows, D. L., and others. *The Limits to Growth: A Report for the Club of Rome's Project on the Predicament of Mankind.* (2nd ed.) New York: Universe Books, 1974.

Merton, R. *Social Theory and Social Structure.* New York: Free Press, 1957.

Merton, R., Fiske, M., and Kendall, P. *The Focused Interview.* New York: Free Press, 1956.

Mesarovic, M., and Pestel, E. *Mankind at the Turning Point: Second Report to the Club of Rome.* New York: Dutton, 1974.

Meyers, W. R. "The Politics of Evaluation Research: The Peace Corps." *Journal of Applied Behavioral Science,* 1975, *11,* 261-280.

Meyers, W. R., and Kempner, M. "Clinical Psychology and Health Planning." In P. Karoly and J. Steffen (Eds.), *Improving the Long-Term Effects of Psychotherapy.* New York: Gardner Press, 1980.

Meyers, W. R., and others. "Methods of Measuring Citizen Board Accomplishment in Mental Health and Retardation." *Community Mental Health Journal,* 1972, *8,* 313-320.

Meyers, W. R., and others. "Organizational and Attitudinal Correlates of Citizen Board Accomplishment in Mental Health and Retardation." *Community Mental Health,* 1974, *10,* 192-197.

Meyerson, M. "Building the Middle-Range Bridge for Comprehensive Planning." *Journal of the American Institute of Planners,* 1956, *22,* 58-64.

Michels, R. *Political Parties.* New York: Dover Books, 1959.

Milgram, S. "The Experience of Living in Cities." *Science,* 1970, *67,* 1461-1468.

Milgram, S. *Obedience to Authority.* New York: Harper & Row, 1974.

Miller, S. M., and others. "Creaming the Poor." *Transaction,* 1970, *8,* 39-45.

Morison, S. E. *History as a Literary Art, An Appeal to Young Historians.* Boston: Old South Association, 1948.

Morison, S. E. "History as a Literary Art." In O. Handlin (Ed.), *Harvard Guide to American History,* Cambridge, Mass.: Belknap Press of Harvard University Press, 1954.

Mosteller, F. "Innovation and Evaluation." *Science,* 1981, *211,* 881-886.

Murphy, R. K., Jr., and others. "Social Adaptations to a Built Environment: Seating in a Public Square." Paper presented at Environmental Design Research Association ninth annual meeting, Tucson, Ariz., University of Arizona, April 1978. [Mimeographed paper available from R. Murphy, Department of Psychology, 429 Dyer Hall, University of Cincinnati, Cincinnati, Ohio 45227.]

Myrdal, G. *Asian Drama: An Inquiry into the Poverty of Nations.* New York: Random House, 1968.

Myrdal, G. *Objectivity in Social Research.* New York: Pantheon Books, 1969.

Newman, O. *Defensible Space.* New York: Macmillan, 1972.

Noble, W. Speech at a Symposium at annual convention of the Evaluation Research Society, Washington, D.C., November 1978.

Orne, M. T. "The Nature of Hypnosis: Artifact and Essence." *Journal of Abnormal and Social Psychology,* 1959, *58,* 277-299.

Orne, M. T. "On the Social Psychology of the Psychological Experiment: With Particular Reference to Demand Characteristics and Their Implications." *American Psychologist,* 1962, *17,* 776-783.

Orne, M. T. "Demand Characteristics and the Concept of Quasi-Controls." In R. Rosenthal and R. L. Rosnow (Eds.), *Artifact in Behavioral Research.* New York: Academic Press, 1969.

Osler, W. O. *The Principles and Practice of Medicine.* (12th ed.) Revised by T. McCrae. New York: Appleton-Century-Crofts, 1935.

Owen, O. *Natural Resource Conservation.* (2nd ed.) New York: MacMillan, 1975.

Parry, A. *Terrorism: State and Private.* New York: Vanguard, 1977.

Parsons, T. *The Social System.* New York: Free Press, 1951.

Patton, M. Q. *Utilization-Focused Evaluation.* Beverly Hills, Calif.: Sage, 1978.

Peattie, L. R. "Drama and Advocacy Planning." *Journal of the American Institute of Planners,* 1970, *36,* 405-410.

Pelto, P., and Pelto, G. *Anthropological Research: The Strategy of Enquiry.* (2nd rev. ed.) Cambridge, England: Cambridge University Press, 1978.

Perloff, R. (Ed.). *Evaluator Interventions: Pros and Cons.* Beverly Hills, Calif.: Sage, 1979.

Peters, C. (Ed.). *The Washington Monthly.* Washington, D.C.: Washington Monthly Company, 1968-1981 (monthly).

Peters, D. F., and Ceci, S. J. "A Manuscript Masquerade: How Well Does the Review Process Work?" *The Sciences,* 1980, *20,* 16-19.

Peters, D. F., and Ceci, S. J. "A Naturalistic Study of the Journal Review Process in Psychology." Unpublished paper, Psychology Department, University of North Dakota, 1981.

Piliavin, I. M., Rodin, J., and Piliavin, J. A. "Good Samaritanism: An Underground Phenomenon?" *Journal of Personality and Social Psychology,* 1969, *13,* 289-299.

Polsky, N. *Hustlers, Beats, and Others.* Garden City, N.Y.: Anchor Books, 1969.

Pressman, J. L., and Wildavsky, A. B. *Implementation: How Great Expectations in Washington Are Dashed in Oakland: or Why It's Amazing That Federal Programs Work at All, This Being a Saga of the Economic Development Administration as Told by Two Sympathetic Observers Who Seek to Build Morals on a Foundation of Ruined Hopes.* Berkeley, University of California Press, 1973.

Redfield, R. *Tepoztlan, a Mexican Village.* Chicago: University of Chicago Press, 1930.

Redfield, R. *The Little Community*. Chicago: University of Chicago Press, 1955.

Reichardt, C. S., and Cook, T. D. "Beyond Qualitative Versus Quantitative Methods." In T. D. Cook and C. S. Reichardt (Eds.), *Qualitative and Quantitative Methods in Evaluation Research*. Beverly Hills, Calif.: Sage, 1979.

Riecken, H. W. "Memorandum on Program Evaluation." In C. H. Weiss (Ed.), *Evaluating Action Programs: Readings in Social Action and Education*. Boston: Allyn & Bacon, 1972.

Riecken, H. W., and Boruch, R. F. (Eds.). *Social Experimentation: A Method for Planning and Evaluating Social Intervention*. New York: Academic Press, 1974.

Riesman, D., and Glazer, N. "Criteria for Political Apathy." In A. W. Gouldner (Ed.), *Studies in Leadership*. New York: Russell and Russell, 1965.

Rist, R. C. "On the Relations Among Educational Research Paradigms." *Anthropology and Education Quarterly*, 1977, *8*, 42-49.

Robinson, I. "Beyond the Middle-Range Planning Bridge." *Journal of American Institute of Planners*, 1964, *31*, 304-312.

Robinson, W. S. "The Logical Structure of Analytic Induction." *American Sociological Review*, 1951, *16*, 812-818.

Rockhoff, M. Speech at a Symposium at annual convention of the Evaluation Research Society, Washington, D.C., November 1978.

Rodman, H., and Kolodny, R. "Organizational Strains in the Researcher-Practitioner Relationship." *Human Organization*, 1964, *23*, 171-182.

Rosenberg, M. *The Logic of Survey Analysis*. New York: Basic Books, 1968.

Rosenhan, D. L. "On Being Sane in Insane Places." *Science*, 1973, *179*, 250-258.

Rossi, P. "Evaluating Educational Programs." *The Urban Review*, 1969, *3*, 17-18.

Russell, B. "On the Notion of Cause." *Proceedings of the Aristotelian Society* (New Series), 1913, *13*, 1-26.

Ryan, W. *Blaming the Victim*. New York: Vintage Books, 1971.

Salasin, S. "Experimentation Revisited: A Conversation with Donald T. Campbell." *Evaluation*, 1973, *1*, 7-13.

Schatzman, L., and Strauss, A. L. *Field Research: Strategies for a Natural Sociology.* Englewood Cliffs, N.J.: Prentice-Hall, 1973.

Schwartz, E. "A Modest Proposal: Letter to Thomas Jefferson from Lord North." *Social Policy,* 1974, *5,* 10-11.

Scriven, M. S. Speech presented at symposium on "Goal-Free Evaluation in Practice," presented at annual meeting of the American Educational Research Association, Toronto, Canada, 1978.

Sechrest, L. "The Psychologist as Program Evaluator." In P. Woods (Ed.), *Career Opportunities for Psychologists: Expanding and Emerging Areas.* Washington, D.C.: American Psychological Association, 1976.

Sherrill, S. B. *Outcomes, Values and Costs in the Evaluation of Governmental Programs.* Santa Monica, Calif.: Goodyear, forthcoming.

Sheuch, E. K. "Cross-National Comparisons Using Aggregate Data: Some Substantive and Methodological Problems." In R. L. Merritt and S. Rokkan (Eds.), *Comparing Nations: The Use of Quantitative Data in Cross-National Research.* New Haven, Conn.: Yale University Press, 1966.

Sills, D. L. *The Volunteers.* New York: Free Press, 1957.

Simon, H. A. "Satisficing and the One Right Way." In S. Kaplan and R. Kaplan (Eds.), *Humanscape: Environments for People.* North Scituate, Mass.: Duxbury Press, 1978.

Sjoberg, G. "Politics, Ethics and Evaluation Research." In M. Guttentag (Ed.), *Handbook of Evaluation Research.* Vol. 2. Beverly Hills, Calif.: Sage, 1975.

Snepp v. *U.S.* 444 U.S. 507 (1980); 100 S. Ct. 763 (1980).

Solomon, M. Speech at a Symposium at annual convention of the Evaluation Research Society. Washington, D.C., November 1978.

Sommer, R. *Personal Space: The Behavioral Basis of Design.* Englewood Cliffs, N.J.: Prentice-Hall, 1969.

Sommer, R. "No, Not Research. I Said Evaluation." *APA Monitor,* 1977, *8,* 1, 11.

Srole, L. "Social Integration and Certain Corollaries: An Exploratory Study." *American Sociological Review,* 1956, *21,* 709-716.

Stouffer, S. A. *The American Soldier.* Vol. 1: *Adjustment During Army Life.* Vol. 2: *Combat and Its Aftermath.* Princeton: Princeton University Press, 1949.

Struening, E. L. (Ed.). *Handbook of Evaluation Research.* Vol. 1. Beverly Hills, Calif.: Sage, 1975.

"Study Finds Turns on Red Cause 20% Accident Rise." *New York Times,* Dec. 11, 1980, p. 13.

"Subway Drama Ends in Death; None Gave Aid." *New York Times,* October 9, 1980, p. 22.

Suchman, E. A. *Evaluative Research: Principles and Practice in Public Service and Social Action Programs.* New York: Russell Sage Foundation, 1967.

Suchman, E. A. "Action for What? A Critique of Evaluative Research." In C. Weiss (Ed.), *Evaluating Action Programs: Readings in Social Action and Education.* Boston: Allyn & Bacon, 1972.

Swift, J. "A Modest Proposal." In R. A. Greenberg and W. B. Piper (Eds.), *The Writings of Jonathan Swift.* New York: Norton, 1973.

Terkel, S. *Working.* New York: Avon, 1975.

Terkel, S. *American Dreams: Lost and Found.* New York: Pantheon Books, 1980.

Thomas, W. I. "On the Definition of the Situation." In M. Truzzi (Ed.), *Sociology: The Classic Statements.* New York: Random House, 1971.

Thomas, W. I., and Znaniecki, F. *The Polish Peasant in Europe and America.* (2nd ed.) New York: Knopf, 1927.

Thompson, J., and McEwen, W. "Organizational Goals and Environment." *American Sociological Review,* 1958, *23,* 23-31.

Tinbergen, J. *R.I.O.: Reshaping the International Order: A Report to the Club of Rome.* New York: New American Library, 1977.

Trend, M. G. "On the Reconciliation of Qualitative and Quantitative Analyses: A Case Study." In T. D. Cook and C. S. Reichardt (Eds.), *Qualitative and Quantitative Methods in Evaluation Research.* Beverly Hills, Calif.: Sage Publications, 1979.

Truzzi, M. (Ed.). *Verstehen: Subjective Understanding in the Social Sciences.* Reading, Mass.: Addison-Wesley, 1974.

U.S. Office of the Federal Register. "The Final Regulations Amending Basic HHS Policy for the Protection of Human Research Subjects." *Federal Register,* 1981, *46* (16), 8366-8392.

van de Ven, A. H. and Delbecq, A. L. "The Effectiveness of Nominal, Delphi, and Interacting Group Decision-Making Processes." *Academy of Management Journal,* 1974, *17,* 605-621.

Veblen, T. *The Instinct of Workmanship, and the State of the Industrial Arts.* New York: B. W. Heubsch, 1918.

Voas, R. B. "Research Programs and Policy at the National Highway Traffic Safety Administration." Paper presented at a Colloquium at the Department of Psychology, University of Cincinnati, April 6, 1979.

Watkins, J. W. N. "Ideal Types and Historical Explanation." In H. Feigl and M. Brodbeck (Eds.), *Readings in the Philosophy of Science.* New York: Appleton-Century-Crofts, 1953.

Wax, M. L. "On Misunderstanding *Verstehen*: A Reply to Abel." In M. Truzzi (Ed.), *Verstehen: Subjective Understanding in the Social Sciences.* Reading, Mass.: Addison-Wesley, 1974.

Wax, R. H. *Doing Fieldwork: Warnings and Advice.* Chicago: University of Chicago Press, 1975.

Webb, E. J., and others. *Unobtrusive Measures: Nonreactive Research in the Social Sciences.* Chicago: Rand McNally, 1972.

Webber, M. "Order in Diversity: Community Without Propinquity." In R. Gutman and D. Popenoe (Eds.), *Neighborhood, City and Metropolis: An Integrated Reader in Urban Sociology.* New York: Random House, 1970.

Weber, M. *The Theory of Social and Economic Organization.* New York: Oxford University Press, 1947.

Weiss, C. "Where Politics and Evaluation Meet." *Evaluation,* 1973, *1,* 37-45.

Weiss, R. S. "Input and Process Studies as Alternatives and Complements to Outcome Evaluation." Unpublished paper, Laboratory of Community Psychiatry, Harvard Medical School, 1971.

Weiss, R. S., and Rein, M. "The Evaluation of Broad-Aim Programs: A Cautionary Case and a Moral." *The Annals of the American Academy of Political and Social Science,* 1969, *385,* 133-142.

Weiss, R. S., and Rein, M. "The Evaluation of Broad-Aim Programs: Experimental Design, Its Difficulties, and an Alternative." *Administrative Science Quarterly,* 1970, *15,* 97-109.

Wholey, J. S. "Evaluability Assessment." In L. Rutman (Ed.), *Evaluation Research Methods: A Basic Guide.* Beverly Hills, Calif.: Sage, 1977.

Whyte, W. H. *The Social Life of Small Urban Spaces.* Washington, D.C.: Conservation Foundation, 1980.

Wiggins, J. S. "Circumplex Models of Interpersonal Behavior." In L. Wheeler (Ed.), *Review of Personality and Social Psychology.* Vol. 1. Beverly Hills, Calif.: Sage, 1980.

Wildavsky, A. "Consumer Report." *Science,* 1973, *182,* 1335-1338.

Wildavsky, A. *The Politics of the Budgetary Process.* (2nd ed.) Boston: Little, Brown, 1974.

Wildavsky, A. *Budgeting: A Comparative Theory of Budgetary Processes.* Boston: Little, Brown, 1975.

Windle, C. Speech at a Symposium at annual convention of the Evaluation Research Society, Washington, D.C., November 1978.

Wirth, L. "Urbanism as a Way of Life." *American Journal of Sociology,* 1938, *44,* 3-24.

Wirth, L. *The Ghetto.* Chicago: University of Chicago Press, 1969.

Wolfe, T. *Radical Chic and Mau-Mauing the Flak Catchers.* New York: Bantam Books, 1971.

Woodward, B., and Bernstein, C. *All the President's Men.* New York: Simon & Schuster, 1974.

Wortman, P. M. "Evaluation Research: New Training Programs for New Careers." *Professional Psychology,* 1977, *8,* 361-367.

Zeisel, H. *Say It With Figures.* New York: Harper & Row, 1968.

Zeisel, J. *Inquiry by Design: Tools for Environment-Behavior Research.* Monterey, Calif.: Brooks/Cole, 1981.

Zimbardo, P. G. "A Field Experiment in Auto Shaping." In C. Ward (Ed.), *Vandalism.* London: Architectural Press, 1973a.

Zimbardo, P. G. "The Human Choice: Individuation, Reason and Order Versus Deindividuation, Impulse and Chaos." In J. Helmer and N. A. Eddington (Eds.), *Urbanman: The Psychology of Urban Survival.* New York: Free Press, 1973b.

Znaniecki, F. *The Method of Sociology.* New York: Holt, Rinehart and Winston, 1934.

Zube, E. H. *Environmental Evaluation: Perception and Public Policy.* Monterey, Calif.: Brooks/Cole, 1980.

Zuckerman, H. *Scientific Elites: Nobel Laureates in the United States.* New York: Free Press, 1977.

Index

~.

A

Abel, T., 176, 178
Accountability, and demand for evaluation, 2-3
Ackoff, R., 19, 184, 212, 217-218
Administrative analyses. *See* Managerial and administrative analyses
Administrators, responsibilities of, for evaluation, 71-90
Advocate evaluation, 76-77
Agency for International Development (AID): basic ordering agreements of, 102; computerized system of, 107-108; management information system of, 214
Alcohol, Drug Abuse, and Mental Health Administration (ADAMHA), and wiring, 96-97

Alinsky, S. D., 8
Altman, D., 136-137
American Statistical Association, 64
Amnesty International, 20
Analytic experiments: advantages of, 146-150; classic types of, 131-137; construct validity in, 135; defined, 131; for evaluation, 137-144; as less labor intensive, 147; logic and scope of, 144-146; and postexperimental inquiry, 148; and program effectiveness, 145-146; and randomization, 149-150; robustness of, 135; and sampling, 149; social context of, 139; and socialization, 147-148
Analytic induction, for data analysis, 190-192

255